Law, Governance and Technology Series

Volume 70

The *Law, Governance and Technology Series* is intended to attract manuscripts arising from an interdisciplinary approach in law, artificial intelligence and information technologies. The idea is to bridge the gap between research in IT law and IT-applications for lawyers developing a unifying techno-legal perspective. The series will welcome proposals that have a fairly specific focus on problems or projects that will lead to innovative research charting the course for new interdisciplinary developments in law, legal theory, and law and society research as well as in computer technologies, artificial intelligence and cognitive sciences. In broad strokes, manuscripts for this series may be mainly located in the fields of the Internet law (data protection, intellectual property, Internet rights, etc.), Computational models of the legal contents and legal reasoning, Legal Information Retrieval, Electronic Data Discovery, Collaborative Tools (e.g. Online Dispute Resolution platforms), Metadata and XML Technologies (for Semantic Web Services), Technologies in Courtrooms and Judicial Offices (E-Court), Technologies for Governments and Administrations (E-Government), Legal Multimedia, and Legal Electronic Institutions (Multi-Agent Systems and Artificial Societies).

Soorya Balendra

Free Speech in the Puzzle of Content Regulation

Insights from the West and the Global South

Springer

Soorya Balendra
Center for Human Rights and Legal Pluralism
McGill University
Montreal, QC, Canada

ISSN 2352-1902 ISSN 2352-1910 (electronic)
Law, Governance and Technology Series
ISBN 978-3-031-75812-6 ISBN 978-3-031-75813-3 (eBook)
https://doi.org/10.1007/978-3-031-75813-3

This Springer imprint is published by the registered company Springer Nature Switzerland AG
The registered company address is: Gewerbestrasse 11, 6330 Cham, Switzerland

Dedicated to Maayavan—*master of illusions and my pillar of strength*

Acknowledgments

As an early-career scholar, publishing a book at the *predoctoral* stage has been a challenge from the very first day I thought about writing.

This project began as my master's thesis at McGill University a huge debt of gratitude goes out to my supervisor Professor Peer Zumbansen. I was fortunate to receive financial support from the Centre for Human Rights and Legal Pluralism (CHRLP) at McGill. Many thanks go to the funders and the O'Brien Graduate Fellowships committee.

I am also deeply thankful to many individuals who offered invaluable guidance and support throughout various stages of my work. I am grateful to the International Society of Public Law for their generous funding, which enabled me to attend the ICON•S Winter/Summer School in June 2023 and stay nearly 3 weeks at the University of New South Wales (UNSW) as a visiting scholar. I also appreciate the UNSW Allens Hub for Technology, Law and Innovation for the opportunity to participate in a panel discussion on my research topic. In particular, I am indebted to Professor Lyria Bennett Moses, Professor Daniel Joyce, Professor Rosalind Dixon, and Siddharth Narrain for their insightful comments and engaging discussions.

Additionally, I extend my gratitude to the organizers and funders of the Jean Monnet Centre of Excellence Just AI, held in Brussels in June 2024. Special thanks to Ljupcho Grozdanovski and all the discussants and colleagues for their valuable insights and feedback, which significantly contributed to the development of this project.

Since my undergraduate days, I have been profoundly influenced and grateful for the mentorship of Janakan S. Muthukumar, David Sanjayan Rajasingham, and Sivakaran Navaratnam. Their encouragement, support, and constructive critique *over nearly a decade* have significantly shaped my academic journey.

Many people have contributed, both directly and indirectly, to the writing of this book. I am especially grateful for the support of Althaf Masroof, Chamila Talagala, Vishakha Wijenayake, Prof. Nandini Ramanujam, Prof. Darren Rosenblum, Kalana Senaratne, Sanduni Wickramasinghe, and Prof. Jennifer Raso.

This book has been enriched by the guidance of series editors Pompeu Casanovas and Giovanni Sartor, who graciously accepted it into the series. Special thanks are also due to publishing editor Manuela Schwietzer for her outstanding management of the manuscript. I am also deeply grateful to the anonymous peer reviewers for their valuable suggestions and insightful comments. My sincere appreciation for their patience with this *first-time author*, as well as their keen advice and insights, which have significantly strengthened this work.

Without the dedication and support of my parents, Balendra and Nirmala, I would never have embarked on my journey as a *first-generation* academic in law. They instilled in me a love for learning, reading, and intellectual curiosity. Amidst constant challenges and deadlines, my wife, Nalina, has been the reason I was able to complete this book on time. I am deeply grateful for her love and unwavering encouragement throughout my lengthy student life.

September 2024

Montreal, QC, Canada Soorya Balendra

The original version of the book has been revised. A correction to this book can be found at https://doi.org/10.1007/978-3-031-75813-3_12

Contents

Abbreviations

AI	Artificial intelligence
BBS	Bulletin board system
CCA	Computer Crimes Act of Sri Lanka
CCTV	Closed-circuit televisions
CEO	Chief executive officer
DDoS	Distributed denial of service
DMA	Digital Markets Act of the European Union
DNS	Domain Name System
DPDP	Digital Personal Data Protection Act of India
DSA	Digital Service Act of the European Union
ECD	E-Commerce Directive of the European Union
ECHR	European Convention on Human Rights
ECtHR	European Court of Human Rights
EU	European Union
FCC	Federal Communications Commission
FOB	Facebook Oversight Board
G2C	Government-to-citizen
GDP	Gross domestic product
GDPR	General Data Protection Regulation of the European Union
HTML	Hyper Text Markup Language
ICCPR	International Covenant on Civil and Political Rights
ISP	Internet service provider
IT	Information technology
MENA	Middle East and North Africa
MIB	Ministry of Information and Broadcasting of India
MIETY	Ministry of Electronics and Information Technology of India
NetzDG	Network Enforcement Act of Germany
OFCOM	The Office of Communications
OHCHR	Office of the United Nations High Commissioner for Human Rights
OSA	Online Safety Act of Sri Lanka

OTT	Over the top
POFMA	Protection from Online Falsehoods and Manipulation Act of Singapore
PTA	Prevention of Terrorism Act of Sri Lanka
SLCERT	Sri Lanka Computer Emergency Readiness Team
SMI	Social media intermediary
SMP	Social media platform
SSMI	Significant social media intermediary
ToS	Terms of service
TRAI	Telecom Regulatory Authority of India
UK	United Kingdom
US	United States
UDHR	Universal Declaration of Human Rights
UN	United Nations
URL	Uniform resource locator

List of Figures

List of Tables

Chapter 1
Introduction

1.1 Free Speech Online

Free speech, one of the oldest and most widely recognized constitutional rights in many countries across the world, is traditionally perceived as the liberty to express oneself and is indispensable as it guarantees the opportunity for citizens to participate in the government (Kentridge, 1996; Meiklejohn, 1961; Stevens, 1993). Also, it has been recognized as a fundamental human right in many of the international and regional instruments.[1] However, when free speech adopts an increasingly *dark and deeply malicious tone*, it plays a conflicting role with other rights, such as the right to privacy, and the right to freedom of thought and religion (Bychawska-Siniarska, 2017; Smet, 2010; Sullivan, 2010). Navigating these conflicts requires a delicate balance between upholding free speech and addressing its potential adverse consequences on other rights and societal values. Different jurisdictions adapt various approaches and preferences in balancing conflicts among these fundamental human rights. For instance, in the United States, a strong preference is placed on protecting free speech, as guaranteed under the First Amendment to the Constitution. For example, in the case of *New York Times Co. v. Sullivan,*[2] where the New York Times published an ad by civil rights activists criticizing the Montgomery, Alabama, police's treatment of protestors, containing some inaccuracies. Police Commissioner

[1] *International Covenant on Civil and Political Rights*, 19 December 1966, 999 UNTS 171, Can TS 1976 No 47, Art. 19 (entered into force 23 March 1976) [ICCPR]; *Universal Declaration of Human Rights*, 10 December 1948, 10 December 1948, General Assembly resolution 217A (III), UN Doc. A/810, Art. 19 (entered into force 10 December 1948) [UDHR]; *European Convention on Human Rights*, 4 November 1950, Art. 10 (entered into force 3 September 1953) (ECHR); *American Convention on Human Rights*, 22 November 1969, Art. 13 (entered into force 18 July 1978) (ACHR); *African Charter on Human and Peoples' Rights,* 27 June *1981* (entered into force 21 October 1986) (ACHPR); ASEAN Human Rights Declaration, 18 November 2012, Art. 23; Arab Charter on Human Rights, 22 May 2004, Article 32.

[2] *New York Times Co. v. Sullivan*, 376 U.S. 254.

S. Balendra, *Free Speech in the Puzzle of Content Regulation*, Law, Governance and Technology Series 70, https://doi.org/10.1007/978-3-031-75813-3_1

L.B. Sullivan, claiming the ad defamed him, won a libel case against the Times in Alabama courts. The New York Times appealed to the U.S. Supreme Court, arguing the ad's content was protected under the First Amendment and not intended to harm Sullivan's reputation. The U.S. Supreme Court unanimously ruled in favor of the New York Times, establishing that the First Amendment protects the publication of statements, even if inaccuracies exist. The Court introduced the standard that a public official claiming libel must prove the statement was made with actual malice, meaning with knowledge of its falsehood or reckless disregard for the truth. This decision emphasized that vigorous debate about government and public affairs is protected under the First Amendment, even if such debate includes vehement criticism and mistakes. The ruling extended First Amendment protections to the press, significantly impacting how libel and defamation are approached legally, particularly in cases involving public figures and officials. In a 2015 Time magazine survey involving over 50 law professors, this decision was named the best Supreme Court decision since 1960 by both Owen Fiss of Yale and Steven Shiffrin of Cornell.[3]

In the last two decades, the Internet has connected millions of people across the globe and not only changed how humans interact with each other but also transformed the online space into a new avenue for enjoying free speech (Barendt, 2005; Godwin, 2003; Warburton, 2009). The digitization of these rights has paved the way for the development of a pattern of democracy through technological advancement—*Digital Democracy*.[4] This concept represents the use of information and communication technologies and strategies by democratic actors within the political and governance processes of local communities, nations, and on the international stage (Beacon, 2021; Berg & Hofmann, 2021). This digital transformation, including the enjoyment of human rights in cyberspace, has made them more accessible, convenient, and affordable than ever before, reaching a wider global audience with ease.

Social media platforms (SMPs) play a crucial role in accommodating free speech in the digital space, facilitating political debate and communication, and offering accessible tools for users to organize and mobilize communities. More particularly, SMPs provide spaces to produce and consume news that is no longer *elite-biased* (Ceron, 2015). Several studies highlight that social media has become a key alternative to traditional media outlets such as television, radio, and newspapers. These traditional platforms are often criticized for promoting various forms of propaganda, bias, and deliberate misinformation, which pose significant challenges in protecting human rights and democratic values (Anderson, 2021; Elejalde et al., 2018). Social media, in contrast, is increasingly seen as a space where these values can be better upheld.

---

[3] See https://time.com/4055934/best-supreme-court-decisions.

[4] According to the Research, the term is credited to digital activist Steven Clift. See https://www.ashoka.org/en-in/fellow/steven-clift.

However, these *"public squares"* often carry content that is harmful, dangerous, untrue, and against values. Recently, several key incidents, including the Christchurch Mosque shootings, Rohingya violence, numerous disinformation campaigns around the *Brexit* referendum, the 2016 U.S. elections, Russia's invasion of Ukraine, and many more, serve as examples. These issues undermine the principles of equality, dignity, tolerance, inclusion, diversity, and fundamental human rights (Gauja, 2021). Though it is necessary to uphold "free speech" in a democratic arena, the problem lies in the fact that democracy is threatened by hate speech, disinformation, and conspiracy theories.

These instances urge that, although the SMPs become avenues for the enjoyment and amplification of free speech, it is necessary to have some form of regulation or oversight to ensure trust, safety, and reliability along with other core values.

1.2 Regulating Social Media Platforms (SMPs)

As social media avenues are an emerging context, often the existing regulatory frameworks are unable to regulate or govern the issues arising from content shared across the SMPs. This issue is more pronounced in majoritarian societies than in developed countries, as developing nations have largely been building their technology infrastructure only within the past couple of decades. Thus, authorities frequently resort to technological measures such as *restricting access* to social media or *shutdowns* of social media within their jurisdiction or *throttling* measures, which slow down Internet access or *de-platforming* the accounts in question to prevent further massacres from spreading through the Internet space. However, these measures are considered serious violations of human rights, as the measures against the restriction of free speech, should be justified under the law, ensuring necessity (Ayalew, 2019; De Gregorio & Stremlau, 2020; Gosztonyi, 2020; Reglitz, 2020). Additionally, these measures intrude on the communication systems that many people rely on to connect with one another, also resulting in the extension of authoritarian regimes by the authorities (Gauja, 2021; Lucchi, 2013).

It is also *alarmed* by many human rights advocates, and organizations, including the Office of the United Nations High Commissioner for Human Rights (OHCHR), which noted that:

> While Internet shutdowns deeply affect many human rights, they most immediately affect freedom of expression and access to information – one of the foundations of free and democratic societies and an indispensable condition for the full development of the person. It is a touchstone for all other rights guaranteed in the International Covenant on Civil and Political Rights and other human rights instruments. Any restriction on freedom of expression constitutes a serious curtailment of human rights (OHCHR, 2022).

In many cases, the European Court of Human Rights (ECtHR) has found that blocking access to or shutting down the Internet and social media constitutes a severe violation of human rights. For example, in the case of *Cengiz and Others v. Turkey,*[5] the ECtHR determined that the measures taken by Turkey violated Article 10 of the European Convention on Human Rights. The Court recognized that YouTube was a crucial platform for the applicants to exercise their right to receive and impart information and ideas via the Internet.

Yet, these measures are still in a growing trend, in 2023, in a record-high 41 of the 70 countries covered by Freedom on the Net, governments blocked websites that hosted political, social, and religious speech (Freedom House, 2023).

Consequently, there is a call for regulating content on social media through some form of regulatory measures. These measures should safeguard free speech while balancing other competing values in cyberspace, including human rights and democratic principles.

1.3 Contemporary Developments on Regulatory Models

The contemporary scholarly and policy debates have highlighted the challenges and repercussions associated with extra-legal measures, which currently lead to regulatory frameworks for content moderation in online spaces. Three models of content governance have emerged worldwide: "*self-regulations*" involves platforms internally regulating with minimal external oversight; "*external regulations*," where the government intervenes in social media governance through policies related to privacy, data protection, content sharing, intellectual property, and competition; and "*co-regulations*," which attempts to democratize aspects of the governance and management of big technology companies (Balkin, 2021; Gauja, 2021; Gorwa, 2024; Gosztonyi, 2023). Each of these models has its own processes, nature, merits, and demerits in regulating social media content.

The Self-Regulation model involves platforms drafting and enforcing their own content policies, often referred to as community standards. Under this model, platforms independently moderate, remove, and regulate content shared on their services, a process commonly known as content moderation or, in some cases, platform-driven censorship. Content moderation involves the systematic review of *user-generated* content on digital platforms to ensure adherence to the platform's established guidelines, often referred to as *community standards*, which define the boundaries of permissible content. I argue that this practice is a successor to telegraphic codes proposed by the International Telecommunication Union in the 1870s, which aimed to exclude specific languages from communication, as well as subsequent attempts by jurisdictions to moderate nudity in the media.

Yet, the increasing reliance on *this model* resulted in numerous challenges, as highlighted in various policy and scholarly works. Specifically, concerns have been raised about the democratic legitimacy of speech regulations being determined by a

[5] *Cengiz and Others v. Turkey* (2015) 48226/10 and 14027/11.

relatively homogeneous group of *Silicon Valley elites* (Gillespie, 2020). The procedural complexities of technology and AI often result in discriminatory treatment of content from different parts of the world, each with its unique values, interpretations, and languages. This issue is especially pronounced in the moderation of online speech, where the intricate, personal, and context-dependent nature of language presents significant challenges (Gorwa et al., 2020).

Censorship typically involves filtering or removing content that is prohibited by law or policy. Platforms often engage in content moderation to enforce these rules, which may involve censoring certain content. Balkin, however, raises a challenge known as "collateral censorship." This occurs when laws and regulations enforced by authorities lead platforms to adopt broad or overly restrictive content moderation policies (Balkin, 1999, 2004). As a result, these policies can inadvertently suppress a wide range of speech, significantly eroding freedom of speech.

The lack of transparency in platform and AI operations, the over-removal of content, occasional negligence in moderation, and the training of AI systems often being influenced by market size are additional challenges inherent in this model of regulation (Gorwa et al., 2020; United Nations, 2019). These factors contribute to the suppression of free speech online, making this self-regulatory approach flawed. These issues will be explored in greater depth in the upcoming chapters of this book.

External regulation typically involves oversight by governmental or state authorities, and in some cases, regional bodies like the European Union (EU). The EU's regulatory frameworks, such as the Digital Services Act (DSA), exemplify this model, imposing specific obligations and requirements on platforms. Other notable examples include Germany's Network Enforcement Act (NetzDG) and India's Information Technology (Intermediary Guidelines and Digital Media Ethics Code) Rules. These frameworks are often rooted in the principle of cyber sovereignty under international law, granting jurisdictions the authority to regulate their digital spaces (Gosztonyi, 2023; Jougleux, 2022). However, this model can also stifle free speech due to overly broad regulations, as seen in countries like China and Russia—extending the authoritarian practices in the digital realm. I argue that some other countries, such as Sri Lanka, are beginning to adopt similar approaches.

Though the objectives of these regulatory frameworks are largely similar, they are shaped by a variety of factors, including government approaches, market size, user base, cultural variations, and power asymmetries between platforms and governments (Finck, 2018; Gillespie, 2020; Gorwa, 2024; Jougleux, 2022; Khan, 2019). As a result, these regulations differ significantly from one another, impacting their effectiveness, interplay with the platforms, efficiency, and, crucially, their influence on free speech rights in online spaces.

Finally, the third model, the Co-Regulation, emphasizes collaboration between authorities, platforms, and other stakeholders (Gorwa, 2019; Hirsch, 2010). Within this regulatory framework, a country may opt for informal, non-binding forms of regulation or co-regulation, which involve working with companies to encourage their commitment to new rules and institutional processes aimed at improving their practices (Criépeau, 2022; Gorwa, 2024; Marsden, 2004, 2011). The EU's Codes of

Conduct[6] and Australia's Code of Practice[7] are examples of the co-regulatory model. Gosztonyi argues that this model is gaining prominence due to the challenges associated with the other two models. He suggests that a regulatory code proposal, adopted by a new agency, could facilitate a combination of public and self-regulation—essentially co-regulation (Gosztonyi, 2023). Like the other two models, the co-regulation model also faces challenges, including lack of accountability, inconsistent enforcement, coordination difficulties, limited public oversight, and the risk of developing weak standards due to the need for consensus among diverse stakeholders (Jougleux, 2022; Marsden, 2011; Weber, 2010).

1.4 Questions

In this context, this book centralizes around and seeks to answer the following question: How do different social media content regulatory models, from Western to Majority world contexts, impact online free speech?

This work is inspired by four broad and interrelated sub-questions that I encountered as an active social media user in Sri Lanka a few years ago, where both social media content and regulatory measures had a rapid and significant impact. First, how do social media platforms interplay with free speech and expression? Second, is there a need to regulate the content shared across these platforms? Third, how can we regulate them in a balanced manner without stifling free speech and the public good? Finally, where do differences in these regulations lie between Western and majoritarian contexts? Engaging with these core questions and addressing various dimensions of social media content regulation through the lens of free speech remains an area yet to be fully explored in scholarship.

First, the relationship between free speech and social media must be examined. What exactly are social media platforms, and how have they evolved? How do these spaces accommodate freedom of speech and expression, and what role do they play in democratic contexts? These sub-questions are crucial for understanding the background of the problem this study seeks to address.

Second, the regulation of these social media platforms is essential to explore. Why is it necessary to regulate the content on social media platforms? What are the implications for a democratic society if content regulation is absent? How has the lack of regulation impacted various jurisdictions? Addressing these questions will help readers navigate the ongoing challenges.

Third, it is important to analyze the strengths and weaknesses of existing regulatory models. What are the current approaches to content regulation, and what are their pros and cons? How do authorities and private platforms engage with these

---

[6] *EU Code of Conduct against online hate speech,* 2016; EU Code of Practice on Disinformation, 2018.

[7] *Consolidated Industry Codes of Practice for the Online Industry*, 2021.

three broader regulatory models? Answering these questions will aid in identifying a balanced approach to social media content regulation.

Finally, the disparities between the Global North and the Majority World must be considered. Are there differences in how Western countries and the Global South regulate social media content? Do developing countries face additional challenges in building regulatory frameworks? How does the struggle to establish these frameworks create obstacles for transitional justice in the Majority World?

By examining these questions, this book aims to address a scholarly gap by analyzing regulatory models with a comparative focus on the Western and Majority world contexts. Although literature exists on the three regulatory models, this study offers a novel perspective by evaluating them through a majoritarian lens. After establishing a foundational discussion of the models, it employs a case study approach to compare how various factors and regulatory frameworks lead to differing approaches between the Western world and the Majority world, particularly regarding their implications for free speech rights.

1.5 Approach and Chapter Outline

This study investigates the variables of free speech, government authorities, and private platforms to identify the challenges associated with various regulatory models and their impact on online free speech. The book lays a foundation by first exploring the role of social media in freedom of speech (Chap. 2) and its recognition in international legal instruments (Chap. 3), underscoring the necessity of a global perspective on the Internet.

Through Chap. 4, the study then navigates through three broader regulatory models, providing readers with a clear understanding of how these models operate concerning platforms, government authorities, and the free speech rights of users. It extends the discussion to various types of intermediary liabilities related to both platforms and governments.

Chapter 5 focuses on the self-regulation model, emphasizing the role of private platforms in content moderation. It offers an in-depth analysis of the processes, pros, and cons of these measures, particularly on free speech rights. Chapter 6 explores external regulations, with a specific reference to the Chinese model, which represents an extreme form of censorship or blanket regulation. This chapter examines how such authoritarian approaches impact free speech and the flow of information online.

After discussing these models and the associated practical challenges, starting from Chap. 7, the study adopts a case study approach to explore different regulatory models developed by authorities within the three broader categories. Chapter 7 examines the U.S. Communication Decency Act—Section 230, which leans towards the self-regulation model. The following Chap. 8 investigates Germany's NetzDG—within the context of the EU, an example of external regulation.

Chapters 9 and 10 shift focus to case studies from the Majority world, highlighting challenges and differences compared to Western models. Chapter 9 analyzes India's IT Rules, a significant effort with broad provisions in the domain of social media regulation. India's case is unique due to its large market size, diverse user base, and the complex interplay between governmental approaches and public interaction with platforms. Chapter 10 examines Sri Lanka's regulatory approach as a representative case from the majority world. Sri Lanka's regulatory framework has faced criticism for heavy-handed approaches related to human rights, particularly in the post-war context. The chapter explores issues such as transitional justice, internal ethnic conflicts, and the fragile nature of Sri Lankan democracy, offering a different perspective on regulatory challenges, and examining the newly passed Online Safety Act.

Chapter 11 concludes the study by summarizing the main observations and arguments regarding content regulation and its role in either amplifying or stifling free speech. It also provides recommendations to address existing challenges in the global content regulation domain.

References

Anderson, C. (2021). Propaganda, misinformation, and histories of media techniques. *Harvard Kennedy School Misinformation Review*, 1–7.

Ayalew, Y. E. (2019). The internet shutdown muzzle (s) freedom of expression in Ethiopia: Competing narratives. *Information & Communications Technology Law, 28*(2), 208–224.

Balkin, J. M. (1999). Free speech and hostile environments. *Columbia Law Review*, 2295–2320.

Balkin, J. M. (2004). Law and liberty in virtual worlds. *New York Law School Law Review, 49*, 63–73.

Balkin, J. M. (2021). How to regulate (and not regulate) social media. *Journal of Free Speech Law*, 71–96.

Barendt, E. (2005). *Freedom of speech*. Oxford University Press.

Beacon, R. (2021, June 10). *What Is the State of Debate on Digital Democracy?* Retrieved from Tony Blair Institute for Global Change: https://institute.global/policy/what-state-debate-digital-democracy

Berg, S., & Hofmann, J. (2021). Digital democracy. *Internet Policy Review, 10*(4).

Bychawska-Siniarska, D. (2017). *Protecting the right to freedom of expression under the European convention on human rights - a handbook for legal practitioners*. Council of Europe Publishing.

Ceron, A. (2015). Internet, news, and political trust: The difference between social media and online media outlets. *Journal of Computer-Mediated Communication, 20*(5), 487–503.

Criépeau, L. (2022). Responding to deficiencies in the architecture of privacy: Co-regulation as the path forward for data protection on social networking sites. *Canadian Journal of Law and Technology, 19*(2), 411–455.

De Gregorio, G., & Stremlau, N. (2020). Internet shutdowns and the limits of law. *International Journal of Communication, 14*, 4224–4243.

Elejalde, E., Ferres, L., & Herder, E. (2018). On the nature of real and perceived bias in the mainstream media. *PLoS One, 13*(3).

Finck, M. (2018). Digital co-regulation: Designing a supranational legal framework for the platform economy. *European law Review*.

Freedom House. (2023). *Freedom on the net - 2023*. Freedom House.

Gauja, A. (2021). Digital democracy: Big technology and the regulation of politics. *University of New South Wales Law Journal, 44*(3), 959–982.

Gillespie, T. (2020). Content moderation, AI, and the question of scale. *Big Data & Society, 7*(2).

Godwin, M. (2003). *Cyber rights: Defending free speech in the digital age*. MIT press.

Gorwa, R. (2019). The platform governance triangle: Conceptualising the informal regulation of online content. *Internet Policy Review, 8*(2), 1–22.

Gorwa, R. (2024). *The politics of platform regulation: How governments shape online content moderation*. Oxford University Press.

Gorwa, R., Binns, R., & Katzenbach, C. (2020). Algorithmic content moderation: Technical and political challenges in the automation of platform governance. *Big Data & Society*, (7), 1.

Gosztonyi, G. (2020). The European court of human rights: Internet access as a means of receiving and imparting information and ideas. *International Comparative Jurisprudence, 6*(2), 134–140.

Gosztonyi, G. (2023). *Censorship from Plato to social media: The complexity of social Media's content regulation and moderation practices* (Vol. 61). Springer Nature.

Hirsch, D. D. (2010). The law and policy of online privacy: Regulation, self-regulation, or co-regulation. *Seattle University Law Review, 34*, 439–480.

Jougleux, P. (2022). *Facebook and the (EU) law. How the social network reshaped the legal framework*. Springer Nature AG.

Kentridge, S. (1996). Freedom of speech: Is it the primary right? *International & Comparative Law Quarterly, 45*(2), 253–270.

Khan, L. M. (2019). The separation of platforms and commerce. *Columbia Law Review, 119*(4), 973–1098.

Lucchi, N. (2013). Internet content governance and human rights. *Vanderbilt Journal of Entertainment and Technology Law, 16*, 809–856.

Marsden, C. T. (2004). Co-and self-regulation in European media and internet sectors: The results of Oxford University's study. *Tolleys Communications Law, 9*, 187–195.

Marsden, C. T. (2011). *Internet co-regulation: European law, regulatory governance and legitimacy in cyberspace*. Cambridge University Press.

Meiklejohn, A. (1961). The first amendment is an absolute. *The Supreme Court Review*, 245–266.

OHCHR. (2022). *Internet shutdowns: Trends, causes, legal implications and impacts on a range of human rights*. United Nations.

Reglitz, M. (2020). The human right to free internet access. *Journal of Applied Philosophy, 37*(2), 314–331.

Smet, S. (2010). Freedom of expression and the right to reputation: Human rights in conflict. *American University International Law Review, 26*(1), 183–236.

Stevens, J. P. (1993). The freedom of speech. *Yale Law Journal, 102*(6), 1293–1314.

Sullivan, K. M. (2010). Two concepts of freedom of speech. *Harvard Law Review, 124*, 143. *Two Concepts of Freedom of Speech, 124*, 143-177.

United Nations. (2019). *Promotion and protection of the right to freedom of opinion and expression*. United Nations.

Warburton, N. (2009). *Free speech: A very short introduction*. Oxford University Press.

Weber, R. H. (2010). Internet of Things–New security and privacy challenges. *Computer Law & Security Review, 26*(1), 23–30.

References

Chapter 2
The Evolution of Free Speech in the Era of Social Media

2.1 Introduction

The term "social media" was initially coined in 1994 by Darrell Berry within the Tokyo online media environment called *Matisse* (Bercovici, 2010). Defining social media is a complex task, with various perspectives proposing different definitions, and the rapidly evolving technology introducing advanced features over time. A universally accepted scholarly or colloquial definition of social media is yet to emerge. Different scholars have defined and identified social media by their function, structure, and nature.

According to Kaplan and Haenlein, social media encompasses *"a group of Internet-based applications that build on the ideological and technological foundations of Web 2.0, allowing the creation and exchange of user-generated content"* (Kaplan & Haenlein, 2010). Suggesting examples of social media such as XING, Facebook, Myspace, Google+, and studiVZ, Gebicka and Heinemann argued that social media *"are web-based services that allow individuals to construct a public or semi-public profile within a limited forum, to articulate a list of other users with whom they share a connection ('friends' on Facebook), and to view and traverse their list of connections and those made by others within the system"* (Gebicka & Heinemann, 2014).

Tuten and Solomon defined social media as *"the online means of communication, conveyance, collaboration, and cultivation among interconnected and interdependent networks of people, communities, and organizations enhanced by technological capabilities"* (Tuten et al., 2015). Anabel Quan-Haase and Lori McCay-Peet offered a definition that *"Social media are web-based services that allow individuals, communities, and organizations to collaborate, connect, interact, and build community by enabling them to create, co-create, modifies, share, and engage with user-generated content that is easily accessible"* (McCay-Peet & Quan-Haase, 2017).

S. Balendra, *Free Speech in the Puzzle of Content Regulation*, Law, Governance and Technology Series 70, https://doi.org/10.1007/978-3-031-75813-3_2

For Jack Balkin, social media serves three distinct roles: facilitating public participation, organizing public conversation, and curating public opinion (Balkin, 2021). He argues that social media plays a pivotal role in public discourse today—particularly by publishing the content of others (users). Balkin further advocates that social media's roles are crucial for a healthy public sphere, which is a space where freedom of speech thrives and the values of freedom of expression are realized (Balkin, 2021). When these values are supported and facilitated by the institute on governing the public sphere, it means the public sphere is functioning well and is healthy.

The use a broad definition of social media, using it to refer to (a) the information infrastructure and tools used to produce and distribute content that has individual value but reflects shared values; (b) the content that takes the digital form of personal messages, news, and ideas that becomes cultural products; and (c) the people, organizations, and industries that produce and consume both the tools and the content (Woolley & Howard, 2017). However, this broader definition carries danger together since it would also include encrypted messaging services such as WhatsApp, Telegram, Direct Messages on Instagram, or X (DMs), Facebook Messenger, and WeChat. Exploring free speech on social media presents a challenge when including encrypted messaging services in research because the encrypted messages are protected, making the data inaccessible for studies. Therefore, this limitation poses a challenge in producing a broader picture of the study.

Therefore, after analyzing the above definitions, this book will adopt the narrower definition of social media as platforms that allow *user-generated* content to be viewed publicly or within a private network, where the nature of the platform facilitates monitoring and supervision. This includes platforms like Facebook, Twitter, YouTube, and Instagram. Consequently, this book excludes content shared through interpersonal messaging applications, as such content is not accessible to technology platforms due to encryption and privacy considerations and thus will not be subject to moderation or content regulation. I trust this limitation will not significantly impact the study, since the content shared on the one-to-one platforms does not have the same level of exposure to a broader audience as social media, given that it is primarily shared in conversations.

2.2 The Evolution of Social Media

As social beings, humans have always sought ways to interact and communicate with others. Technology has played a pivotal role in facilitating communication among people, transcending borders, and contributing to the development of digital communities worldwide. The peak of social media occurred around 2003 in the digital arena, marking a significant shift in the landscape of communication. Before that, only a few platforms enabled communication through the facilitation of technology.

Before the advent of platforms like LiveJournal, early Internet services such as the Bulletin Board System (BBS), Prodigy, America Online (AOL), CompuServe, and later, Yahoo and MSN Messengers, played a foundational role in the evolution of online communication. These platforms primarily focused on providing personal messaging services, news updates, and other utilities to users, establishing crucial elements that would later be integral to social media. However, they do not entirely fit within the scope of social media as defined in this book, which adopts a more precise definition centered on broader social interaction and community-building features.

LiveJournal could be considered a very *early-stage* social media platform that began in 1999. The platform allowed users to share posts in a diary format within the online space. A technical term introduced by LiveJournal was "friend," which enabled users to view each other's protected entries on the platform. According to Wikipedia, "*As of 2014, LiveJournal in the United States had 10 million monthly uniques, 30 million monthly visitors, and 170 million pageviews.*"[1]

As a social media, LiveJournal has faced allegations of data breaches affecting its users[2] and has been victimized by Distributed Denial-of-Service (DDoS) attacks.[3] In 2007, the Chinese government blocked LiveJournal within its jurisdiction[4] as an extreme form of censorship. Surprisingly, LiveJournal has encountered relatively few instances of Internet censorship globally. In a landmark decision, a Russian court imposed a one-year suspended sentence on Mr. Terentyev under Article 282 of the Russian Criminal Code for his comment in a blog post published on LiveJournal (Voorhoof, 2018). However, this decision was later overturned by The European Court of Human Rights (ECtHR) in the case of *Savva Terentyev v. Russia,*[5] as it was deemed to be a violation of the right to freedom of expression under Article 10 of the European Convention on Human Rights (ECHR), provides:

> 1. Everyone has the right to freedom of expression. This right shall include freedom to hold opinions and to receive and impart information and ideas without interference by public authority and regardless of frontiers. This Article shall not prevent States from requiring the licensing of broadcasting, television, or cinema enterprises.

As the early 2000s approached, the social media landscape began to evolve rapidly with new platforms emerging to build on the foundation laid by pioneers like LiveJournal. Gosztonyi, G. pointed out that in the early to mid-2000s, the emergence of Web 2.0—which included social media, was seen as a revolutionary shift in how the Internet was used and perceived since it introduced interactive, user-

[1] See https://web.archive.org/web/20140806134445/http://www.fastcompany.com/1809674/return-livejournal.

[2] See https://www.zdnet.com/article/26-million-livejournal-credentials-leaked-online-sold-on-the-dark-web.

[3] See https://www.netcraft.com/blog/sustained-livejournal-ddos-attack-continues.

[4] See https://boingboing.net/2007/03/06/china-blocks-livejou.html.

[5] *Savva Terentyev v. Russia,* 10692/09 ECHR (2018).

generated content platforms that allowed for greater participation and collaboration (Gosztonyi, 2023).

Jougleux, P. also argues on the same point:

> The most intimate technological device in history, a companion of each moment and a vault of its owner's activities, thoughts, feelings and sentiments, the mobile phone fuses with social media in an exponential amplification of the influence of social media in the everyday life of individuals (Jougleux, 2022).

One such platform was Friendster, launched in 2002, which introduced new ways for users to connect and share media, reflecting the growing demand for more interactive and visually rich online experiences. Friendster was introduced in 2002 with features such as media sharing, including photos and videos, text posts, and the ability to link to other posts via Uniform Resource Locator (URL). Attracting a substantial market, Friendster experienced significant growth, surpassing three million users by early 2003.[6] However, due to the competitive landscape with the emergence of later social media giants, Friendster gradually faded out. In 2011, Friendster attempted a rebranding as a gaming platform[7] but eventually shut down in 2018.

Launched in 2003, MySpace remained a notable social media platform for an extended period. Particularly from 2005 to 2008, it held the distinction of being the most widely used social media platform worldwide. A key and unique feature of the platform was its ability to allow users to insert music or video into their profiles using customized Hyper Text Markup Language (HTML) coding. This feature served as a precursor to modern platforms centered around music, such as Instagram and TikTok. Despite its prolonged competition, MySpace ultimately could not sustain its dominance, facing challenges from newer social media platforms, particularly Facebook. Statistics indicate a decline of over 30 million users in 2010–11, marking a significant downturn for the platform.

Despite its prolonged competition, MySpace ultimately could not sustain its dominance, facing challenges from newer social media platforms, particularly Facebook. Statistics indicate a decline of over 30 million users in 2010–2011, marking a significant downturn for the platform.

After MySpace, modern social media platforms were introduced one after another, each serving different purposes, addressing various objectives, and providing new features and technologies. Introduced in 2003, the LinkedIn platform remains the only and biggest professional community social media platform to date. As of March 2023, over 900 million users have registered on the platform.[8] LinkedIn offers a range of features such as connection options, messaging tools, and an interactive job board. Since 2015, LinkedIn has been owned by Microsoft and

[6] See https://myaffiliaterockstar.com/how-to-crush-your-enemies-facebook-vs-friendster.

[7] See https://techwireasia.com/2011/06/friendster-relaunched-as-gaming-platform.

[8] See https://thenextscoop.com/linkedin-biggest-professional-social-media-platform/.

ceased its operations in China in 2021, citing difficulties in complying with Chinese regulatory frameworks.[9]

As professional networking solidified its place in the digital world with platforms like LinkedIn, the broader social media landscape was also transforming. In parallel, a new contender emerged that would soon redefine how people connect and share across the globe—Facebook. Launched by Mark Zuckerberg in 2004, initially to connect his Harvard Campus colleagues and friends (Boyd, 2019). It later expanded to include other colleagues, and by 2004, Facebook had amassed more than a million registered users. With its globally appealing features, Facebook reached 2.3 billion users by the end of 2018, representing half of the world's online population (Richter, 2019). Following numerous updates, Facebook currently provides facilities to publish notes, media (including music, photos, and videos), texts, advertisements, job openings, suggestions, and more. Facebook also ensures security algorithms and verification mechanisms to guarantee users' privacy and authenticity. Recently, Facebook introduced a paid-blue tick verification system for users,[10] along with additional account protection upon submission of identity documents to identify verified users. Since 2021, Facebook has been rebranded as Meta, with the goal of building the "metaverse." Facebook has experienced several data breaches worldwide, leading to numerous lawsuits and imposed penalties for their breaches. The *Cambridge Analytica* data breach (Confessore, 2018) stands out as one of the most severe in the history of social media, significantly impacting major elections, including Brexit (Ball, 2020), and the 2016 United States presidential election (Detrow, 2018). Facebook has faced bans in several countries due to controversies surrounding its content and conflicts with national public policies. Notably, countries such as Russia, China, North Korea, and others have restricted access to the platform, citing concerns over its influence on public discourse and its alignment with their regulatory frameworks.

As Facebook continued to expand its reach and influence, new platforms began to emerge, each offering unique features that catered to different aspects of social interaction. Among these, Twitter, launched in 2006 and recently rebranded as "X" by Elon Musk in July 2023,[11] holds a significant place in contemporary social media. It is predominantly used by high-profile personalities worldwide, replacing the concept of friends with a follower setup. Since Elon Musk acquired the platform in 2022, it has undergone major updates and changes. By the end of 2022, Twitter introduced paid blue tick verifications for its users.[12] Comparatively, Twitter has faced very minimal data breach allegations but remains subject to controversies, such as the banning of the account of the former President of the United States,

[9] See https://www.bbc.com/news/technology-58911297.

[10] See https://www.hindustantimes.com/technology/meta-announces-paid-blue-verification-tick-on-facebook-and-instagram-details-101676822202511.html.

[11] See https://www.cnn.com/2023/07/24/tech/twitter-rebrands-x-elon-musk-hnk-intl/index.html/.

[12] See https://www.thehindu.com/sci-tech/technology/twitter-launches-8-monthly-subscription-with-blue-checkmark/article66101737.ece.

Donald Trump.[13] To date, Twitter boasts approximately 450 million active users, solidifying its position as a major player in the social media landscape.

While platforms like Twitter revolutionized real-time communication and public engagement, the rise of video content began to reshape the way people consumed and shared information online. Leading this shift was YouTube, which quickly became the go-to platform for video streaming after its launch in 2005 and acquired by Google in 2006, stands as the most popular video-streaming website. Undergoing several updates over time, the platform allows users to upload video content, comment on videos, express preferences through likes or dislikes, and subscribe to channels. With more than 2.70 billion active users as of 2023, YouTube offers viewers the opportunity to watch a vast array of videos for free. Launched in 2017, TikTok has rapidly emerged as one of the fastest-growing social media platforms, facilitating the sharing of short-form video content with its audience. However, due to criticisms related to privacy and cybersecurity risks, as well as its ties to China, numerous governments are in the process of blocking the application within their jurisdictions.[14]

In addition to these widely used social media for content sharing, Instagram—a platform that facilitates the sharing of media, including photos and videos, along with messaging—Thread, introduced by Meta recently in July 2023, enables users to primarily share text updates and join conversations. Snapchat, an application that allows the sharing of short-form content with *"friends,"* incorporates the use of multiple filters. Pinterest, a platform that facilitates the sharing of images and allows users to "*pin*" them to collections, is also widely used by a considerable number of users today.

Social media have a long history, not only in terms of the number of platforms involved but also concerning the updates they periodically implement. These technical updates and features enable users to share their ideas, thoughts, and personal updates from their accounts across various platforms, facilitating the flow of information and amplifying users' freedom of speech and expression.

2.3 Free Speech on Social Media

The advent of "Information and Communication Technology" has an effect on almost all the spheres of human life (Soorya, 2021), and the enjoyment of fundamental human rights is not an exception to it. The right to free speech, as one of the widely recognized human rights, has undoubtedly amplified with the development of information technology, particularly after the evolution of social media.

[13] See https://www.bbc.com/news/technology-55657417.

[14] See https://apnews.com/article/tiktok-ban-privacy-cybersecurity-bytedance-china-2dce297f0aed056efe53309bbcd44a04.

In examining the question of the prohibition of sex offenders from accessing various websites as a violation of the *First Amendment* to the Constitution of the United States, the Supreme Court, in the case of *Packingham v. North Carolina*[15] addressed social media as the modern public square explaining,

> These websites can provide perhaps the most powerful mechanisms available to a private citizen to make his or her voice heard.[16]

Social media, as the new avenue, accommodates the content shared by the users—the individuals become journalists—citizens' journalism in the modern era. This nature of social media has paved the way to the contribution towards the emergence and development of digital democracy (Ashwin, 2022). As the term "democracy" denotes the participation of people, social media has tremendously facilitated participation in the electronic form. It has paved the way for the creation of a new form of democracy—digital democracy (Bastien et al., 2020) (also known as e-democracy).

On the outreach of the content shared across the social platforms, Guiora and Park argue that:

> The later social media platforms disseminate information almost instantaneously to a vast audience and inevitably have the impact to marginalize those targeted by the speech (Guiora & Park, 2017).

Digital democracy is an emerging idea that believes, because of Information and Technology innovation, online spaces have replaced physical spaces as venues for political argument and social interaction (Papacharissi, 2010). Digital tools have both democratized access to information and created barriers, transforming how people, engage with the world. As online spaces have broadened and deepened participation, while others talk of promoting empowerment by enabling citizens to make decisions directly through online tools (Simon et al., 2017)—as the practice of democracy using digital tools and technologies.

In addition to mainstream media, the role of social media and its contents in amplifying movements promoting Human Rights, Sustainability, and Good Governance has been immense in the recent past (Granillo, 2020). Although social media platforms were initially developed and influenced by Western jurisprudence, their contemporary engagement extends globally, reaching across regions from the West to the Global South. For example, the contents shared during the recent "fall of Kabul" (Afghanistan) and the role of the International Community,[17] the Easter Sunday Attacks, and the Constitutional Coup against the Government of Sri Lanka (Democracy Reporting International, 2019) are a few incidents where the social media contents have amplified the issue in a global scale in advocating for the values of human rights, rule of law, and democracy.

---

[15] *Packingham v. North Carolina*, 582 U.S. 98 (2017).

[16] Ibid., p. 1736.

[17] See https://timesofindia.indiatimes.com/videos/news/watch-visuals-of-kabuls-fall-to-taliban-go-viral-on-social-media/videoshow/85367308.cms.

2.3.1 Election Campaigning

Elections are a pivotal part of the political process in a democracy, and the fair and free nature of elections is fundamentally important in the realm of electoral democracy. The ubiquitous nature of the Internet and social media allows the candidates and the political party to communicate their agendas and ideologies with the voters and the international community across the globe. Social media platforms have become the paradigm for political campaigning, accommodating various forms, such as posts, tweets, videos, and sometimes commercials. Additionally, these social media sites facilitate the organization of physical campaigning, the mobilization of communities, the recruitment of volunteers, fundraising efforts, and interactions with the public. This phenomenon has been observed globally during electoral periods, including in jurisdictions such as the United States (U.S.), the United Kingdom (U.K.), Italy, India, and many others.

In the U.S., in what now seems a long time ago, Barack Obama's first presidential campaign in 2008 strategically leveraged the potential of social media sites, recognizing a shift from conventional media to these platforms. Evidently, around 74% of Internet users sought election news online during Obama's initial campaign. Aaron Smith writes that this is the first time more than half the voting-age population used the Internet to connect to the political process during an election cycle (Smith, 2019). Instrumentalizing the Internet during a campaign is a great example of how social media can be used as a tool to assist governance. Beyond conventional media, social media platforms provide individuals with the opportunity to interact with shared content through comments and retweets. As a result, candidates employ various strategies in their social media campaigns. It is noted that Clinton's campaign strategy was rooted in traditional media, while Trump adopted a more informal style, with a predominant focus on social media outlets (Marx, 2017; Phillips, 2024).

However, a recent study by Fujiwara et al. found that Twitter had a negative impact on the Republican Party's vote share in both the 2016 and 2020 U.-S. presidential elections, pointing out:

> This pattern of results suggests that, in 2016 and 2020, Twitter became a vehicle for spreading opinions, particularly from Democratic-slanted users, on Trump. This may, in turn, have persuaded voters with weaker priors—independents and perhaps more moderate Republicans—to vote against Trump in the presidential election (Fujiwara et al., 2024).

This conclusion challenges the widely accepted narrative that social media played a central role in Donald Trump's electoral victories. Instead, the evidence suggests that social media users were less inclined to vote for Trump in 2016 and were also less likely to hold polarized political views.

Observing a similar trend, the political parties in India, particularly during the 2019 general elections, adapted to the growing influence of social media, targeting the approximately 15 million voters aged between 18 to 19 years. The BJP, led by Prime Minister Narendra Modi, embraced routinized communication through social media, significantly contributing to political agenda-building, policy crowdsourcing, and publicity, evident in pan-India campaigns like *Swachh Bharat* (Clean India) and the *Fit India Movement* (Rao, 2019). After declaring in 2017 that the 2019 election would be fought on smartphones, Modi and the BJP won their second term with a full majority in 2019 (Bansal, 2019).

Sharma rightly pointed out the difference in approaches between the 2014 and 2019 elections, wherein Narendra Modi was a first-time candidate, arguing that:

> "It is plausible that populist communication will not adhere to one ideology or strategy per leader in an online age. As a first-time contender for the post, Modi used the populist strategy of attacking elites, positioning himself as a savior of the people, and presenting himself as a development guru, among other tactics. As an incumbent, he shifted his populist strategy to focus on establishing an emotional connection and promoting his own image online, while still attacking elites and political rivals (albeit on a smaller scale)" (Sharma, 2022).

Social media campaigns gradually became a crucial tool in election strategies, particularly following the BJP's successful campaign in the 2019 general elections. Sarma and Hazarika explain that, consequently, for the 2021 Assam assembly election, the BJP invested heavily in social media advertising, focusing their online campaign strategy on highlighting their achievements since the 2016 victory and portraying Assam as a progressive state under their governance (Sarma & Hazarika, 2023).

A study of the 2019 U.K. general election revealed that online sources, including news websites and social media, were more widely used than any other source (Fletcher et al., 2020). Conventional media was more popular among the older audience, while the younger generation consumed more information from online platforms. Similarly, another study conducted by Bright et al. identified that broadcast communication on social media is likely to remain a prominent feature of local electoral campaigns (Bright et al., 2020). Particularly, Twitter contributes to the increasing localism within electoral politics, where national campaigns are reframed to address local issues.

Wring and Ward pointed out this trend:

> Digital platforms continue to grow and are now as integral to campaigning as they are to journalism. The notion of a distinct so-called "internet election" is redundant; the 2019 campaign experienced flows of information between online, social and traditional news media, and vice-versa (Wring & Ward, 2020).

Beyond serving as platforms for electoral campaigns, social media played an active role in countering misinformation during the election timeline. For example, as Vaccari et al. point out in their study, the UK's main independent fact-checker, Full Fact, is a small charity organization with only a handful of staff that partnered with Facebook as a Third Party Fact Checker during the 2019 general election and was frequently cited by journalists in their campaign coverage (Vaccari et al., 2023).

In Italy, the decline in popularity of traditional Italian news media is attributed to poor journalistic practices. Time Magazine in 2009 labeled Italian newspapers as *"untrusted sources,"* criticizing their insular reporting and lack of background in stories, catering to an elite rather than the general public. Marco Alloni adds that Italian journalism often reduces news to political gossip, failing to engage the electorate meaningfully. Michele Serra criticizes the practice of *"ambush"* journalism in political reporting, which sacrifices in-depth analysis of complex issues for quick, sensational stories (LSE Blog, 2013). On this backdrop, social media provided an effective alternative to the public. The impact of Beppe Grillo's *Movimento 5 Stelle* (Five Star Movement) during the 2013 Italian elections serves as compelling evidence of the multiplier effects of social media campaigns (Davies, 2014). In the 2013 elections, the party secured 25.6% of the vote and became the second largest party in Italy.

With this foundation, the contemporary political landscape of Italy reveals that social media communication is increasingly becoming a powerful tool for political leaders to gain momentum in electoral campaigns. Leaders use social media to influence mainstream media, implement their agendas, make their issues central to political debate, garner public support by spreading their messages, and engage supporters in campaigning (Bracciale et al., 2023). As evidence of user engagement with social media content related to political parties, a recent study by Ceron et al. demonstrated that Facebook posts explicitly referencing crises or using crisis rhetoric are associated with higher levels of user engagement. The study found that citizens are particularly attentive to emergencies and closely monitor how political parties respond to various crises (Ceron et al., 2024).

In the current trend, during the election period, social media has become a paradigm for political communication, allowing diverse forms of content sharing and fostering engagement with the public—an essential in free and fair elections. From the perspective of candidates, voters, and democratic countries, social media play a significant role in reaching a wider audience, distributing content, mobilizing, and engaging through various features of these platforms, understanding the pulse and the trends of the current generation of voters.

2.3.2 Political Discussions

In today's world, the traditional format of in-person discussions has become more nuanced and complex, often subject to various restrictions, such as those imposed for safety and public health reasons. For instance, physical political discussions are typically limited to a certain number of attendees. However, the transition to digital platforms has significantly enriched political discourse worldwide. This shift introduces a new paradigm, leveraging virtual tools like social media and online meeting platforms such as Zoom, which offer greater convenience, accessibility, and cost-effectiveness. This transformation is particularly noteworthy in weak democratic states or those with vulnerable human rights jurisprudence. The shift has tremendously contributed to bringing forth arguments, dissenting voices, and speeches onto the online sphere through social media.

Not only during electoral periods, but online social media spaces also accommodate public participation in expressing political views. Replacing mass or conventional media, social websites have become tools for individuals. In 2015, Barack Obama's State of the Union address grabbed the attention of social media users, and there were around 2.6 million tweets in this context (Twitter, 2015). The expression of views has significantly captured the attention of the global community (Bailo, 2013). Observatories, as well as human rights organizations, consistently consider such matters and respond when there are violations against human rights, democratic values, or the rule of law.

Shirazi points out about the movements amplified across the Middle East and North Africa (MENA) region:

> Despite the differences in each of these countries' level of social, cultural, political and economic developments, the events in the MENA region share many similarities and characteristics including the massive presence of youths and women in street demonstrations and the widespread use of the internet, including the use of social media web sites as a communication channel for organizing protest events (Shirazi, 2013).

#BlackLivesMatter is a pivotal social media movement that has heightened discussions on police brutality and racial abuse against the black community. The movement originated in the aftermath of the acquittal of George Zimmerman in the shooting death of Trayvon Martin in 2012. Over time, it evolved into a national voice, gaining prominence on various occasions. In 2020, the movement experienced a significant surge, particularly after a video depicting police officer Derek Chauvin kneeling on the neck of a black man, George Floyd, went viral. This incident propelled the movement to a global scale, connecting millions of users on social media platforms (Buchanan et al., 2020).

In 2017, the #MeToo movement went viral globally, gaining significant traction, particularly among Black and Brown women. Founded in 2006 by Tarana Burke, the movement aimed to support survivors of sexual violence, with a specific focus on young women. While the reception of this movement in America has been varied, marked by both support and opposition, its impact has been notably influential in Global South countries (Brown, 2022). Particularly, India serves as a significant example, where millions of people shared their experiences of surviving sexual harassment on social media following the peak of the #MeToo movement in October 2017. Many of these accounts emerged from the media and entertainment industries (Marathe, 2020). These movements have also brought attention to and criticized the framework, enforcement mechanisms, and lacunas of Indian Sexual Harassment Laws.

In response to the urgent need to protect the Earth and address climate change, the #FridaysForFuture movement was initiated by then-15-year-old Greta Thunberg and other young activists in 2018 (Igini, 2022). The movement quickly garnered global attention, coinciding with an era that demands necessary climate actions. In September 2021, protests were organized in 1400 locations worldwide, attracting the participation of over four million people (Mlaba, 2021). As of August 2023, the movement marked its fifth anniversary and is recognized as one of the most successful global movements, overcoming the challenges posed by the COVID-19 pandemic, which affected in-person gatherings for a few years (Euronews Green, 2023).

Social media has become a pivotal platform in facilitating political discussions, especially after the COVID-19 outbreak and the subsequent restrictions on social movements imposed by authorities. Additionally, in fragile democratic states, these platforms have played a crucial role in amplifying suppressed voices that are stifled through various in-person measures.

2.3.3 Cyber Governance

Particularly after the COVID-19 pandemic, governments across the world are slowly moving into cyber governance in their administrative, governmental, and judicial functions. In such background, social media with advanced features contribute to the wider population in assisting these mechanisms without any delay or interruptions.

As the world transitions into digital governance, social media handles play an integral role in advancing cyber governance across multiple layers. Primarily, these platforms empower the public to interact with governments, contributing to the sharing and facilitation of various administrative and governmental functions. For instance, in the communication of emergencies, weather conditions, and service interruptions, social media handles serve as efficient tools to disseminate information rapidly to a broad audience, functioning as a one-to-many communication tool. The provision of real-time information enhances community safety by delivering alerts, evacuation orders, and other essential information swiftly and effectively (Barnhart, 2022).

While social media became prominent in the dissemination of news and updates across the public, in August 2023, in response to new legislation, Meta removed news stories from Facebook and Instagram, blocking users in Canada from sharing news links, including important updates about ongoing wildfires in Kelowna, British Columbia, and Yellowknife. Prime Minister Trudeau criticized Meta's action as unacceptable, highlighting that it prevents fair compensation for local journalists reporting on critical events like wildfires, and restricts access to news on its platforms.[18]

In contemporary times, these platforms play a crucial role in facilitating virtual meetings for government representatives, especially amid the COVID-19 pandemic outbreak and the corresponding measures implemented. For example, in 2020, the Government of Canada organized a virtual meeting through Facebook Live featuring the Prime Minister and Deputy Prime Minister, allowing real-time interaction with citizens.[19]

Social media features, including the ability to create surveys, questions, and polls, empower governments to collect feedback from citizens when formulating policies, projects, and addressing ongoing issues. An illustrative example is the City of

[18] See https://www.cbc.ca/news/politics/trudeau-meta-wildfires-news-1.6942458.

[19] See https://www.facebook.com/watch/?ref=embed_video&v=197614948519509.

New York, which utilizes platforms like Twitter to invite residents to participate in surveys on significant occasions.[20] These advanced features enable governments to gain insights into the concerns and opinions of the public, facilitating the development of tailored policies for communities.

Social media serve as a boon for cyber governance by addressing delayed responses in traditional government systems. Post-pandemic, countries worldwide have transitioned to online services, particularly in processes such as registrations, obtaining certifications, and reserving government services in person. These digital arrangements not only enhance the efficiency of services but also save considerable time for the public.

2.4 Free Speech As a *"Double Edged Sword"*

The debate surrounding free speech on social media exemplifies the quintessential *double-edged* sword for public discourse. On one hand, the unprecedented freedom of expression and access these platforms provide has democratized information dissemination, empowering individuals worldwide, a few of them are discussed above. Yet, this very freedom breeds significant challenges, particularly as the darker, unchecked aspects of these platforms come to light. The informational chaos resulting from such unfettered expression, as studies have shown (Cinelli et al., 2020; Prier, 2020), poses a substantial threat to democratic values.

It is not merely the existence of specific threats within the digital sphere that concerns scholars and policymakers, but the broader implications of unchecked freedom. This includes the rampant dissemination of false information (Baek et al., 2019) and the proliferation of hate speech, which undermine the very foundations of democratic societies. The consequences of such unrestricted sharing are not trivial, occasionally leading to severe societal rifts. These issues underscore the growing discourse on the necessity of regulating social media, highlighting a critical juncture in balancing the benefits of free expression with the imperative to protect democratic integrity and social harmony.

While social media accommodate and amplify free speech values, they also present significant challenges to democracy due to their wide range of free access. Despite offering unprecedented freedom and access, these platforms contribute to the spread of *"informational chaos,"* posing a threat to democratic societies. Key issues include the proliferation of disinformation content that is intentionally false or manipulated and misinformation, which consists of unintentional errors. These

[20] See https://twitter.com/nycgov/status/1602754474791116803?ref_src=twsrc%5Etfw%7Ctwcamp%5Etweetembed%7Ctwterm%5E1602754474791116803%7Ctwgr%5E138f73ab3d7ff9ea409d4d15faf2a92fb40341ca%7Ctwcon%5Es1_&ref_url=https%3A%2F%2Fstatusbrew.com%2Finsights%2Fsocial-media-for-government%2F.

problems, along with the spread of untrue statements and hate speech, pose critical challenges to democratic values and processes.

Lidsky points out, the unmediated nature of social media speech significantly heightens its potential to incite violence (Lidsky, 2011). Galli et al. argue problems related to unauthorized publication, copyright violations, privacy breaches, and data protection can arise, while further issues may include the distribution of unlawful or antisocial content, such as hate speech, child pornography, incitement to crime, libel, slander, fake news, and content promoting incivility, aggression, or cruelty (Galli et al., 2022).

Gillespie, T. identified the reasons why social media pose challenges in terms of public and policy concerns, noted:

> Public and policy concerns around illicit content, at first largely focused on sexually explicit and graphically violent images, have expanded in recent years: to include with additional categories like hate speech, self-harm, and extremism; and to deal with the enormous problem of user behavior targeting other users, including misogynistic, racist, and homophobic attacks, trolling, harassment, and threats of violence (Gillespie, 2017).

However, these standards often vary among jurisdictions worldwide, as each is influenced by its own culture, lifestyle, and traditions. For example, as Suzor points out, Europeans generally tolerate sex and nudity more than Americans, who are more accepting of violence and hate (Suzor, 2019).

Prohibited content on social media not only impacts personal rights and affects Internet safety but also significantly erodes culture, morals, and values across borders.

Suzor further mentions:

> Others believe in a democratic right to create cultural rules that reflect our collective moral values, rules that signal that their society does not tolerate hate speech, pornography, sacrilege, or violence, for example. These moral claims are not generally based on harm to any individual, but in a sense that certain types of content are harmful to a society's collective moral well-being (Suzor, 2019).

This section highlights the discussion on the flip side of free speech and expression, particularly within the realm of democratic society.

2.4.1 As a Tool of Manipulation

While social media is recognized as a platform that facilitates the dissemination of information during crises and in democratic environments, its free-flowing nature has also made it susceptible to the manipulation of information. This manipulation, especially during electoral periods, has significant detrimental effects.

In this chapter, I have previously discussed how these platforms have enabled features that allow candidates and voters to connect virtually. This section analyzes how social media have been inciteful during electoral periods, thereby negatively impacting the democratic process.

A prominent illustration of social media's impact on manipulating elections is evident in the 2016 United States presidential election. In 2017, The New York Times reported that Facebook acknowledged companies linked to Russia had purchased $100,000 worth of ads with the intent of disseminating *disinformation and propaganda* (Shane & Goel, 2017). The role of Facebook, including the potential imposition of civil liability, became a focal point of discussion. Also, the Cambridge Analytica Scandal, involving the use of harvested data from over 50 million Facebook users to target and manipulate content, campaigns, and advertisements toward American voters, significantly influenced the 2016 election results (Ghosh & Scott, 2018).

This manipulation of information through social media poses a serious threat to democracy, as online platforms emerge as new avenues for expressing democratic values in the information era. A 2020 Oxford study revealed that 76 countries worldwide, including the United States and the United Kingdom, employed disinformation and media manipulation as part of their campaigns (Bradshaw et al., 2021).

In Russia, the social media platform *VKontakte* was utilized to promote or discredit candidates, targeting a domestic audience (Fredheim et al., 2022). Similar tactics were observed during the conflict between Russia and Ukraine, where posts were shared to discredit either party in the war and capture global attention (Al-Saied, 2023).

In the digital age, social media information manipulation has reached new heights with the advent of Artificial Intelligence (AI). AI-powered bots and fake accounts now play a substantial role in manipulating information through social media channels. Authors have voiced criticism regarding the efficacy of existing content moderation frameworks in effectively addressing these challenges (Ienca, 2023). A recent study has identified that 57 countries have employed bots to disseminate disinformation through social media (Bradshaw et al., 2021).

On one hand, the free flow of information across social media, and the unlimited, easy access have been used as a tool of manipulation in a number of occasions, with the advanced features of technology. They leverage the ease with which information can be disseminated to achieve their goals, whether political, economic, or social. This underscores the need to reconsider regulating the content and information shared across social media to make the Internet more resilient.

2.4.2 Scaling up the Tensions Among Communities

The widespread nature of social media often becomes the avenue to disseminate and share content, intensifying tensions among different communities. On such occasions, it leads to communal clashes, extremist violations, and many threats against public order and national security. These results occur due to external factors and internal elements of the platforms, such as Filter Bubbles, Algorithmic Amplification, and Polarization.

Social media has been utilized as a platform for expressing individual ideas and opinions. However, it has also been exploited by various organizations and individuals to disseminate content that fuels communal, racist, and sociological tensions. This content often takes the form of misinformation, prejudice, and xenophobia. The dissemination of such material goes beyond the boundaries of the platforms and spills over into the public domain. The threats posed by these conflict drivers are exacerbated by the content circulated on social media, significantly impacting fragile democratic states such as South Sudan, Ethiopia, Myanmar, and Nigeria.

In Russia, authorities tightened legal restrictions on organizations labeled as "*undesirable*," "extremist," and "foreign agents," leading to heightened Internet and social media censorship and the shutdown of the notable human rights group Memorial International. Like the fragile democratic States, Russia also extensively restricts the Internet platforms—predominantly social media from public access. Since the 2014 Russian invasion of Ukraine, pervasive propaganda and political repression have significantly stifled open and free private discourse. This effect is worsened by increasing state attempts to regulate online expression. Authorities have introduced laws that penalize actions such as insulting the state, spreading misinformation, committing libel, and discussing personal details of judges and law enforcement on social media, among others, to curb and penalize dissent (Freedom House, 2023).

In a recent study examining the Russian Case Laws in the backdrop of the Russia-Ukraine war, Sherstoboeva points out:

> During the initial phase of the war in 2022–2023, Russian judicial application of fake news bans and their legal parameters, despite their vagueness, uniformly and systemically interpreted law in favour of the government's interference with freedom of expression (Sherstoboeva, 2024).

Sherstoboeva further argues that Russian courts have manipulated legal interpretations to favor the government's narrative and suppress dissent, particularly regarding the war in Ukraine, by making "truth" conditional—alterable or dismissible based on the government's interests and demanding unconditional loyalty to the state, which has effectively monopolized public discourse and led to labeling dissenting views as "fake news" or expressions of "hatred towards Russia," thereby stifling free speech and independent journalism (Sherstoboeva, 2024).

Few other studies also point out that during the invasion of Ukraine in 2022, Russia controlled social media, and created targeted efforts to spread *pro-Russian* narratives on the platforms. These narratives have played a significant role in international law and international affairs. For example, a study conducted by Geissler et al. illustrated that Bots were pivotal in disseminating pro-Russian messages, making up over 20% of the spreaders, especially early in the diffusion process. Many were created at the invasion's outset, significantly boosting pro-Russian content. This effect was notably strong in countries like India, South Africa, and Pakistan, which abstained from a UN vote condemning the invasion (Geissler et al., 2023). Russian approach towards social media is not only repressive but also invading the platforms' spaces and creating massive Infodemics across the world favoring *pro-Russian* narratives.

In India, the extensive social media outreach employed by the Bharatiya Janata Party (BJP) as part of its election strategy has made social media a contested space (Bhatnagar, 2022). The platform is frequently used for the publication and dissemination of Hindu nationalism, contributing to *anti-Muslim* and *anti-Christian* sentiments that, in turn, lead to communal tensions across the country. The digital discussions often revolve around fears of the perceived loss of Hindu identity, seeking support for Hinduism concepts and the BJP (Bhatia, 2022). However, this approach inadvertently results in heightened tensions among various societies and communities in India.

In the aftermath of the Easter Sunday attacks and hotel bombings claimed by ISIS in Sri Lanka in 2019,[21] disturbing content was widely shared on social media, targeting the Muslim community (Minority Rights Group, 2019). This influx of content significantly heightened racial tensions in Sri Lanka, a nation that had recently emerged from a prolonged internal conflict and was undergoing a transitional justice era. Notably, not only the general public but also certain extremist politicians and religious leaders from the majority communities propagated hateful content against the Muslim community.

For example, a study conducted by Democracy Reporting International identified:

> A photo posted on the "Sinhala Buddhist" page and presumably showing a young Muslim woman sitting on a Buddha statue generated the highest number of shares exceeding 38,000. The text accompanying the post says "This woman is sitting on the lotus base of the respected Buddha statue. Whether they worship statues or not is irrelevant to us. But disrespecting our teacher is not acceptable." This post entails misleading content because it does not provide any context (when, where, is it real?) and assumes malicious intentions on the part of the women, while generalising the behaviour of one individual to represent the entire community of Sri Lankan Muslims (Democracy Reporting International, 2019).

This troubling trend persisted even during the COVID-19 pandemic, following the Easter Sunday attacks. Incidents ranged from attacks on the houses of Muslim communities in Sri Lanka (Amnesty International, 2020) to controversial practices such as the cremation of the first Muslim COVID-19 patient (Haaris, 2020).

Social media, due to its open nature, freely provides access to all users and significantly contributes to information sharing worldwide by amplifying free speech. However, from the flip side, the serious challenges, and repercussions it presents to the democratic community highlight the need for cyberspace to be more responsible and ethical. This discussion underscores the necessity of regulating social media to mitigate the negative impact of social media content on communal harmony. While free speech is an integral part of a democratic society, dangerous speech should be stifled through legal measures and regulatory mechanisms.

[21] See https://edition.cnn.com/interactive/2019/04/world/sri-lanka-attacks.

References

Al-Saied, N. (2023, Mar 12). *Social media as a propaganda tool in the Russia-Ukraine Conflict*. Retrieved from The Cairo Review: https://www.thecairoreview.com/essays/social-media-as-a-propaganda-tool-in-the-russia-ukraine-conflict

Amnesty International. (2020). *From burning houses to burning bodies: Anti-Muslim violence, discrimination and harassment in Sri Lanka*. Amnesty International.

Ashwin. (2022, March 28). *Role of Social Media in a Democracy*. Retrieved from Enhelion Blogs: https://enhelion.com/blogs/2022/03/28/role-of-social-media-in-a-democracy

Baek, Y. M., Kang, H., & Kim, S. (2019). Fake news should be regulated because it influences both "others" and "me": How and why the influence of presumed influence model should be extended. *Mass Communication and Society, 22*(3), 301–323.

Bailo, F. (2013, June 9). *Social media and political engagement in the World Today*. Retrieved from Australian Institute of International Affairs: https://www.internationalaffairs.org.au/australianoutlook/social-media-and-political-engagement-in-the-world-today

Balkin, J. M. (2021). How to regulate (and not regulate) social media. *Journal of Free Speech Law, 1*, 71–96.

Ball, J. (2020, Oct 11). *The real story of Cambridge Analytica and Brexit*. Retrieved from The Spectator: https://www.spectator.co.uk/article/were-there-any-links-between-cambridge-analytica-russia-and-brexit

Bansal, S. (2019, June 12). *How the BJP used technology to Secure Modi's Second Win*. Retrieved from Centre for International Governance Innovation: https://www.cigionline.org/articles/how-bjp-used-technology-secure-modis-second-win

Barnhart, B. (2022, Jan 13). *Social media and government: How to keep citizens engaged*. Retrieved from Sprout Social: https://sproutsocial.com/insights/social-media-and-government

Bastien, F., Koop, R., Small, T. A., Giasson, T., & Jansen, H. (2020). The role of online technologies and digital skills in the political participation of citizens with disabilities. *Journal of Information Technology & Politics, 17*, 218–231.

Bercovici, J. (2010, Dec 09). *Who coined social media? Web pioneers compete for credit*. Retrieved from Forbes: https://www.forbes.com/sites/jeffbercovici/2010/12/09/who-coined-social-media-web-pioneers-compete-for-credit/?sh=6998344151d5

Bhatia, K. V. (2022). Hindu nationalism online: Twitter as discourse and interface. *Religions, 13*(8), 739–755.

Bhatnagar, S. (2022). Social media and Hindu extremism in India. In I. A. Ahmed (Ed.), *Religion, extremism and violence in South Asia* (pp. 79–99). Palgrave Macmillan.

Boyd, J. (2019, Jan 25). *The History of Facebook: From BASIC to Global Giant*. Retrieved from Brand Watch: https://www.brandwatch.com/blog/history-of-facebook.

Bracciale, R., Andretta, M., & Martella, A. (2023). Does populism go viral? How Italian leaders engage citizens through social media. In D. Mercea (Ed.), *Understanding movement parties through their communication* (pp. 151–168). Routledge.

Bradshaw, S., Bailey, H., & Howard, P. N. (2021). *Industrialized disinformation: 2020 global inventory of organized social media manipulation*. Computational Propaganda Project at the Oxford Internet Institute.

Bright, J., Hale, S., Ganesh, B., Bulovsky, A., Margetts, H., & Howard, P. (2020). Does campaigning on social media make a difference? Evidence from candidate use of twitter during the 2015 and 2017 U.K. elections. *Communication Research, 47*(7), 988–1009.

Brown, A. (2022, Sept 29). *More Than Twice as Many Americans Support Than Oppose the #MeToo Movement*. Retrieved from Pew Research Center: https://www.pewresearch.org/social-trends/2022/09/29/more-than-twice-as-many-americans-support-than-oppose-the-metoo-movement

Buchanan, L., Bui, Q., & Patel, J. K. (2020, July 3). *The New York Times*. Retrieved from Black Lives Matter May Be the Largest Movement in U.S. History: https://www.nytimes.com/interactive/2020/07/03/us/george-floyd-protests-crowd-size.html

Ceron, A., Berloto, S., & Rosco, J. (2024). What are crises for? The effects on users' engagement in the 2022 Italian Election. *Politics and Governance.*

Cinelli, M., Quattrociocchi, W., Galeazzi, A., Valensise, C. M., Brugnoli, E., Schmidt, A. L., et al. (2020). Scientific reports. *The COVID-19 Social Media Infodemic, 10*(1), 1–10.

Confessore, N. (2018, Apr 4). *Cambridge Analytica and Facebook: The Scandal and the Fallout So Far.* Retrieved from The New York Times: https://www.nytimes.com/2018/04/04/us/politics/cambridge-analytica-scandal-fallout.html

Davies, R. (2014). *Social media in election campaigning.* European Parliamentary Research Service.

Democracy Reporting International. (2019). *Social media analysis: What Facebook tells us about social cohesion in Sri Lanka.* Democracy Reporting International.

Detrow, S. (2018, Mar 20). *Cambridge analytica and Facebook: The Scandal and the Fallout So Far.* Retrieved from National Public Radio: https://www.npr.org/2018/03/20/595338116/what-did-cambridge-analytica-do-during-the-2016-election

Euronews Green. (2023, Aug 21). *From solo protest to global movement: Five years of Fridays for Future in pictures.* Retrieved from Euro News: https://www.euronews.com/green/2023/08/21/from-solo-protest-to-global-movement-five-years-of-fridays-for-future-in-pictures

Fletcher, R., Newman, N., & Schulz, A. (2020). A mile wide, an inch deep: Online news and media use in the 2019 UK general election. *Available at SSRN 3582441.*

Fredheim, R., Bay, S., Dek, A., Stolze, M., & Haiduchyk, T. (2022). *Social media manipulation 2022/2023: Assessing the ability of social media companies to combat platform manipulation.* NATO Strategic Communications Centre of Excellence.

Freedom House. (2023). *Freedom in The World 2022: Russia.* Retrieved from Freedom House: https://freedomhouse.org/country/russia/freedom-world/2022

Fujiwara, T., Müller, K., & Schwarz, C. (2024). The effect of social media on elections: Evidence from the United States. *Journal of the European Economic Association, 22*(3), 1495–1539.

Galli, F., Loreggia, A., & Sartor, G. (2022). The regulation of content moderation. In *International conference on the legal challenges of the fourth industrial revolution* (pp. 63–87). Springer International Publishing.

Gebicka, A., & Heinemann, A. (2014). Social Media & Competition law. *World Competition, 37*(2), 149–172.

Geissler, D., Bär, D., Pröllochs, N., & Feuerriegel, S. (2023). Russian propaganda on social media during the 2022 invasion of Ukraine. *EPJ Data Science, 12*(1), 35–54.

Ghosh, D., & Scott, B. (2018, Mar 19). *Facebook's New Controversy Shows How Easily Online Political Ads Can Manipulate You.* Retrieved from Time: https://time.com/5197255/facebook-cambridge-analytica-donald-trump-ads-data

Gillespie, T. (2017). Governance of and by platforms. *SAGE handbook of social media*, 254–278.

Gosztonyi, G. (2023). *Censorship from Plato to social media: The complexity of social Media's content regulation and moderation practices* (Vol. 61). Springer Nature.

Granillo, G. (2020, June 10). *The role of social media in social movements.* Retrieved from Portland Monthly: https://www.pdxmonthly.com/news-and-city-life/2020/06/the-role-of-social-media-in-social-movements

Guiora, A., & Park, E. A. (2017). Hate speech on social media. *Philosophia, 45*, 957–971.

Haaris, M. (2020, Apr 2). *Anti-muslim hatred: Clouding the fight against corona!* Retrieved from Colombo Telegraph: https://www.colombotelegraph.com/index.php/anti-muslim-hatred-clouding-the-fight-against-corona

Ienca, M. (2023). On artificial intelligence and manipulation. *Topoi, 42*(3), 833–842.

Igini, M. (2022, Mar 25). *Fridays for future: How young climate activists are making their voices heard.* Retrieved from Earth.Org: https://earth.org/fridays-for-future

Jougleux, P. (2022). *Facebook and the EU law: How the social network reshaped the legal framework.* Springer.

Kaplan, A. M., & Haenlein, M. (2010). Users of the world, unite! The challenges and opportunities of social media. *Business Horizons, 53*(1), 59–68.

Lidsky, L. B. (2011). Incendiary speech and social media. *Texas Tech Law Review, 44*, 147–164.

LSE Blog. (2013, Apr 26). *Italian journalism is the real loser from Italy's elections*. Retrieved from LSE Blog: https://blogs.lse.ac.uk/europpblog/2013/04/26/italian-journalism-is-the-real-loser-from-italys-elections

Marathe, H. (2020, Oct 14). *"No #MeToo for Women Like Us" Poor Enforcement of India's Sexual Harassment Law*. Retrieved from Human Rights Watch: https://www.hrw.org/report/2020/10/14/no-metoo-women-us/poor-enforcement-indias-sexual-harassment-law

Marx, J. (2017). Twitter and the 2016 presidential elections. *Critique: A Worldwide Student Journal of Politics*, 17–37.

McCay-Peet, L., & Quan-Haase, A. (2017). What is social media and what questions can social media research help us answer. *The SAGE handbook of social media research methods*, 13–26.

Minority Rights Group. (2019). *Peoples under threat 2019*. Minority Rights Group.

Mlaba, K. (2021, Sept 24). *Fridays for future: Young climate activists around the world take to the streets*. Retrieved from Global Citizen: https://www.globalcitizen.org/en/content/fridays-for-future-climate-protest-cop26/?gclid=Cj0KCQjw0bunBhD9ARIsAAZl0E1mQSIck5JkH

Papacharissi, Z. (2010). *A private sphere: Democracy in a digital age*. Routledge.

Phillips, N. E. (2024). Edel Rodriguez takes on Donald Trump. Interrogating the Visual Culture of Trumpism. In N. E. G. Hamming (Ed.), *Interrogating the visual culture of Trumpism*. Routledge.

Prier, J. (2020). Commanding the trend: Social media as information warfare. In A. T. C. Whyte (Ed.), *Information warfare in the age of cyber conflict* (pp. 88–113). Routledge.

Rao, A. (2019, Dec 28). *How did Social Media Impact India's 2019 General Election?* Retrieved from Economic and Political Weekly: https://www.epw.in/index.php/engage/article/how-did-social-media-impact-indias-2019-general

Richter, F. (2019, Feb 5). *How Facebook grew from 0 to 2.3 billion users in 15 years*. Retrieved from World Economic Forum: https://www.weforum.org/agenda/2019/02/how-facebook-grew-from-0-to-2-3-billion-users-in-15-years/?DAG=3&gclid=Cj0KCQjwxuCnBhDLARIsAB-cq1pvlZKFa81wN969

Sarma, P. P., & Hazarika, T. (2023). Social media and election campaigns: An analysis of the usage of twitter during the 2021 Assam assembly elections. *International Journal of Social Science Research and Review, 6*(2), 96–117.

Shane, S., & Goel, V. (2017, Sept 6). *Fake Russian Facebook Accounts Bought $100,000 in Political Ads*. Retrieved from New York Times: https://www.nytimes.com/2017/09/06/technology/facebook-russian-political-ads.html

Sharma, N. (2022). Populism and social media use: Comparing the Indian prime minister Narendra Modi's strategic use of twitter during the 2014 and the 2019 election campaigns. *Media Asia, 50*(2), 181–203.

Sherstoboeva, E. (2024). Russian bans on 'fake news' about the war in Ukraine: Conditional truth and unconditional loyalty. *International Communication Gazette, 86*(1), 36–54.

Shirazi, F. (2013). Social media and the social movements in the Middle East and North Africa: A critical discourse analysis. *Information Technology & People, 26*(1), 28–49.

Simon, J., Bass, T., Boelman, V., & Mulgan, G. (2017). *Digital democracy: The tools transforming political engagement*. Nesta.

Smith, A. (2019, Apr 15). *The Internet's Role in Campaign 2008*. Retrieved from Pew Research Center: https://www.pewresearch.org/internet/2009/04/15/the-internets-role-in-campaign-2008

Soorya, B. (2021). Revitalizing 'digital democracy': Regulating social media discourses in Sri Lanka. In *Paper delivered at SICASH 2021 - SLIIT international conference on advancements in sciences & humanities* (pp. 423–432). Faculty of Humanities and Sciences, SLIIT.

Suzor, N. P. (2019). *Lawless: The secret rules that govern our digital lives*. Cambridge University Press.

Tuten, T., Solomon, M., & Ladik, D. (2015). The teaching of social media marketing. In *Marketing Dynamism & Sustainability: Things change, things stay the same… proceedings of the 2012 academy of marketing science (AMS) annual conference* (p. 475). Springer International Publishing.

Twitter. (2015, Jan 21). *#SOTU visualized: see how the nation reacted on Twitter*. Retrieved from Twitter: https://blog.twitter.com/official/en_us/a/2015/sotu-visualized-see-how-the-nation-reacted-on-twitter.html

Vaccari, C., Chadwick, A., & Kaiser, J. (2023). The campaign disinformation divide: Believing and sharing news in the 2019 UK general election. *Political Communication, 40*(1), 4–23.

Voorhoof, D. (2018, Oct 9). *Savva Terentyev V. Russia: Criminal conviction for inciting hatred against the police violated a blogger's freedom of expression*. Retrieved from Strasbourg Observers: https://strasbourgobservers.com/2018/10/09/savva-terentyev-v-russia-criminal-conviction-for-inciting-hatred-against-the-police-violated-a-bloggers-freedom-of-expression/

Woolley, S., & Howard, P. (2017). *Computational propaganda worldwide: Executive summary*. University of Oxford - Computational Propaganda Project.

Wring, D., & Ward, S. (2020). From bad to worse? The media and the 2019 election campaign. *Parliamentary Affairs, 73*, 272–287.

Chapter 3
International Standards on Free Speech and Intermediaries

3.1 Introduction

As the previous chapter examines the role of social media in freedom of speech and expression, it also emphasizes the importance of regulating these platforms due to the nature of the content shared. However, the complex Internet landscape and the cross-border nature of social media pose significant challenges to traditional regulatory measures, creating hurdles in establishing effective regulatory frameworks. The Internet's global reach impacts both regulatory models and the foundational principles of law. Ladeur points out that traditional private international law is often ill-suited to address issues arising from social networks (Ladeur, 2022). Moreover, cyberspace and the Internet have been widely criticized for violating a core principle of international law: state sovereignty. Moynihan argues that state cyber intrusions are frequently conducted remotely, from outside the target state's territory, rather than by agents physically present within the affected state, thereby infringing on sovereignty and non-intervention principles of international law (Moynihan, 2019). Liaropoulos further notes that the inability to attribute cyber-attacks undermines state sovereignty, as it hampers the effective exercise of power in cyberspace by preventing the identification and tracing of malicious actors (Liaropoulos, 2013).

On the other hand, from a domestic or national perspective, Internet regulation has yielded different approaches and outcomes across various countries. Each country's approach to regulating online content at the domestic level is distinct and shaped by factors such as user base, cultural values, platform power, government policies, and more. For instance, the United States adopts a relatively relaxed framework, providing platforms with certain immunities, such as those granted under Section 230 of the Communications Decency Act (CDA), allowing them some autonomy in developing their own measures. In contrast, the European Union takes a stricter approach, mandating that major tech platforms comply with stringent requirements prescribed by regulations like the Digital Services Act (DSA). Meanwhile, countries like China implement an extreme level of governmental

S. Balendra, *Free Speech in the Puzzle of Content Regulation*, Law, Governance and Technology Series 70, https://doi.org/10.1007/978-3-031-75813-3_3

regulation, amounting to blanket censorship—comprehensive, indiscriminate, and widespread banning of Internet services based on their legal and political frameworks (Gosztonyi, 2023).

Therefore, due to the recurring challenges in regulating digital spaces, this chapter aims to lay the foundation before exploring different regulatory models in the following chapters. It introduces the crucial variables this book will discuss freedom of speech and Internet intermediaries—primarily the platforms examined in the following chapters of this book. I argue that international standards serve as a framework for navigating these issues in a way that respects free speech and other competing values online. These standards act as guidelines for platforms, governments, and regulatory institutions when adopting various measures and regulations. They are essential for balancing competing values in online spaces. While these standards generally recognize the importance of open discourse and the free flow of information, they also assist in content moderation, addressing harmful content, and accommodating legal and cultural differences across jurisdictions.

3.2 International Standards on Free Speech

This section of the chapter examines key international instruments and their definitions or accommodations of free speech within their respective contexts. It explores the recognition of free speech across various documents, from the Convention on the Use of Broadcasting to the International Bill of Human Rights, highlighting the significance of freedom of speech and its global acknowledgment across various instruments. The chapter underscores the importance of free speech and expression as fundamental rights while addressing its universal recognition and protection.

3.2.1 International Convention Concerning the Use of Broadcasting in the Cause of Peace

The discussion of competing rights, particularly on the right to free speech, has a *deep-rooted* history within international law, stretching back to the early twentieth century. This dialogue saw a significant development with the introduction of the International Convention concerning the Use of Broadcasting in the Cause of Peace in 1936. This convention marked the first international attempt, under the auspices of the League of Nations, to regulate speech through a formal treaty.

The Conference for the Adoption of a Convention on the Use of Broadcasting in the Cause of Peace was held on September 17, 1936, at the Palace of Nations in Geneva, chaired by *Raestad*. It saw participation from delegates of over 30 countries across Europe, Latin America, along with Turkey, Egypt, India, New Zealand, and the USSR. Observers from Estonia, Latvia, Siam, the Rockefeller Foundation, the

International Broadcasting Union (IBU), and an unofficial representative from the USA's Federal Communications Commission were also present. Notably, Germany, a country then widely associated with using broadcast propaganda for aggressive purposes, did not attend (Potter, 2023).

Specifically, Article 3 and Article 4 of the convention prohibited the deliberate broadcasting of false news.

Article 3 of the International Convention Concerning the Use of Broadcasting in the Cause of Peace provides that:

> The High Contracting Parties mutually undertake to prohibit and, if occasion arises, to stop without delay within their respective territories any transmission likely to harm good international understanding by statements the incorrectness of which is or ought to be known to the persons responsible for the broadcast.

Article 4 states that:

> The High Contracting Parties mutually undertake to ensure, especially in time of crisis, that stations within their respective territories shall broadcast information concerning international relations the accuracy of which shall have been verified - and that by all means within their power - by the persons responsible for broadcasting the information.

Yet, the convention aimed at regulating broadcast in the interest of peace largely failed to have a practical impact. Although initially ratified by seven countries (the UK, Brazil, Denmark, France, India, Luxembourg, and New Zealand), and reportedly accepted by ten governments by June 1938, it remained ineffective (Potter, 2023).

This convention is one of the significant instruments since while the free speech protections are enshrined in many of the frameworks, it is essential to prescribe certain provisions that spell out the limitations of the right, such as resulting in fake news, as discussed above.

3.2.2 Convention on the International Right of Correction

Along the same line, the Convention on the International Right of Correction in 1953 is also a key attempt that recognize the *"Right of Correction"* or *"Right to Reply,"* which is the right to defend oneself against public criticism regarding the publication on their platform. While some countries recognize the right to reply as a constitutional right (e.g., Brazil), some media outlets adopt them as part of their editorial policy (e.g., BBC). So far, the convention has been signed by 12 states, and 17 countries are parties to the convention.[1] This convention contributed to the recognition of free speech by permitting parties to rectify false information, thus

---

[1] See https://treaties.un.org/Pages/ViewDetails.aspx?src=TREATY&mtdsg_no=XVII-1&chapter=17&clang=_en.

reducing the need for external regulatory intervention that could impinge upon the freedom of speech.

Balancing with free speech, the convention is an effort to improve the standards of global news communication and make a valuable contribution toward achieving this goal. Whitton appreciates this effort as:

> It offers a practical means of conciliating the imperative need of states in their mutual relations for reliable, non-subversive, non-incendiary news, with the democratic principle of freedom of information (Whitton, 1950).

3.2.3 The Universal Declaration of Human Rights (UDHR)

The Universal Declaration of Human Rights (UDHR) (1948), is the very first attempt when the countries came together to recognize inalienable rights—which laid the solid foundation for the further development of the international human rights law.

Article 19 of the UDHR recognizes the right to freedom of opinion and expression in a right-based approach. It provides that:

> Everyone has the right to freedom of opinion and expression; this right includes freedom to hold opinions without interference and to seek, receive and impart information and ideas through any media and regardless of frontiers.

UDHR further established the grounds on which the recognized rights can be limited as enshrined in Article 29(2), which states that:

> In the exercise of his rights and freedoms, everyone shall be subject only to such limitations as are determined by law solely for the purpose of securing due recognition and respect for the rights and freedoms of others and of meeting the just requirements of morality, public order and the general welfare in a democratic society.

The UDHR also attempts to safeguard individuals against unlawful attacks, such as defamatory publications. Article 12 lists that on such occasions, the individual has the right to seek the protection of the law.

Article 12 of UDHR reads as follows:

> No one shall be subjected to arbitrary interference with his privacy, family, home or correspondence, nor to attacks upon his honour and reputation. Everyone has the right to the protection of the law against such interference or attacks.

The UDHR does not explicitly address *hate speech*, but given the context of its creation, state practices reviewed by the drafting commission, and its focus on equality and non-discrimination, it is implied that the Declaration does not protect hate speech (Defeis, 1992). Thus, the arrangement under which UDHR settled is an indirect one rather than a direct regulatory measure, which is one of the challenges when countering hate speech and identifying the key elements of hate speech.

3.2.4 *The International Bill of Rights: ICESCR and ICCPR*

In December 1966, the UN General Assembly adopted two key international treaties that significantly influenced global human rights: the International Covenant on Economic, Social, and Cultural Rights (ICESCR) and the International Covenant on Civil and Political Rights (ICCPR). Together, these are commonly known as *the International Covenants*.

ICESCR addresses a wide range of economic, social, and cultural rights, including the right to social security, health, education, participation in social life, and few more. The idea of ICESCR is to ensure the enjoyment of these rights, without any discrimination and interference.

On the other hand, ICCPR, which is a major guideline to the state parties related to the constructions of civil and political rights in their national instruments, mandates that hatred content should be prohibited by law.

Article 20(2) of ICCPR provides that:

> Any advocacy of national, racial or religious hatred that constitutes incitement to discrimination, hostility or violence shall be prohibited by law.

Yet, in the meantime, as a pillar of recognition of freedom, the ICCPR also recognizes the freedom and the right to expression through Article 19(2), which provides that:

> Everyone shall have the right to freedom of expression; this right shall include freedom to seek, receive and impart information and ideas of all kinds, regardless of frontiers, either orally, in writing or in print, in the form of art, or through any other media of his choice.

However, it balances the challenges often caused by such rights (such as defamation and fake news) by regulating the exercise of the rights with certain limitations lawfully, as outlined in the immediately following subsection.

Article 19(3) reads as follows:

> The exercise of the rights provided for in paragraph 2 of this article carries with it special duties and responsibilities. It may therefore be subject to certain restrictions, but these shall only be such as are provided by law and are necessary.

In addition, Article 17 of the ICCPR provides protection against attacks on one's dignity or reputation made unlawfully.

Article 17(1) provides that:

> No one shall be subjected to arbitrary or unlawful interference with his privacy, family, home or correspondence, nor to unlawful attacks on his honour and reputation.

It grants an opportunity to seek legal remedy when reputation is harmed by disinformation, and thereby attempts to safeguard free speech while protecting the other competing rights.

The ICCPR specifically prohibits any advocacy of national, racial, or religious hatred that incites discrimination, hostility, or violence, yet it also aims to balance freedom of expression with protection against its abuse, ensuring respect for privacy and reputation.

The three major regional human rights treaties—the European Convention on Human Rights (ECHR),[2] the American Convention on Human Rights (ACHR),[3] and the African Charter on Human and Peoples' Rights (ACHPR)[4]—each guarantee the right to freedom of expression. This right is enshrined in Article 10 of the ECHR, Article 9 of the ACHR, and Article 13 of the ACHPR. These protections are largely consistent and similar to those found in ICCPR, reflecting a shared commitment to upholding freedom of expression across different regions.

However, the ACHR goes further by explicitly prohibiting hate speech. Article 13(5) of the ACHR specifically provides for the banning of hate speech, as follows:

> Any propaganda for war and any advocacy of national, racial, or religious hatred that constitute incitements to lawless violence or to any other similar illegal action against any person or group of persons on any grounds, including those of race, color, religion, language, or national origin, shall be considered as offenses punishable by law.

ICCPR, and UDHR clearly articulate the right to free speech while also delineating specific restrictions on the exercise of this right to address concerns such as the spread of fake news and hate speech. These instruments ensure that while the right to free expression is protected, there are also provisions for safeguarding against abuses of this liberty, promoting a balance between freedom and responsibility.

3.2.5 The Budapest Convention on Cybercrime and Joint Declaration

The Budapest Convention on Cybercrime, which came into force in 2004, is especially relevant in today's digital era, where much of our communication and publishing take place online. This convention offers critical guidance for the development of national legal frameworks to combat cybercrime, covering a wide range of online offenses. While it attempts to effectively address various forms of cybercrime, the Budapest Convention does not expressly categorize defamation or the dissemination of fake news as criminal activities. Further, the Budapest Convention does not provide any standards related to free speech online. Legal recourse under this convention is typically available when fake news is part of cyber offenses like hacking, phishing, or fraud. However, in cases where the spread of fake news or defamatory content does not involve other cybercriminal activities, the Budapest Convention may not provide an adequate legal basis for action. To date, more than sixty (60) countries ratified the convention, including many of the non-European countries such as the United States, Sri Lanka, Japan, and Australia.

[2] Article 10, European Convention on Human Rights (1953).

[3] Article 9, American Convention on Human Rights (1978).

[4] Article 13, African Charter on Human and Peoples' Rights (1986).

However, from a free speech perspective, it has been extensively criticized that the broad power vested in law enforcement, often ends up with the suppression of free speech and expression (Article 19, 2022).

This challenge on empowering the governments and law enforcement has also been raised by Wilkinson in the recent scholarship exploration on cybercrime treaty, stating that:

> Some states have used cybercrime laws to criminalize online content and limit free speech by targeting journalists, activists and political opposition, or to police behaviour through so-called 'morality clauses' (Wilkinson, 2023).

In 2017, key representatives from various international organizations—the United Nations Special Rapporteur on Freedom of Opinion and Expression, the OSCE Representative on Freedom of the Media, the OAS Special Rapporteur on Freedom of Expression, and the ACHPR Special Rapporteur on Freedom of Expression and Access to Information—collaborated to issue a Joint Declaration.[5]

This declaration focused on freedom of expression and addressed concerns related to fake news, disinformation, and propaganda. It outlined a set of principles for publishers across various platforms in the digital age, set standards for tackling disinformation, discussed the balance between freedom of expression and responsible communication, and emphasized the protection of intermediaries and stakeholders in the media sector, among other critical points.

A few of the international standards are given below.

The Joint Declaration underlines several principles regarding restrictions on the freedom of speech and expression online including:

(i) Restrictions of free expression must be legal, serve a legitimate interest under international law, and be necessary and proportionate.[6]
(ii) Restrictions are permissible to prevent advocacy of hatred that leads to violence, discrimination, or hostility, in line with international human rights law.[7]
(iii) These standards apply internationally, affecting not only domestic jurisdictions but also foreign media outlets and communication systems.[8]
(iv) Individuals should be protected from liability for simply sharing or promoting content they did not create or alter.[9]
(v) Blocking entire websites or other broad online measures is a severe action only justifiable under strict conditions, including necessity, proportionality, and due process.[10]

[5] See https://www.ohchr.org/Documents/Issues/Expression/JointDeclaration3March2017.doc.

[6] Joint Declaration 2017 Clause 1(a).

[7] Joint Declaration 2017 Clause 1(b).

[8] Joint Declaration 2017 Clause 1(c).

[9] Joint Declaration 2017 Clause 1(e).

[10] Joint Declaration 2017 Clause 1(f).

(vi) Government-imposed content filtering systems not controlled by end-users are not acceptable restrictions on free speech.[11]

(vii) The right to freedom of expression spans international borders; jamming or restricting broadcasts from foreign jurisdictions is only legitimate when the content significantly violates legitimate content restrictions and all other less intrusive measures have failed.[12]

The Declaration is not a legally binding treaty or law. Rather, it is a statement of principles and recommendations issued by expert bodies tasked with monitoring and promoting freedom of expression internationally.

International standards specifically recognize free speech online and establish criteria for its limitation, aiming to protect the core values of a democratic society, including public order, morality, security, harmony, and dignity. These standards ensure that restrictions on free speech and expression are legally justified and used only in situations of extreme necessity, thus preventing authoritarian misuse of such limitations.

However, these standards have not been effectively applied at these junctures, due to the *"international soft"* nature of the laws.

In the case of Yahoo! Inc., the United States Court of Appeals for the Ninth Circuit observed that:

> Absent a body of law that establishes international standards with respect to speech on the Internet and an appropriate treaty or legislation addressing enforcement of such standards to speech originating within the United States, the principle of comity is outweighed by the Court's obligation to uphold the First Amendment.[13]

Due to this soft law nature, despite ongoing progress in the standardization of various human rights, scholars argue that these rights are often more difficult to translate into concrete legal obligations compared to civil and political rights, making their practical application and adjudication more complex (Lagoutte et al., 2016). Sun also makes this point, as follows:

> The first major obstacle to the implementation of human rights norms is the contradiction between repressive states' sign onto policies and treaties and their lack of willingness or capacity to comply (Sun, 2023).

Further, Strossen argued that the content moderation policies of online platforms, particularly those concerning hate speech, may not fully comply with the international free speech standards. Yet, he hopes, these policies are frequently updated, and their alignment with these guidelines is still a developing process (Strossen, 2021). Edwards pointed out that allowing censorship without the need for legislation or judicial oversight, relying on ISP collaboration prioritizes ISP interests and risk management over freedom of expression values (Edwards, 2006).

---

[11] Joint Declaration 2017 Clause 1(g).

[12] Joint Declaration 2017 Clause 1(h).

[13] *Yahoo!, Inc. v. La Ligue Contre le Racisme et L'Antisemitisme*, 169 F.Supp.2d.

Another challenge of applying international standards online is the cultural variation among jurisdictions. Furthermore, as a *cross-border* streamline, the Internet often seems *redundant* in applying uniform standards for interpreting speech.

Sangsuvan wrote about this challenge, noting that:

> However, the Internet has not converged all different cultures in the world into one single culture. While they may operate in a global culture, people remain members of their subcultures or cultural groups. They may have "the distinctive lifestyles, values, norms, and beliefs of certain segments of the population with a society." Their own culture manages their way of behaving or living. For instance, some Internet users in one country may still value traditional religious beliefs whereas other users in another country may prefer high technologies. Some users may prefer material comfort and success whereas others might favor simplicity and a quiet life (Sangsuvan, 2014).

While the recognition of free speech is enshrined in various international instruments, significant challenges remain in the practical application of these standards due to their non-binding nature. The voluntary compliance with these international norms has resulted in varying standards across jurisdictions. The following chapters of this book will explore how this voluntary nature of compliance influences these discrepancies and impacts the implementation of free speech protections globally when regulating social media.

3.3 International Standards on Intermediary Liability

Struggling to manage the countless individuals empowered by the global Internet, governments frequently turn to online intermediaries as a pathway to impose control over digital spaces (Chander, 2016).

As online platforms become the primary means of disseminating content to global users, international authorities have periodically addressed various standard measures concerning the responsibilities and liabilities of Internet intermediaries. In 2011, a joint declaration among the United Nations (UN) Special Rapporteur on Freedom of Opinion and Expression, the Organization for Security and Co-operation in Europe (OSCE) Representative on Freedom of the Media, the Organization of American States (OAS) Special Rapporteur on Freedom of Expression and the African Commission on Human and Peoples' Rights (ACHPR) Special Rapporteur on Freedom of Expression and the Internet,[14] enshrined the recommendations on General Principles, Intermediary Liability, Filtering and Blocking, Criminal and Civil Liability, Network Neutrality, and Access to the Internet.

It provides that:

> No one who simply provides technical Internet services such as providing access, or searching for, or transmission or caching of information, should be liable for content generated by others, which is disseminated using those services, as long as they do not

[14] See https://www.oas.org/en/iachr/expression/showarticle.asp?artID=848.

specifically intervene in that content or refuse to obey a court order to remove that content, where they have the capacity to do so.[15]

It clearly enshrines a shield of protection to the intermediaries against the liability to the content generated or shared by their platforms unless it fails to comply with the judicial orders and interventions. Also, it prescribes that the restrictions placed on the content generated in the online space should adhere the international standards—particularly complying with the three-part test of *legality, necessity, and proportionality*. Oster argues, in legal analysis, that a restriction must first pursue a legitimate aim, then be necessary with no less severe alternatives, and finally, be proportionate by balancing its severity against the importance of the goal (Oster, 2015).

This three-part test has been examined in numerous cases, particularly when it intersects with the right to free speech and expression. In an earlier case of *Handyside v. United Kingdom,*[16] the European Court of Human Rights addressed the issue of freedom of expression. Richard Handyside, who had acquired the British rights to a book intended to educate teenage readers about sex—including topics such as masturbation, pornography, homosexuality, and abortion—was convicted under the Obscene Publications Act for possessing obscene publications for gain. The Court held that the confiscation of the book did not violate the right to freedom of expression. It concluded that the Act's aim to protect minors, along with its measured and precise application, was consistent with the state's margin of appreciation in determining what is *"necessary in a democratic society."* This case established an important precedent in the Court's approach to freedom of expression, setting a robust standard that continues to guide its decisions today.

Similarly, In the case of *Animal Defenders International v. United Kingdom,*[17] the European Court of Human Rights (ECtHR) addressed the issue under Article 34 of the Convention for the Protection of Human Rights and Fundamental Freedoms. The court emphasized that restrictions on political speech may be upheld if the government can satisfy the requirement of proportionality, balancing the necessity of the regulation against the potential threat to freedom of speech rights.

The joint declaration further suggests that corporations commit to upholding freedom of expression in various aspects of their operations, including internal policies, product engineering, business development, and staff training. Additionally, the recommendation includes a call for private actors to establish transparent human rights assessment procedures, considering the potential impact of their policies.[18]

To protect Internet users' freedom of expression and privacy rights, it is recommended that intermediaries should only limit these rights following judicial

[15] Joint Declaration 2011 Clause 2(a).

[16] *Handyside v United Kingdom* (5493/72).

[17] *Animal Defenders International v. United Kingdom* [2013] ECHR 362, (2013) 57 EHRR 21.

[18] Joint Declaration 2011 Clause 6(c).

orders.[19] Intermediaries should be transparent about the actions taken, informing the affected user and, when appropriate, the public. Additionally, intermediaries should give advance notice to users before implementing restrictions and should aim to minimize the impact of these measures on the specific content in question.[20] To enhance the transparency requirements, it is suggested that states should engage in action plans and plan to improve public reporting and monitoring.[21]

It further establishes the role of intermediaries in upholding the transparency values,

> Internet intermediaries should be required to be transparent about any traffic or information management practices they employ, and relevant information on such practices should be made available in a form that is accessible to all stakeholders.[22]

When discussing international standards, it is relevant to mention the efforts of the United Nations Educational, Scientific and Cultural Organization (UNESCO). UNESCO has adopted the concept of *"Internet Universality"* as a holistic framework for developing the Internet in the public interest. UNESCO proposes four guiding principles, summarized as R-O-A-M: Rights-based (ensuring human rights and freedom), Open (promoting openness), Accessible (ensuring accessibility), and multi-stakeholder driven (encouraging participation from various stakeholders) (Souter & Van der Spuy, 2019). These principles aim to guide the regulation and development of the Internet, fostering a knowledge society.

The Manila Principles on Intermediary Liability, proposed by global civil society organizations,[23] establish a foundational framework of essential safeguards and optimal practices for states concerning intermediary liability, guided by international human rights instruments. These principles advocate for states to limit intermediaries' liability for content generated by third parties (Principle 1), emphasize the necessity of a court order following due process for content restriction or removal (Principles 2 &3), and recommend that laws align with the three-part test on freedom of expression while incorporating transparency and accountability principles (Principles 5 & 6).

Although international standards prescribe good practices, they have been influenced or shaped by numerous factors in the international ecosystem. Therefore, this conflict often leads to undue delays in creating regulatory frameworks that comply with international standards. Recently, concerns have arisen that Internet intermediaries might manipulate the information on their platforms. These companies must ensure they do not unfairly influence the information we receive through their services (Chander, 2016).

Fagin noted that:

---

[19] Joint Declaration 2011 Clause 2(a).

[20] Joint Declaration 2011 Clause 2(b).

[21] Joint Declaration 2011 Clause 6(f).

[22] Joint Declaration 2011 Clause 5(b).

[23] See https://manilaprinciples.org/index.html#:~:text=Any%20liability%20imposed%20on%20an,not%20comply%20with%20this%20principle.

> Admittedly nations face a difficult decision between over-inclusive and inclusive measures. If they under-enforce as before, they will find their regulatory goals are frustrated. If states choose to over-enforce, then they encourage legal and political conflicts with other players in the international system. However, a combination of cooperation, externally with other states, and restraint, as an internal public policy, may lead to enhanced cooperation overall (Fagin, 2003).

As Fagin suggests, international cooperation is essential in establishing standards for intermediaries, given their often cross-border nature. International standards on intermediary liability reflect the universal and cross-jurisdictional nature of the Internet. These standards set forth basic principles that Internet intermediaries must follow, typically offering them certain protections or immunities while imposing obligations to ensure their operations, particularly regarding online content, comply with these guidelines.

References

Article 19. (2022). *The Council of Europe Convention on Cybercrime and the First and Second Additional Protocol.* Article 19.

Chander, A. (2016). *Internet intermediaries as platforms for expression and innovation*. Global Commission on Internet Governance.

Defeis, E. F. (1992). Freedom of speech and international norms: Response to hate speech. *Stanford Journal of International Law, 29*(1), 57–130.

Edwards, L. (2006). From child porn to China, in one cleanfeed. *SCRIPTed: Journal of Law, Technology and Society, 3*(3), 174–175.

Fagin, M. (2003). Regulating speech across borders: Technology vs. values. *Michigan Telecommunications and Technology Law Review, 9*(2), 395–456.

Gosztonyi, G. (2023). *Censorship from Plato to social media: The complexity of social Media's content regulation and moderation practices* (Vol. 61). Springer Nature.

Ladeur, K. H. (2022). Cyber courts for social media as a new institutional dimension of media freedom? In G. F. C. B. de Morais (Ed.), *The rule of law in cyberspace* (pp. 387–401). Springer International Publishing.

Lagoutte, S., Gammeltoft-Hansen, T., & Cerone, J. (2016). Introduction: Tracing the roles of soft law in human rights. In S. G.-H. Lagoutte (Ed.), *Tracing the roles of soft law in human rights* (pp. 1–13). Oxford University Press.

Liaropoulos, A. (2013). Exercising state sovereignty in cyberspace an international cyber-order under construction? *Journal of Information Warfare, 12*(2), 19–26.

Moynihan, H. (2019, Dec 2). *The application of international law to state cyberattacks.* Retrieved from Chatham House: https://www.chathamhouse.org/2019/12/application-international-law-state-cyberattacks/2-application-sovereignty-cyberspace

Oster, J. (2015). *Media freedom as a fundamental right*. Cambridge University Press.

Potter, S. J. (2023). Broadcasting in the cause of peace: Regulating international radio propaganda in Europe, 1921–1939. *The International History Review, 45*(6), 843–864.

Sangsuvan, K. (2014). Balancing freedom of speech on the internet under international law. *North Carolina Journal of International Law and Commercial Regulation, 39*(3), 701–756.

Souter, D., & Van der Spuy, A. (2019). *UNESCO's internet universality indicators: A framework for assessing internet development*. UNESCO Publishing.

Strossen, N. (2021). United nations free speech standards as the global benchmark for online platforms' hate speech policies. *Michigan State International Law Review, 29*(2), 307-[xxviii].

Sun, Q. (2023). The enforcement of international human rights law: Challenges and solutions. *Journal of Education, Humanities and Social Sciences, 8*, 491–498.

Whitton, J. B. (1950). An international right of reply. *American Journal of International Law, 44*(1), 141–145.

Wilkinson, I. (2023, Aug 04). *What is the UN cybercrime treaty and why does it matter?* Retrieved from Chatham House: https://www.chathamhouse.org/2023/08/what-un-cybercrime-treaty-and-why-does-it-matter

Chapter 4
Regulating Social Media Platforms

4.1 Introduction

Over the last decade, governments worldwide have become less tolerant of the idea that the Internet should govern itself, moving away from a hands-off approach to more active regulation. Initially, there were only minor regulatory efforts, but these have significantly increased over time. Bradford refers to this growing trend of government intervention in Internet governance as a "*cascade of regulation*" exploring the various conflicts that have arisen between regulatory bodies and tech companies, as well as disputes among the regulators themselves (Bradford, 2023).

However, technological advancements and their roles in *day-to-day* human interactions compel the urgency of regulating the Internet sphere. Predominantly, the rapid advancement of generative AI has led to increased calls for government regulation, notably from prominent figures within the AI industry itself, such as Mustafa Suleyman (Bremmer & Suleyman, 2023), Sam Altman of OpenAI,[1] and Elon Musk.[2] Generative Artificial Intelligence (AI) can propel humanity into new frontiers of knowledge and productivity, fostering economic growth and societal advancement. However, the accelerated pace of AI development raises apprehensions among technologists, citizens, and regulators due to the unsettled nature of the AI (Bradford, 2023).

The contemporary foundational efforts in the current regulatory regime might not fully embrace or promote the original values of freedom, solidarity, and equitable access the Internet was supposed to uphold. The shift from a libertarian approach to potentially heavy-handed government control, or "*reflexive statism*," is being debated and legislated across numerous countries and states, indicating a significant

[1] See https://www.nytimes.com/2023/05/16/technology/openai-altman-artificial-intelligence-regulation.html.

[2] See https://www.bnnbloomberg.ca/elon-musk-calls-for-ai-regulations-in-chat-with-uk-prime-minister-1.1993354.

S. Balendra, *Free Speech in the Puzzle of Content Regulation*, Law, Governance and Technology Series 70, https://doi.org/10.1007/978-3-031-75813-3_4

moment of transition in how digital technology and AI are governed globally (Kapur, 2024).

The legal challenge of regulating global social media is complex because it operates across multiple jurisdictions, each with its own legal culture and norms. These platforms, predominantly owned by American companies, are influenced by US legal principles, particularly strong free speech protections, which often clash with the laws and values of other countries (Gosztonyi, 2023).

Understanding that numerous regulatory frameworks and models have been developed by authorities to address platforms from a corporate perspective—given that these platforms are corporate entities—and that compliance laws such as competition, data protection, and regulatory frameworks also apply, this chapter and book focus specifically on content regulation. The primary aim is to explore how the content shared across these platforms is regulated, rather than delving into broader corporate compliance issues.

In this chapter, I explore the underlying reasons behind the urge to regulate Social Media Platforms (SMPs) and then delve into an examination of three broad models of social media regulations. By doing so, I intend to present a comprehensive overview of the opportunities and challenges associated with these models, related to free speech online.

4.2 Why Regulate Social Media Platforms?

In the global debate on whether to regulate social media platforms—considered bastions of free speech online—there is a growing inclination towards regulating these platforms due to their widespread impact on a global scale, stretching across various norms and values.

A study by Pradel et al. highlighted how different types of *toxic speech* on SMPs provoke varied reactions from users. This research questions the effectiveness of a *"minimalist approach"* that focuses on removing only extreme content while allowing less severe toxic speech to persist. It further points out the complexities in finding a balance between safeguarding free speech and protecting users from harm, especially given the limited support for content moderation in the face of toxic speech. The findings emphasize the necessity for platforms to adopt nuanced, multi-layered strategies that consider user preferences and the potential impacts on marginalized communities to maintain a healthy public discourse (Pradel et al., 2024).

It is evident that the content disseminated on SMPs functions as a *double-edged* sword, as discussed in the Chap. 2 of the book. This nuanced interplay underscores the delicate balance between the principles of free speech and the perils of dangerous speech, presenting profound implications for democratic societies. While these platforms serve as catalysts for amplifying human rights and democratic values in the digital realm, paradoxically, they also pose a threat to these foundational principles when the content disseminated spirals beyond control. Unlike other Internet-based technologies, social media exerts a pervasive influence on communities globally (Wickramanayake, 2020), underscoring the imperative to uphold rigorous standards for the content shared on these platforms.

Therefore, it is inevitable that some form of governance mechanisms be implemented to ensure trust, reliability, and safety for both platforms and users. Without such measures, social media platforms risk becoming hubs for the propagation of hate speech and manipulative content, thereby significantly influencing and impacting the public.

4.3 What Are the Social Media Regulations?

What are the social media regulations? Regulations is generally understood as the government's ability to make and enforce rules over subjects to maintain law and order in their jurisdiction (Weiss, 2000). However, social media regulation is a broader concept, shaped by numerous factors, and the accessibility of platforms is cross-border due to the nature of the Internet. Some scholars articulate that platform regulations are engaged from the grassroots level as it is shaped by individuals—users of these social media platforms (Gillespie, 2017). These platforms' regulations are shaped by a variety of policy and regulatory constraints, including regulations in the United States—where most social media platforms are headquartered—overseas operation regulations, regional requirements, the respective countries' regulations where they operate, and many more (Gillespie, 2017). In addition to all these external regulatory compliances, these platforms have their own policies and measures, such as *"community standards."*

Underlying the argument of scholars in global governance, social media regulations exist in various layers—finding out the hierarchy of actors is extremely hard (Dingwerth & Pattberg, 2006) and would vary among jurisdictions based on power asymmetry variations between the platforms and governments. Compared with other sectors such as share markets, companies, and properties, social media platforms are under-regulated. Vaidhyanathan argues that this happens due to unfettered sovereign power—the private power of social media platforms that exist globally (Vaidhyanathan, 2018). However, the platforms are subject to laws and regulations globally and locally. Along with the internal regulations of these platforms, externally, regulation is primarily framed by telecommunication, Internet laws, and occasionally media laws and policies.

4.4 Combating Social Media Turbulence

In the absence of social media regulations, government authorities often resort to the strategy of extreme censorship of social media and Internet disruptions to get rid of content *Infodemics*—an excessive amount of information flow during an outbreak, typically unreliable, that rapidly disseminates in digital or physical spaces.[3] While the need to control Infodemics is widely acknowledged, the practice of extreme censorship and Internet disruptions have faced global criticism for being a serious violation of human rights in cyberspace. Such measures are seen as impinging on the freedom of expression, the free flow of information, and the freedom and pluralism of the media (Commissioner for Human Rights - COE, 2012).

As of May 19, 2023, Access Now reports a concerning trend, with 80 instances of Internet shutdowns recorded across 21 countries in the year 2023, and notably, 18 of these shutdowns have persisted since 2022 (Rosson & Felicia, 2023). For example, after the Russian military occupation in Ukraine, Russia implemented widespread Internet blackouts, presumably to control the narrative and restrict the flow of information regarding the truth beyond Ukraine. The extreme censorship was more severe than that experienced within Russia, and Google, YouTube, and the messaging app Viber have been blocked in the territories occupied by Russia.

A study conducted by Access Now observed that:

> Since the start of a full-scale war, Russia has blocked 2,696 news websites, 584 of which are Ukrainian, as well as dozens of Ukrainian government domains (Anastasiya, 2022).

In 2022 April, the Sri Lankan government imposed Internet disruption across the island restricting access to platforms including Twitter, Facebook, WhatsApp, YouTube, and Instagram as an emergency was declared amid widespread protests, which lasted over sixteen (16) hours.[4] A similar incident was witnessed in Sri Lanka in 2019, immediately following the Easter Sunday attacks. The government reported that it took such measures to control content deemed hateful, misinformation, and posing threats to the security of the state.

An Internet shutdown was also recorded in Pakistan recently, following the arrest of former Prime Minister Imran Khan.[5] Especially in a jurisdiction like Pakistan, social media and the Internet serve as the primary avenues for sharing *unbiased* news. Consequently, blocking access to these platforms results in widespread information censorship across the country, constituting a violation of fundamental human rights. Further, the social media ban disconnects the public from one another and impacts information sharing during the protests—which is a violation of human rights, including the right to peaceful assembly and protest.

In Myanmar, following the 2021 Myanmar coup, the authorities exhibit dictatorship over the digital space, predominantly through the shutdowns of the Internet.

These Internet shutdowns hush down the voices against serious human rights violations—equivalent to war crimes. Frequently, it was criticized by different

---

[3] See https://www.who.int/health-topics/infodemic#tab=tab_1.

[4] See https://netblocks.org/reports/social-media-restricted-in-sri-lanka-as-emergency-declared-amid-protests-JA6ROrAQ.

[5] See https://www.bbc.com/news/world-asia-65541769.

international organizations including the Office of the United Nations High Commissioner for Human Rights (OHCHR).[6]

Countries such as Pakistan, Sierra Leone, Turkey, Cuba, etc. have recorded social media bans during the electoral period. Since free and open political communication is an essential element in ensuring fair and democratic electoral processes, these *Internet shutdowns* severely vanish the democratic values of the states.

I emphasize that the prevalence of social media censorship and Internet shutdowns underscore the inadequacy of existing regulatory measures or their inefficacy in addressing ongoing issues. These strategies are increasingly wielded by authorities as an extension of an authoritarian approach to the digital space. Remarkably, fragile democratic authorities often justify such measures by citing concerns related to public safety or the need to curb the spread of misinformation. However, in practice, these measures are frequently stretched beyond their original purposes to suppress dissent and hinder the free flow of information. The above-presented case studies compel a nuanced discussion about the comprehensive regulatory regime that strikes a delicate balance in regulating social media. It becomes evident that a comprehensive and well-crafted regulatory framework is essential to curtail the arbitrary use of power and to ensure that measures ostensibly designed for public safety do not encroach upon the fundamental principles of free expression and the open exchange of ideas in the digital sphere.

4.5 Emergence of Regulatory Models

While the response to the question of *"should we regulate social media?"* has predominantly been affirmative, contemporary scholarly discussions have transitioned to a new query: *"how to regulate social media?"* This shift reflects a growing recognition that the necessity for regulation is widely acknowledged, prompting a nuanced exploration of the strategies, mechanisms, and frameworks that can be employed to effectively govern social media platforms.

In response to the challenges discussed above, both social media giants and state authorities are gradually transitioning toward a regulatory framework for social media. Governments worldwide are increasingly involved in overseeing social media activities, and concurrently, tech platforms are also proactively enhancing self-regulatory measures (Cusumano et al., 2021). This evolving landscape reflects a collective effort to strike a balance between preserving the positive aspects of free expression and mitigating the risks associated with unbridled dissemination of content in the digital age.

Critics have argued that these social media platforms have been subject to the regulations already such as the laws they would compile to operate within a

[6] See www.ohchr.org/en/press-releases/2022/06/myanmar-un-experts-condemn-militarys-digital-dictatorship.

jurisdiction. Therefore, additional regulations would stifle the innovation of these platforms. Predominantly, studies have also noted that government-centered regulations of social media threaten free speech in the digital arena (Kumar, 2019; Samples, 2019; Santuraki, 2019) and frequently lead to digital authoritarian regimes (Shahbaz, 2020). Few other scholars identify the challenges of regulating social media platforms—excessive restrictions, diversity of languages, anonymity, cross-border, new technology, power asymmetry among social media companies and governments, etc. as obstacles in developing the regulatory regime (Battista & Uva, 2023; Beausoleil, 2019; Paulos & Çelik, 2021; Repucci, 2019), almost making regulating social media impossible.

The transparency, authenticity, and trustworthiness of policy frameworks come under scrutiny, especially when considering online free speech. Considering this issue of regulating social media platforms, governments and policy developers across the globe have faced challenges (Gauja, 2021) since existing regulatory frameworks are outdated and incapable of regulating the features of these modern platforms.

Acknowledging the pressing need for online regulations, scholars propose various models of social media regulatory regimes. These models are envisioned as balanced measures that not only safeguard free speech online but also effectively address the challenges associated with the *"deception of technology."* This includes tackling issues such as hate speech, misinformation, violence, and online defamation. The objective is to strike a careful equilibrium where regulatory actions enhance accountability without compromising the essential principles of open expression in the digital realm.

Underlying this regulatory argument, Balkin advocated the urge for an intermediate institution on the way to the regulation of social media.

He argued that:

> You need more than a legal norm that the state doesn't censor. You need more than the formal ability to speak free of government sanction. You need intermediate institutions that can create and foster a public sphere... (Balkin, 2021).

Concerns about the need for regulation have also been acknowledged by the platforms themselves, too. For example, in 2019, Mark Zuckerberg, Facebook's chief executive, expressed his opinion on regulating Facebook by Congress and discussed four policy areas: harmful content, election integrity, privacy, and data portability, seeking the attention of the government.[7]

The following discussion aims to explore three primary models of social media regulations, namely, "self-regulations," "external regulations," and "co-regulations." In doing so, it seeks to address how existing laws can be reformed within an environment that prioritizes the protection of free speech. Key questions include who should bear the responsibility for regulating the platforms and what policy

[7] See https://www.nytimes.com/2019/03/30/technology/mark-zuckerberg-facebook-regulation-explained.html.

developments ought to be pursued. These are some of the critical inquiries in this context.

4.5.1 Self-regulations

In light of the dominance and influence of social media platforms, this regulatory model aims to internally regulate platforms with minimal external oversight (Suzor, 2018). This approach emerges largely in response to public scandals, with platforms increasingly taking on the responsibility and accountability for their governance (Gorwa, 2019). For example, the US is a good example of the internal regulations—as acknowledged in various legislations such as the Communication Decency Act of the United States,[8] the law provides certain protections to platforms from liability, outlining the relationship between governmental authorities and the platforms.

Stockmann pointed out that:

> As of 2021 this self-regulatory approach that grants a high degree of autonomy and flexibility to technology companies is still reflected in most national-level regulations (Stockmann, 2022).

While transparency on these platforms is *often voluntary*, recent policy changes reflect a trend toward greater accountability and transparency. For instance, Meta (Facebook) updated its privacy policy in 2022, emphasizing strong protections for user privacy (O'Flaherty, 2022). Also, Meta is expanding its horizon across the globe in the verification process—recently expanded this to New Zealand as well (Meta, 2023a, b), after the Christchurch Mosque shootings went viral on the Facebook platform. The X (previously Twitter) in updating the personalized experience and security of the users, started collecting biometric and demographic data from the premium users in September 2023.[9] Also, to limit the comments in the space, X has introduced the option to the creators to limit the post-reply feature only to verified users (Hutchinson, 2023). TikTok, the most popular video creation platform, updated its data usage policy in accordance with the emerging rules across the regions.[10]

These time-to-time policy improvements by platforms increase the trust, reliance, and authenticity of these social media platforms and think forefront to shift the regulatory responsibilities to them. Further, these platforms address the contemporary challenges and ongoing issues and try to respond at the best level to take down those issues across their platform issues. For instance, at the time of writing this

[8] Section 230, *Communications Decency Act*, United States (1996).

[9] See https://dig.watch/updates/x-modifies-privacy-policy-to-collect-biometric-and-demographic-data-from-premium-users#:~:text=X%20informs%20of%20its%20intent,premium%20users%2C%20depending%20on%20content.

[10] See https://www.competitionpolicyinternational.com/tiktok-updates-data-usage-regulations-to-fit-eu-laws.

chapter, during the Israel-Hamas war, social media has become a prevalent space—the information chaos is spread out. The European Union also has requested the platforms to be cautious over the contents—illegal and misinformation.[11] In quickly responding to the issue, Meta has taken several measures against the violating content spread across the platform. These measures include establishing a special operation center with Hebrew and Arabic speakers—to identify and understand a wide array of content that is non-English, restricting Live from Instagram and Facebook, increasing user controls, and many more (Meta, 2023a, b). In three days, the Meta removed contents of more than 795,000 violating the policies.[12] X has also removed contents and numerous accounts that are affiliated with the spread of harmful and disinformation contents related to the war.[13]

Previously, Meta openly acknowledged the failure of its AI system to detect posts related to the Christchurch terror attack livestream[14] and took corrective action by updating its algorithms in 2019. Another significant event was the unprecedented decision to permanently suspend the account of former US President Donald Trump in 2021.[15] This action was taken based on the allegation that the content shared by the account had incited violence.

These contemporary efforts attract the attention of lawmakers, policy developers, scholars, and the public. Scholars like Suzor advocated that the term of service of these platforms should be treated equally to the legislative arrangements of a government since they accommodate a regulatory regime through these terms (Suzor, 2018). As regulating social media remains a complex issue for policy developers, the self-regulation model seems an advantageous one as its direct, speedy, and keeping away the governments from the core content moderation decisions would enable to control the suppression of free speech, and political debate leads to the rise of a digital authoritarian regime (Keller, 2018).

However, the limitations of these models also should be discussed since most of the platforms' initiatives are *voluntary basis*, as discussed above. Also, since these platforms are companies at the core, their movements would be driven by commercial perception most of the time (Gorwa, 2019). The deliberate changes suggested by the policy frameworks should also be carefully analyzed since most of them are shaped by the normative values of the United States (Haggart, 2021). It is argued that most of the policies of social media platforms create a massive imbalance of powers and lead to a discriminative treatment towards Global South (Waldron & Cornell, 2023).

[11] See https://www.bbc.com/news/technology-67073956.

[12] Ibid.

[13] See https://www.cbsnews.com/news/hamas-war-gaza-twitter-x-removes-content-israel-palestinians.

[14] See https://abcnews.go.com/Technology/facebook-admits-ai-failed-flag-nz-terror-attack/story?id=61835501.

[15] See https://www.cnn.com/2021/01/08/tech/trump-twitter-ban/index.html.

Griffin also points out that discrimination is likely to continue, partly due to biases that are present in AI systems. These AI classifiers are often used to automate decisions on social media platforms, among other applications. The biases in AI could stem from a variety of factors, including biased training data or flawed algorithms, leading these systems to make discriminatory choices (Griffin, 2023).

For example, during the 2017 genocide of Rohingya Muslims in Myanmar, Facebook algorithms boosted hate speech, and there was negligence to "take down" the posts, which subsequently led to legal action filed by the Rohingya Muslims in the UK and the US.[16]

Amnesty International—a leading international organization working for human rights, documented that:

> Over 1000 posts, comments, images and videos attacking the Rohingya and other Muslims in Myanmar—some of which had been up on the platform since 2012—were documented and analysed by Reuters news agency and the Human Rights Center at UC Berkeley School of Law in August 2018. One illustrative post cited by the Reuters investigation which had been on Facebook since 2013 stated, "We must fight them the way Hitler did the Jews, damn kalars!"; another example cited a post which stated, "These non-human kalar dogs, the Bengalis, are killing and destroying our land, our water and our ethnic people" (Amnesty International, 2022).

Under this model, the decisions of platforms are subject to very minimal laws or any regulatory measures. Therefore, on what basis these decisions are made and what due process is followed during the decision-making are few of the challenging questions (Gauja, 2021) that may create serious repercussions to the application of the rule of law and due process. As the terms of service, and the community standards are the only transparent information available to the public, vesting the absolute authority to the private entities—social media platforms, may create the challenges above discussed, is a fallback of this regulatory model.

Self-regulation models also create challenges related to collateral censorship, where the responsibility and risk of censoring speech are transferred to private entities. Balkin apprised about this issue in his earlier work, pointing out that:

> Collateral censorship occurs when A censors B out of fear that the government will hold A liable for the effects of B's speech. I believe that the question of when collateral censorship is a permissible effect of regulation and when it is unconstitutional will be increasingly important in the law of telecommunications and cyberspace (Balkin, 1999).

While state authorities possess the power to regulate speech through various laws, collateral censorship shifts this burden to Internet intermediaries such as platforms. These intermediary laws often lead to the suppression or stifling of free speech, as platforms may over-censor content to avoid legal liability or comply with regulatory demands (De Gregorio, 2022; Land, 2020).

Nevertheless, the transparency requirements, privacy controls, content moderation, and community guidelines of private entities, specifically private platforms, are

[16] See https://www.theguardian.com/technology/2021/dec/06/rohingya-sue-facebook-myanmar-genocide-us-uk-legal-action-social-media-violence.

undergoing significant evolution in the contemporary world. This transformation is driven by the mounting pressure from both internal and external organizations advocating for responsible practices. While acknowledging that some imbalances may persist in internal regulation structures, I contend that improving this model and addressing the present challenges associated with the algorithms and AI would represent a viable approach to counter the challenges posed by authoritarian regimes as they intersect with government initiatives.

4.5.2 External Regulations

Under the external regulatory model, the government intervenes in the realm of social media through policies related to privacy, data protection, content sharing, intellectual property, and competition. This model has emerged and gained attraction due to the larger scale of scandals and privacy breaches of social media platforms (Foronda & Iwańska, 2023). Gorwa argued that governmental interventions would arise in three major ways: privacy and data protection regulations; the repudiation of intermediary liability protections; and competition law (Gorwa, 2019).

These policy and regulatory frameworks are the outcome of the inefficiency, inadequacy, and low performance of the self-regulations of social media platforms. The General Data Protection Regulation (GDPR)[17] is an example of the data protection regulatory framework prescribed by the European Union. While the GDPR focuses on transparency and data protection from a fundamental rights perspective, it also addresses issues related to targeted advertising (Arcila & Griffin, 2023). Most of the time, these regulatory frameworks are more efficient and more calculative towards the risks associated with the platforms. For example, GDPR is regarded as one of the pivotal proactive attempts, rather than a reactive model related to the risks associated with in context of personal data (De Gregorio, 2022).

GDPR is a significant framework that comprehensively applies to all Internet platforms that operate in the European Union region. Recently, the European Data Protection Board upheld a ruling against Meta, stating that:

> Meta could not continue targeting ads based on user's online activity without affirmative, opt-in consent, and that it could not rely on contract as a legal basis, as targeted advertising is not a core element of its service and thus not necessary for the performance of its contract with users.[18]

The German Network Enforcement (NetzDG) law is another example of this external regulation, which mandates platforms to remove content *"evidently lawful"* within 24 h after the complaint.[19] The act compels platform companies to remove

[17] General Data Protection Regulation, European Union (2016).

[18] See https://iapp.org/news/a/edpb-issues-binding-decisions-banning-metas-targeted-advertising-practices.

[19] *Section 2 of the Network Enforcement Act*, Germany (2017).

content violating German law, with the threat of substantial fines (up to €5 million).[20] However, NetzDG has been criticized by many as it leads to an authoritarian kind of framework. The United Nations also pointed out that nearly 13 countries have engaged in regulating cyberspace using the model of NetzDG, including Turkey, Venezuela, Australia, Russia, India, Kenya, the Philippines, and Malaysia (Baghdasaryan & Gullo, 2021).

Compared to the self-regulation model, this seems intriguing and effective since the application of this model is not complex as it passes through the respective jurisdictions. It also helps to have proper checks and balances along with establishing the Rule of Law since it is derived from the authority and most of the time includes the role of a judiciary in making decisions, unlike self-regulation. But Gauja pointed out that it will incur high costs if laws need to be enforced through the court system, which would be a challenge for developing economies (Gauja, 2021).

Also, difficulties arise when evolving advances in digital technologies, but the framework's response is slow (Burgess, 2022) due to the procedural gateways, such as parliamentary bill stages that differ within the jurisdictions. On the other hand, the frameworks occasionally lead to the extension of the authoritarian regime in the digital space, causing serious violations of fundamental human rights, including free speech, expression, and political debates.

For example, NetzDG has been widely criticized for its nature that could curb free speech online. The UK's Online Safety Act has also faced criticism, notably due to the significant concerns it raises. Primarily, these concerns stem from the broad powers bestowed upon the Secretary of State in defining the scope of regulated services, and the act imposes disproportionate sanctions on companies for non-compliance, including hefty fines, criminal liability, and the possibility of service blocking (Caster, 2021). Although the regulatory frameworks of Germany and the UK cannot be equivalent as the UK is no longer a member of the European Union, the comparative snapshot illustrates the challenges of external regulations.

In addition to GDPR, to regulate online platforms, the European Council has introduced the Digital Services Act (DSA) and the Digital Markets Act (DMA). The introduction of DSA replaced many of the provisions of the NetzDG, which is extensively discussed in Chap. 8 of this book. However, in contrast with the GDPR, the DSA does not oblige platforms to proactively review user content (Heldt, 2022), but instead, DSA introduced notice and action mechanisms (NAM), which significantly diverge from the existing EU regulatory model (Gosztonyi, 2023).

DMA has been introduced with the objective of:

> Contribute to the proper functioning of the internal market by laying down harmonised rules ensuring for all businesses, contestable and fair markets in the digital sector across the Union where gatekeepers are present, to the benefit of business users and end users.[21]

[20] *Section 4 of the Network Enforcement Act*, Germany (2017).

[21] Article 1(1) of DMA.

As an external regulatory model, DMA is designed to regulate a broad range of technologies and business models that vary significantly in their nature and development—evolve rapidly, driven by differing market dynamics (Alexiadis & De Streel, 2023).

From an abstract perspective, external regulation introduces a nuanced dimension by involving governmental authorities in regulating private platforms. However, certain jurisdictions exhibit reluctance to cede absolute power to these platforms, particularly concerning the intricate determination of content linked to free speech and its limitations. The shift in decision-making on free speech, from authority to private platforms, is critical. Yet, at times, this attitude may result in governmental controls over online content related to free speech. External regulations often fail to clearly define the limitations of government authorities, leading to extensive empowerment that can curtail free speech and democratic discourse online, thereby extending their agendas and authoritarian approaches.

4.5.3 Co-regulations

The co-regulation model emphasizes collaboration between authorities, platforms, and other stakeholders, within the regulatory framework. This combined model of public and self-regulation aims to balance the flexibility and industry insight of self-regulation with the formal oversight and enforcement provided by the public agency, creating a more effective and responsive regulatory framework (Gosztonyi, 2023; Marsden, 2011). Buiten et al. argue that while liability hard-law rules provide a strict legal framework for regulating tech companies, they can be complemented by co-regulation or self-regulation, such as industry codes of conduct (Buiten et al., 2019).

In co-regulation, both government and private parties share responsibility for regulatory tasks. This can involve dividing the roles, such as the government setting overall objectives while the industry establishes and enforces specific standards. Alternatively, government and private sector entities often work together on various aspects, such as negotiating regulatory goals, jointly drafting standards, and collaboratively enforcing these standards against firms that do not comply (Hirsch, 2011). The European Union's code of conducts are examples of these models of regulations, as it collaborates with certain actors, including the private platforms—which develops a co-regulatory model of framework. For example, the Code of Conduct on Countering Illegal Hate Speech Online was established in May 2016 by the European Commission in collaboration with major tech companies like Facebook, Microsoft, Twitter, and YouTube. Over the years, additional platforms have joined this initiative.

Few scholars endorse that this model is considered the *principal-based* framework among these three models (Gauja, 2021; Helberger et al., 2018). It has emerged out of the outcry over the drawbacks of the prior two models and presents an intermediate approach. While the previous two models share the authority and responsibility in regulating the platforms among platforms and governments, this model attempts to democratize aspects of the governance and management of big technology companies (Gauja, 2021).

This model addresses the existing issue of accountability associated with the first couple of models and proposes a third party in this system to ensure checks and balances. This third party can include academics, civil societies, or media and press councils in this model. Gorwa extends this, suggesting that the model would propose best practices from a human rights and transparency perspective, such as reporting, third-party audits, and other relevant mechanisms (Gorwa, 2019). The involvement of the third party would standardize the co-regulatory models, suggesting and developing ethical considerations of technology platforms and inclusive democratic values in decision-making. From a participatory regulatory perspective, this model accommodates and amplifies user participation in policymaking. For example, Facebook initiating user voting on policy changes would fall under this limb and enhance the efficacy and standards of the frameworks (Gillespie, 2018).

Gorwa supported this model among the three, elaborating his view that co-regulations might offer more transformative alternatives in the future because it aligns with a philosophy that shifts focus from large, corporate-controlled platforms to diverse forms of platform cooperatives, decentralized networks, and other types of community self-regulations (Gorwa, 2019).

Co-regulation establishes a delicate equilibrium between digital platforms and governmental oversight. This approach grants platforms the flexibility to delineate their standards through terms of service (ToS). Simultaneously, co-regulation serves as a catalyst for harmonizing government interests within the overarching framework, fostering the development of a robust regulatory structure. This collaborative model ensures that platforms retain the autonomy to define their internal guidelines while facilitating a synergistic alignment with governmental objectives in the broader regulatory landscape.

However, there is also the concern that industry representatives might not enforce regulations rigorously, leading to some firms benefiting from others' compliance without contributing themselves. Also, platforms may be conflicted, as their primary obligation is to their shareholders, potentially prioritizing profit over public interest (Hirsch, 2011). Further, Stockmann notes that strengthening content moderation through legal means is especially favored in countries where institutional challenges complicate ad hoc measures, such as temporary Internet blocking (Stockmann, 2022). He further argues that this approach aligns with criticisms of integrating content moderation into co-regulatory frameworks for platform regulation—highlighting that legal regulations can lead to delays in addressing problematic content or result in *"over blocking,"* where platforms excessively remove content to avoid legal repercussions, even if the content does not actually violate any rules.

While self-regulation is purely an industry-driven approach, external regulation is imposed by government authorities. Co-regulation represents a hybrid model that combines elements of both self-regulation and external regulation. This hybrid nature can sometimes lead to differing perceptions among scholars about where to place a regulatory framework between external and co-regulation. For example, while the NetzDG is often seen as an external regulation due to its governmental enforcement mechanisms, scholars like Stockmann classify it as co-regulation (Stockmann, 2022). This classification is based on the Act's emphasis on public consultation, involvement of policy experts, and its provisions for transparency and oversight. Regardless of these distinctions, the model chosen plays a critical role in content regulation while aiming to protect freedom of speech. Since these models often incorporate overlapping elements, categorizing them can be challenging.

4.6 The Concept of Intermediary Liability

In the ongoing efforts to develop co-regulatory models for content moderation, the role of Internet intermediaries, such as platforms, and intermediary liabilities plays a crucial role in significantly influencing the content moderation process. The concept of "intermediary liability" assigns legal accountability to various Internet entities such as Internet Service Providers (ISPs), SMPs, search engines, and media companies for hosting or disseminating certain types of content that are unpublishable or unlawful. This principle is pivotal because these intermediaries play a crucial role in enabling the exchange and accessibility of information online. ISPs facilitate data exchange, curate search engines, and deliver information snippets, while social networks provide platforms for user-generated content, and media companies offer spaces like comment sections for public discourse, thereby broadening the reach of third-party content. This implies that intermediaries are instrumental in disseminating information to a broad audience.

In light of challenges presented by both internal and external regulations previously discussed in this book, there is a global shift towards developing a co-regulatory model. This model emphasizes collaboration between authorities and platforms, transferring specific liabilities and responsibilities to private entities under certain conditions. Such a shift is motivated by the desire to balance the promotion of free expression and innovation on digital platforms with the need to mitigate the spread of illegal or harmful material. Governments generally refrain from imposing heavy liabilities on platforms that host user-generated content, recognizing the role these platforms play in the expansive growth of the Internet and mobile communications worldwide.

Generally, there is a reluctance among governments to place this liability on platforms that host user-generated content, as doing so is believed to support the freedom of expression for users and encourage innovation among platforms. This stance is considered a crucial element in the global expansion of Internet and mobile communication networks. The rationale behind imposing liability on Internet intermediaries is based on the idea that these entities are best equipped to handle problematic material due to their technical and financial resources. From a fairness standpoint, it is argued that intermediaries should address the challenges arising from their operations, aiding law enforcement and other bodies in the process. Since intermediaries gain from the distribution of third-party content online, they are deemed responsible for preventing the dissemination of illegal or harmful material (Article 19, 2019).

There are three principal models of liability for Internet intermediaries, which determine the circumstances under which these platforms may be held accountable for unlawful or prohibited content shared on their services. These models are the strict liability model, the conditional immunity model, and the broader immunity model.

The broader immunity model affords a wide-ranging shield to intermediaries, effectively treating them as mere conduits or "messengers" rather than publishers of the content. This approach exempts platforms from the duty of screening the content posted by users, placing the responsibility solely on the individual who uploaded the content. Section 230 of the Communication Decency Act (CDA) of the United States is a quintessential example of this model.

The conditional immunity model offers a degree of protection to Internet intermediaries, provided they adhere to certain regulatory requirements. This typically involves a "Notice and Take Down" procedure, where the intermediary must remove content flagged by authorities or risk losing their immunity. This model has been observed in several jurisdictions, including through the European Union's E-Commerce Directive, Germany's Network Enforcement Act, and India's Intermediary Guidelines and Digital Media Ethics Code Rules. However, the new Digital Service Act of the EU has replaced the E-Commerce Directive's Notice and Take Down Procedure with the Notice of Action System (Gosztonyi, 2023).

Finally, under the strict liability model, intermediaries are held directly responsible for any illegal content disseminated through their platforms. This model imposes a significant obligation on these platforms to actively monitor and regulate the content to avoid facing penalties. China is often cited as a prominent example where this model is applied.

This section analyses the three models of intermediary liability and their effects on free speech within the SMPs. It explores how each model either enhances or hinders the full enjoyment of platform features related to free speech.

4.6.1 Broader Immunity Model of Intermediary Liability

The broader immunity model provides extensive protections to platforms regarding objectionable content posted by users. Currently, this model is primarily practiced in the United States. Section 230 of the CDA, commonly referred to as the *"safe harbor"* provision, offers significant immunities to intermediaries from lawsuits, including those for negligence, violations of federal civil rights laws, and defamation. Rooted in a commitment to human rights, particularly as underscored by the *First Amendment*, the United States champions this model to bolster online free speech and innovation. The government and courts have long maintained a stance that prioritizes free speech rights over competing interests. For example, in earlier cases such as *Smith v California*[22] and *Bantam Books v. Sullivan,*[23] the court held that the bookstores are not liable for selling books with obscene content.

By offering greater protections to intermediaries, the broader immunity model creates more room for free speech online. It allows intermediaries to *voluntarily* remove harmful or objectionable content from their platforms. While this arrangement can enhance free speech, the voluntary nature of intermediary obligations also presents challenges by potentially conflicting with interests in the online environment, such as instances where offensive or illegal content is overlooked by platforms. This *"voluntary"* approach to content moderation by intermediaries brings forth significant challenges and can have serious implications for accountability, democracy, due process, and transparency in the modern digital age.

Contemporary research and scholars argue that the Internet and intermediaries, as regulated under Section 230 of the CDA, have undergone significant changes over the years. Consequently, they advocate for updated amendments to be integrated into this framework to address current challenges effectively.

In Chap. 7 of this book, I explore the broader immunity model under CDA Section 230, examining social media content moderation and its effects on free speech.

4.6.2 Conditional Immunity Model of Intermediary Liability

The "conditional immunity" model provides intermediaries and platforms with immunity from liability, contingent upon their compliance with specific statutory conditions outlined in domestic laws. This model governs the regulation of Internet intermediaries and platforms within local or domestic contexts, assigning them certain responsibilities and obligations. Under this framework, platforms and intermediaries can achieve immunity from lawsuits, proceedings, and penalties related to the sharing or publishing of unlawful content on their platforms, provided they meet the conditions set by the regulatory frameworks. However, the specific conditions and the extent of immunity may vary across jurisdictions, influenced by the legal context and various cultural, political, societal, and other factors.

Under this umbrella, two distinct approaches are typically identified:

(i) The fault-based approach; and
(ii) The knowledge-based approach.

The fault-based approach holds intermediaries liable when they fail to adhere to specified conditions, such as exercising "due diligence" or fulfilling a "duty of care." For instance, the proposed Online Safety Act in the United Kingdom[24] sets out

[22] *Smith v. California*, 361 U.S. 147 (1959).

[23] *Bantam Books, Inc. v. Sullivan*, 372 U.S. 58 (1963).

[24] *Online Safety Act*, United Kingdom (2023).

duties and obligations based on the principle of *"Duty of Care"* for service providers, who act as Internet intermediaries. These obligations encompass a range of responsibilities, including conducting risk assessments of illegal content, implementing safety measures specifically designed to protect children, and establishing reporting and complaint procedures. The act aims to address various online harms, including child abuse and exploitation, terrorist content, cyberbullying, suicide or self-harm, as well as online disinformation and manipulation. I believe the newly enacted Online Safety Act in the UK will significantly contribute to combating various online content violations, similar to those experienced during historical events like the *Brexit Referendum*. During this period, the role of social media in the sharing and manipulation of information significantly impacted free speech and democratic values.

The knowledge-based approach imposes a slightly lesser degree of obligation on intermediaries compared to the fault-based approach. It holds intermediaries liable only if they become aware or have knowledge that the content shared or published is illegal or forbidden under any regulations and fail to remove this content within a reasonable or stipulated timeframe. The challenge, however, lies in determining how an intermediary's *"knowledge"* of such content can be assessed. The European Union's (EU) E-Commerce Directive serves as a prominent example of this model. Under the Directive, intermediaries, including hosting providers, ISPs, and online platforms, are generally not held liable for content transmitted or stored by their users, as long as they act as neutral intermediaries and take appropriate actions once they become aware of illegal activities.[25] The leading case on this is the *Google France*[26] case where Vuitton filed a suit against Google's search engine since it directed to other websites—to sell the products as *"sponsored links"* which amounted to a trademark infringement. However, the European Court of Justice upheld that Google may be held liable only if it plays an "active" role as a service provider which essentially has the knowledge or control over the data results it generates. Therefore, Google cannot be held liable in this case.

Similarly in the case of *L'Oréal SA v. eBay International AG,*[27] L'Oréal filed infringement actions against eBay in various EU states, including the UK, alleging eBay's liability for trademark use. The dispute involved the sale of 17 items, two of which were allegedly counterfeit L'Oréal cosmetics. Some items were not intended for sale or meant for sale only in North America. L'Oréal claimed eBay was responsible for displaying its trademarks on its European websites and sponsored links on search engines. These links, triggered by trademark-related keywords, directed users to eBay listings, raising issues of trademark infringement. Hearing

---

[25] Article 11 to 15 of the E-commerce Directive (Directive 2000/31/EC of the European Parliament and of the Council of 8 June 2020 on certain legal aspects of information society services, in particular electronic commerce, in the Internal Market ("Directive on Electronic Commerce")) is available at https://eur-lex.europa.eu/legal-content/EN/TXT/PDF/?uri=CELEX:32000L0031.

[26] *Google France, Google Inc. v Louis Vuitton Malletier* C-236/08.

[27] *L'Oréal SA v. eBay International AG* C-324/09.

this, the Court determined that according to Article 5(1)(a) of Directive 89/104 and Article 9(1)(a) of Regulation No. 40/94, a trademark owner has the right to prevent an online marketplace from promoting products identical to its trademarks, particularly when the advertising makes it challenging for reasonably informed and observant Internet users to determine whether the goods genuinely originate from the trademark owner. Further, the Court ruled that eBay may not be exempt from liability provided under Article 14(1) of Directive 2000/31 when it plays an active role in the sale of goods by optimizing the presentation of the offers or promoting them.

The Digital Services Act (DSA) of the EU, which came into effect on November 16, 2022, marks a departure from the EU's traditional regulatory approach (as in the e-commerce directive) by introducing due diligence obligations for certain online platforms. Under the DSA, platforms are required to take proactive measures to address illegal content, enhance transparency, and foster cooperation with regulatory authorities.[28] While it might seem that imposing such stringent obligations could dissuade platforms from engaging in content moderation, the DSA's framework of conditional immunity, combined with significant financial penalties for non-compliance, effectively ensures that platforms remain motivated to fulfill their responsibilities (Nunziato, 2023).

Through retaining the *"safe harbour"* framework, which offers limited liability to platforms for user-generated content, contingent upon their adherence to specific conditions. Importantly, the DSA introduces a "Notice and Action Mechanism" (NAM), superseding the previous Notice and Take Down System (NTDS). Under the NAM, once a service provider receives a notification that meets established criteria, it is deemed to have *"actual knowledge"* of the unlawful content in question (Gosztonyi, 2023).

Few other scholars argued that conditional immunity is based on the principle of corporate social responsibility (CSR)—as corporates these intermediaries and platforms should have some kind of obligation on the content shared or published on their platforms. Corporate social responsibility theory has been extended to the digital realm, applying human rights principles to non-public entities operating largely beyond traditional human rights law. Advocates argue that obligations endorsed by the UN Human Rights Council for states should also encompass online platforms (Giancarlo & Martin, 2020). Also, there are challenges exist in applying CSR in the online context, where these rights are more intricate, requiring a delicate balance between conflicting rights, unlike well-established CSR areas like the environment and labor (Laidlaw, 2017).

Frosio and Husovec further addressed the drawback of CSR in online platforms, pointing out that:

[28] Chapter Two and Three of Digital Service Act (Regulation (EU) 2022/2065, DSA of the European Union) is available at https://eur-lex.europa.eu/legal-content/EN/TXT/PDF/?uri=CELEX:32022R2065.

> The obvious downside of the corporate social responsibility approach is that it does not prescribe any specific steps and rather tries to create environment in which companies will act in a responsible way. The expectations are very often very vague and thus hard to measure or evaluate (Giancarlo & Martin, 2020).

Compared to the other two models of intermediary liabilities—the strict liability and broader immunity models—the conditional immunity model represents a moderate approach. It offers a level of protection to intermediaries that support the promotion of free speech online and fosters innovation. Simultaneously, by raising standards, this model imposes additional obligations on intermediaries concerning the nature of the content for which they could be held liable, such as content that is illegal or forbidden on any basis. However, the specific standards set by this model of regulation can vary significantly among jurisdictions, adopting their own criteria. This variation sometimes results in more stringent regulations, leaning towards the principles of the strict liability model.

For example:

Thailand introduced its Computer Crimes Act (CCA) in 2007. The act bestowed powers to the government including the authority to block the website under certain circumstances, along with shifting certain liabilities including criminal liability to the Internet intermediaries. Section 15 of the CCA empowers authorities to charge ISPs for intentionally supporting or consenting to offenses under Section 14. The term "intentionally" protects ISPs unaware of illegal content on their systems, but this defense is void once informed. Making ISPs liable may lead to indiscriminate Internet censorship, as claims of illegality could prompt ISPs to remove content to avoid liability, a concern addressed by protective laws in other countries (Sinfah & Toby, 2010). However, on the other hand, this arrangement often leads to threatening free speech content shared across online platforms and may lead to "over blocking" or "over removal" of content.

Like China's regulatory regime, the act of Thailand also has certain wide and ambiguous terms, such as *"likely to cause damage to the public," "false or partially false"* data, *"distorted or partially distorted"* data, or data likely to *"cause public panic"* or harm *"maintenance of national security, public safety, national economic security, public infrastructure serving the public interest."*[29] The criminalization of fake news and defamation was heavily criticized by scholars, human rights defenders, and organizations.

Smith and Perry argued that:

> As has been shown, Thailand has a very aggressive approach to the prosecution of propagators of what Thai authorities consider to be lèse-majesté; criminal deformation; or fake news (Robert & Mark, 2020).

Following the criticisms, a wide range of incidents clearly reflected the danger of the flip-edged notions of the act—within free speech and media freedom. A landmark issue in 2017, the CCA was approached and applied to silence the political opposition against the government. The conviction of *Chiranuch Premchaiporn,*

[29] See https://www.hrw.org/news/2016/12/21/thailand-cyber-crime-act-tightens-internet-control.

Director of Prachatai, an online newspaper in Thailand, under the CCA for failing to remove content on Prachatai's forum that was deemed to be *lèse-majesté* is one of the examples of the dangerous application of this act to silence dissent and stifling the free speech online. After the wider criticism within and beyond Thailand, the CCA was further amended in 2017. Still, the Internet intermediaries are held accountable and liable to penalties similar to the offender upon failing to comply with the regulations prescribed by the authorities.

While Thailand's regulatory approach ostensibly aligns with the conditional immunity model, it distinctly highlights the challenges this framework poses to online free speech and democratic values. Therefore, categorizing Thailand's regulatory measures simply as "conditional immunity" does not aptly reflect a commitment to upholding free speech values. A more fitting approach would incorporate principles enshrined in law-making and procedural fairness to truly support and protect these fundamental rights.

4.6.3 Strict Liability Model of Intermediary Liability

The strict liability model, often referred to as the *"Blanket"* model of liability, places extensive obligations on Internet intermediaries for any unlawful content they publish, share, or distribute. This model demands that platforms not only prevent the dissemination of illegal material but also actively monitor, remove, or report any law violations. The consequences for failing to meet these responsibilities are severe and can include fines, criminal liabilities, and even the suspension or cancellation of licenses.

However, the broad and sometimes ambiguous nature of these regulations can lead to overzealous content removal, inadvertently stifling legitimate criticism of the government. This has raised concerns about the balance between enforcing laws and preserving freedom of expression.

China and North Korea are notable examples where the blanket model of liability is in practice. In China, the effectiveness of industry-based self-regulation has been heavily criticized, leading to the introduction of new laws and regulations aimed at addressing these shortcomings. These measures underscore the challenges faced by countries adopting the strict liability model in regulating online content without compromising the principles of free speech and expression.

A long way back, in the case of Zhang *Fu* vs *Tianya Online Network Technology Co., Ltd,*[30] where the online platform Tianya.cn has permitted the publishing of user information about Zhang's home address, mobile phone number, home phone number, IP address, and family members' information, and failed to remove them within a reasonable time.

---

[30] *Zhang Fu* vs *Tianya Online Network Technology Co., Ltd.*; available at: http://oldfyb2009.chinacourt.org/public/detail.php?id 1/4104467 last accessed on 2 August 2023.

The court upheld against the platform, decided that it has an obligation to the content, and stated that:

> It is true that the website operator is not able to edit and control the user generated contents before they are posted by users, but they can monitor after that, and stop the dissemination of unlawful contents by taking the contents down expeditiously or taking some technological measures to filter or screen them. This postmonitoring should be active and comprehensive, rather than passive. If the service provider's responsibility to take down unlawful information is only based on notification by the victim, it is unfair for the victim because his right to complain is treated as an obligation in order to protect his legitimate right.

China has implemented stringent regulations on Internet intermediaries concerning the content published on their platforms. The core challenge in cyberspace governance involves striking a delicate balance between facilitating online expression and protecting privacy. Contrary to the approaches in the US and EU, where specific immunity provisions for intermediaries exist—like Section 230 of the CDA in the US or the E-Commerce Directive in the EU, Chinese laws do not offer a clear immunity framework. This lack of clarity leads to interpretative challenges for judges, which could negatively affect free speech on the Internet. The absence of explicit immunity provisions introduces a level of legal uncertainty, potentially hindering the open exchange of ideas and information online (Tao, 2011).

Platforms exert significant *quasi-legislative* influence through their internal rules, thereby expanding the scope of content moderation. However, this expansion brings uncertainty due to the use of vague language, reducing the predictability and transparency of these rules. Additionally, platforms often infuse their own values into both the creation of house rules and the enforcement of content moderation processes (Xiao, 2023). Under a strict liability governance model, the role of platforms in content moderation becomes both futile and challenging. As a result, the capabilities, potential, and efforts of platforms to moderate content are significantly undermined. The in-house rules, which are built upon the strict liability model, negatively impact the platforms' ability to effectively moderate content as well.

In contrast to the clear policies on Internet intermediary liabilities found in the US and EU, Chinese regulations remain ambiguous. The US focuses on protecting the free flow of information, a principle enshrined in its constitutional amendments, whereas the EU prioritizes the protection of personal information as a fundamental human right. China, on the other hand, has yet to make a definitive policy decision, increasingly emphasizing consumer protection. The question remains whether consumer protection can provide a robust policy foundation in China, in comparison to the constitutional support for freedom of speech and personal information protection seen in the US and EU (Huang, 2020). The ambiguity surrounding consumer protection contrasts with the constitutionally grounded principles in the US and EU and is often seen as a mechanism for blanket censorship and intermediary liability in China.

The strict liability regimes in China are known to significantly chill free speech. The broad application of these regimes leads to excessive content blocking on Internet platforms, adversely affecting free speech, expression, and the flow of information—key components of a democratic society (Wenguang, 2018). This approach raises concerns about the balance between regulating content and preserving essential democratic values.

The strict liability model, while often criticized for its negative impact on free speech, has also seen support from some scholars advocating for a nuanced approach. These advocates propose integrating principles of due diligence on the part of intermediaries, such as gatekeepers, into the strict liability framework. For instance, years back, Partnoy suggested that Section 11 of the Securities Exchange Act of 1933 (United States) be revised to include modified strict liability principles, emphasizing the due diligence of intermediaries to address emerging conflicts (Partnoy, 2001). Similarly, Friedmann argued for holding intermediaries more accountable beyond the existing "safe harbour" provisions, especially in the protection of personal data and user privacy (Friedmann, 2014).

However, some concerns incorporating elements of strict liability could stifle technological innovation. The trend is gradually shifting away from broadening the scope of strict liability, driven by worries that such an approach could hinder industrial development and economic growth (Henderson Jr, 2016). On another note, gated communities, often seen as providing safety and stability with designated authorities to address concerns, may inadvertently limit innovation from a creative standpoint. These enclosed environments may not outright prevent the flow of ideas and services but could dampen the potential for external contributions. This restriction could affect the capacity of both users and creators to influence the future without navigating regulatory barriers (Zittrain, 2008).

The application of strict intermediary liability, often referred to as *over-blanket* screening, poses significant challenges to online free speech and innovation. This approach has led to major Western social media platforms ceasing operations in China. The consequences are twofold: economically and technologically, these platforms face setbacks, and the broader public is impacted as well. Given these considerations, re-evaluating the strict liability model does not seem advisable unless effective solutions can be found within alternative models.

The comparative analysis of the three models, focusing on their impact on free speech and innovation, as well as how they shift responsibilities and liabilities onto platforms, is illustrated in Fig. 4.1 below.

In an abstract view, the strict liability model adopts a comprehensive approach to Internet censorship for intermediaries, imposing significant penalties. This model poses a severe threat to online free speech, other digital rights, and innovation. The conditional immunity model represents a middle ground, granting immunity to intermediaries provided they meet certain conditions, such as exercising due diligence or unknowingly sharing content of a prohibited nature. The broader immunity model promotes maximum free speech; however, contemporary scholars suggest it undermines certain values within the Internet space and advocate for amendments that would assign specific obligations to platforms. The concept of intermediary liability must be evaluated in the context of its role in preventing harm, protecting free speech and access to information, and encouraging innovation and creativity. Despite the growing concern over online harms and illegal content, a comprehensive

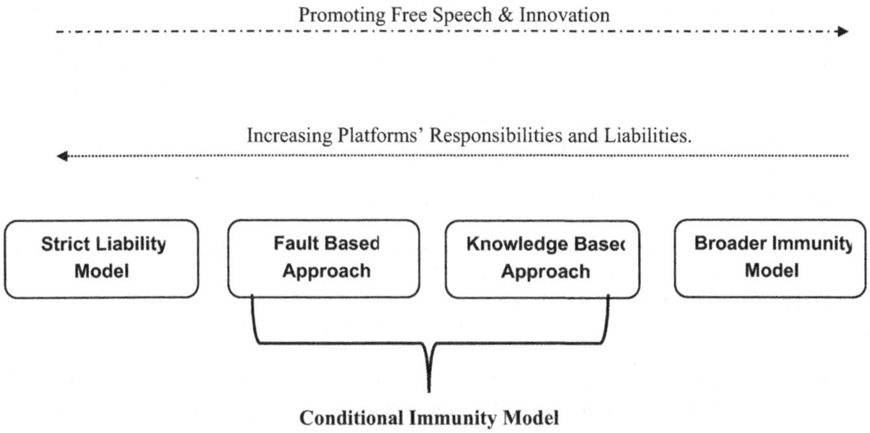

Fig. 4.1 Snapshots of the three intermediary liability models

understanding of intermediary liability is crucial. Nonetheless, the application of intermediary liability models is often shaped by various factors, including the power dynamics between platforms and government authorities.

References

Alexiadis, P., & De Streel, A. (2023). The European way to regulate big tech: The EU's digital markets act. In D. M. Vicente (Ed.), *The legal challenges of the fourth industrial revolution: The European Union's Digital strategy* (pp. 91–125). Springer.

Amnesty International. (2022). *The social atrocity : Meta and the right to remedy for the ROHINGYA*. Amnesty International.

Anastasiya. (2022, Dec 15). *#KeepItOn: Who is shutting down the internet in Ukraine?* Retrieved from Access Now: https://www.accessnow.org/who-is-shutting-down-the-internet-in-ukraine/#skip-to-content

Arcila, B. B., & Griffin, R. (2023). *Social media platforms and challenges for democracy, rule of law and fundamental rights*. European Parliament.

Baghdasaryan, M., & Gullo, K. (2021, Nov 23). *UN Human Rights committee criticizes Germany's NetzDG for letting social media platforms police online speech*. Retrieved from Electronic Frontier Foundation: https://www.eff.org/deeplinks/2021/11/un-human-rights-committee-criticizes-germanys-netzdg-letting-social-media

Balkin, J. M. (1999). Free speech and hostile environments. *Columbia Law Review, 99*(8), 2295–2320.

Balkin, J. M. (2021). How to regulate (and not regulate) social media. *Journal of Free Speech Law, 1*, 71.

Battista, D., & Uva, G. (2023). Exploring the legal regulation of social Media in Europe: A review of dynamics and challenges—Current trends and future developments. *Sustainability, 15*(5), 4144.

Beausoleil, L. E. (2019). Free, hateful, and posted: Rethinking first amendment protection of hate speech in social media world. *Boston College Law Review, 60*(7), 2101–2144.

Bradford, A. (2023). *Digital empires: The global battle to regulate technology*. Oxford University Press.

Bremmer, I., & Suleyman, M. (2023, 12). *Building Blocks for AI Governance*. Retrieved from International Monetary Fund (IMF): https://www.imf.org/en/Publications/fandd/issues/2023/12/POV-building-blocks-for-AI-governance-Bremmer-Suleyman

Buiten, M., De Streel, A., & Peitz, M. (2019). *Rethinking liability rules for online hosting platforms: discussion paper No. 074 Project B 05.*

Burgess, M. (2022, May 23). *How GDPR is failing?* Retrieved from Wired: https://www.wired.co.uk/article/gdpr-2022

Caster, M. (2021, Sept 16). *OPINION: UK Online Safety Bill risks emboldening digital authoritarians around the world.* Retrieved from Thomson Reuters Foundation News: https://news.trust.org/item/20210916100925-8syij/

Commissioner for Human Rights - COE. (2012). *Social media and human rights.* Council of Europe.

Cusumano, M. A., Gawer, A., & Yoffie, D. B. (2021, Jan 15). *Social media companies should self-regulate. Now.* Retrieved from Harvard Business Review: https://hbr.org/2021/01/social-media-companies-should-self-regulate-now

De Gregorio, G. (2022). *Digital constitutionalism in Europe: Reframing rights and powers in the algorithmic society.* Cambridge University Press.

Dingwerth, K., & Pattberg, P. (2006). Global governance as a perspective on world politics. *Global Governance: a Review of Multilateralism and International Organizations, 12*(2), 185–204.

Foronda, F. H., & Iwańska, K. (2023, Feb 2). *A thousand Facebook-Cambridge Analytica scandals every day.* Retrieved from Euractiv: https://www.euractiv.com/section/digital/opinion/a-thousand-facebook-cambridge-analytica-scandals-every-day/

Friedmann, D. (2014). Sinking the safe harbour with the legal certainty of strict liability in sight. *Journal of Intellectual Property Law & Practice*, 148–155.

Gauja, A. (2021). Digital democracy: Big technology and the regulation of politics. *University of New South Wales Law Journal, 44*(3), 959–982.

Giancarlo, F., & Martin, H. (2020). Accountability and responsibility of online intermediaries. In G. Frosio (Ed.), *The Oxford handbook of online intermediary liability* (pp. 612–630). Oxford University Press.

Gillespie, T. (2017). Governance of and by platforms. In *SAGE handbook of social media* (pp. 254–278). Academia.

Gillespie, T. (2018). *Custodians of the internet: Platforms, content moderation, and the hidden decisions that shape social media.* Yale University Press.

Gorwa, R. (2019). What is platform governance? *Information Communication and Society, 2*(2), 1–18.

Gosztonyi, G. (2023). *Censorship from Plato to social media: The complexity of social Media's content regulation and moderation practices* (Vol. 61). Springer Nature.

Griffin, R. (2023). From brand safety to suitability: Advertisers in platform governance. *Internet Policy Review, 12*(3), 1–25.

Haggart, B. (2021, May 5). *American internet, American platforms, American values.* Retrieved from Centre for International Governance Innovation: https://www.cigionline.org/articles/american-internet-american-platforms-american-values/

Helberger, N., Pierson, J., & Poell, T. (2018). Governing online platforms: From contested to cooperative responsibility. *The Information Society, 34*(1), 1–14.

Heldt, A. P. (2022). EU digital services act: The white hope of intermediary regulation. In F. R. T. Flew (Ed.), *Digital platform regulation: Global perspectives on internet governance* (pp. 69–84). Springer International Publishing.

Henderson, J. A., Jr. (2016). Tort vs. Technology: Accommodating disruptive innovation. *Arizona State Law Journal*, 1146–1180.

Hirsch, D. D. (2011). The law and policy of online privacy: Regulation, self-regulation, or co-regulation. *Seattle University Law Review, 34*(2), 439–480.

Huang, E. (2020). Internet (Un)immunity: Where does China stand? *Asian. Journal of Law and Society*, 345–368.

Hutchinson, A. (2023, Oct 9). *X Launches option to restrict post replies to verified users*. Retrieved from Social Media Today: https://www.socialmediatoday.com/news/x-launches-new-option-restrict-post-replies-verified-users-only/696066/

Kapur, A. (2024, Feb 5). *Can the internet be Governed?*. Retrieved from The New Yorker: https://www.newyorker.com/magazine/2024/02/05/can-the-internet-be-governed

Keller, D. (2018, Sept 10). *Don't force google to export other countries' laws*. Retrieved from The New York Times: https://www.nytimes.com/2018/09/10/opinion/google-right-forgotten

Kumar, R. (2019, Nov 15). *Government should not regulate social media*. Retrieved from Observer Research Foundation: https://www.orfonline.org/expert-speak/government-should-not-regulate-social-media-57786

Laidlaw, E. B. (2017). *Regulating speech in cyberspace: Gatekeepers, human rights and corporate responsibility*. Cambridge University Press.

Land, M. K. (2020). Against privatized censorship: Proposals for responsible delegation. *Virginia Journal of International Law, 60*(2), 363–432.

Marsden, C. T. (2011). Internet co-regulation as part of the broader regulatory debate. In *Internet co-regulation: European law, regulatory governance and legitimacy in cyberspace* (pp. 221–242). Cambridge University Press.

Meta. (2023a, Sept 19). *Expanding Meta Verified to Businesses*. Retrieved from Meta: https://about.fb.com/news/2023/09/meta-verified-for-businesses/

Meta. (2023b, Oct 13). *Meta's ongoing efforts regarding the Israel-Hamas War*. Retrieved from Meta: https://about.fb.com/news/2023/10/metas-efforts-regarding-israel-hamas-war/

Nunziato, D. C. (2023). The digital services act and the Brussels effect on platform content moderation. *Chicago Journal of International Law*, 115–128.

O'Flaherty, K. (2022, May 27). *Facebook's new privacy policy—what you need to know*. Retrieved from Forbes: https://www.forbes.com/sites/kateoflahertyuk/2022/05/27/facebooks-new-privacy-policy-what-you-need-to-know/?sh=57a19b2ff84c

Partnoy, F. (2001). Barbarians at the gatekeepers: A proposal for a modified strict liability regime. *Washington University Law Quarterly*, 491–547.

Paulos, B., & Çelik, S. (2021). The challenges of regulating hate speech on social media in light of the theory of freedom of expression. *Süleyman Demirel Üniversitesi Hukuk Fakültesi Dergisi, 11*(1), 97–134.

Pradel, F., Zilinsky, J., Kosmidis, S., & Theocharis, Y. (2024). Toxic speech and limited demand for content moderation on social media. *American Political Science Review*, 1–18.

Repucci, S. (2019). *Media freedom: A downward spiral*. Freedom House.

Robert, S., & Mark, P. (2020). "Fake news" legislation in Thailand: The good, the bad and the ugly. *Athens Journal of Law*, 243–264.

Rosson, Z., & Felicia. (2023, June 6). *Who is shutting down the internet in 2023? A mid-year update*. Retrieved from Access Now: https://www.accessnow.org/publication/internet-shutdowns-in-2023-mid-year-update/#skip-to-content

Samples, J. (2019, Apr 9). *Why the Government should not regulate content moderation of social media*. Retrieved from CATO Institute: https://www.cato.org/policy-analysis/why-government-should-not-regulate-content-moderation-social-media

Santuraki, S. U. (2019). Trends in the regulation of hate speech and fake news: A threat to free speech? *Hasanuddin Law Review, 5*(2), 140–158.

Shahbaz, A. (2020). *The rise of digital authoritarianism, online:* https://freedomhouse.org/sites/default/files/2020-02/10192018_FOTN_2018_Final_Booklet.pdf. Freedom House.

Sinfah, T., & Toby, M. (2010). *Analysis of computer crime act of Thailand*. Center for Law and Democracy.

Stockmann, D. (2022). Tech companies and the public interest: The role of the state in governing social media platforms. *Information, Communication & Society, 26*(1), 1–15.

Suzor, N. (2018). Digital constitutionalism: Using the rule of law to evaluate the legitimacy of governance by platforms. *Social Media + Society, 4*(3).

Tao, Q. (2011). Intermediary liability of website operators in privacy cases in China. *Masaryk University Journal of Law and Technology*, 105–118.

Vaidhyanathan, S. (2018). *Antisocial media: How Facebook disconnects us and undermines democracy*. Oxford University Press.

Waldron, P., & Cornell, A. S. (2023, Apr 13). *One-size-fits-all content moderation fails the Global South*. Retrieved from Cornell Chronicle: https://news.cornell.edu/stories/2023/04/one-size-fits-all-content-moderation-fails-global-south

Weiss, T. G. (2000). Governance good Governance & global Governance: Conceptual & actual challenges. *Third World Quarterly, 21*(5).

Wenguang, Y. (2018). Internet intermediaries' liability for online illegal hate speech. *Frontiers of Law in China*, 342–356.

Wickramanayake, S. A. (2020). *Battling online harms: Can social media platforms ensure a safer online environment through private regulation?* Tilburg University.

Xiao, B. (2023). Making the private public: Regulating content moderation under Chinese law. *Computer Law & Security Review*, 1–16.

Zittrain, J. L. (2008). *The future of the internet — And how to stop it*. Yale University Press & Penguin UK.

Chapter 5
Content Regulations by Platforms: Enduring Challenges

5.1 Introduction

Content regulation measures relocate the primary obligations of moderating content to the Internet intermediaries and online platforms—including Facebook, Twitter, and Google. Due to the expansions of authoritarian regimes and the unique challenges posed by online platforms (Popiel, 2022), there has been a shift in the governance of online content, particularly across social media. While the United States and China are at the two extreme poles of Internet freedom (Fontaine & Rogers, 2011), many countries have passed different content regulation laws within a short period—especially in the last decade. As discussed in the previous chapter, these models are pitched between the extreme poles of the US and China, and regulations by the platforms fall under the broader model of "self-regulations." At present, the internal regulatory approaches include content policies, Terms of Service (ToS), algorithmic designs, and many more—the users of these platforms have little choice to decide (Schneier, 2015).

Traditional regulations have been criticized for their criminal provisions and for suppressing free speech in content regulation. On the other hand, platform-led regulatory measures often result in stifling free speech such as collateral censorship (Gosztonyi, 2023), as discussed in the previous chapter.

Further, Jougleux points out the criticism about Facebook's (Meta) self-regulatory measures:

> This is problematic, first, because, due to the high number of notifications and the related costs, Facebook surely does not employ staff with sufficient qualifications in communications law to monitor the content. Second, there is an obvious conflict of interest in requiring that the company that profits from the existence of the content determine whether it should remove it or not (Jougleux, 2022).

After the prolonged issues surrounding the 2016 US presidential election and the *Brexit* referendum, state authorities are no longer interested in relying on or developing regulations primarily through the platforms (Gosztonyi, 2023).

S. Balendra, *Free Speech in the Puzzle of Content Regulation*, Law, Governance and Technology Series 70, https://doi.org/10.1007/978-3-031-75813-3_5

Despite these concerns, various factors necessitate involving Social Media Platforms (SMPs) in a participatory role in content regulation. In the contemporary digital regulatory landscape, states are increasingly concerned about preserving their sovereignty in the face of big tech's power, leading them to delegate traditional regulatory powers to social media platforms. This shift introduces new obligations focused on preventing potential harm, rather than reacting to actual harm, as was common in the early Internet era (Kretschmer et al., 2022). These obligations are likely to be enforced through platforms' Terms of Service (ToS) and content moderation policies.

Klonick argues that this shift into the platforms' content regulations is influenced by the economic viability and the community standards of these platforms (Klonick, 2018). In addition, few platforms moderate the contents underlying the obligations posed by the corporate social responsibility of the companies. Gorwa advocates for the development of a transnational regulatory model for content shared across social media, arguing that the social media revolution has transformed this model, driving it into complex layers of regulation that involve both private and state actors (Gorwa, 2019).

Further, the recognition of *safe harbor* arrangements in state laws and regulations—such as Section 230 of the CDA—often indirectly influences platform decision-making through their policies and procedures. For instance, as Gillespie pointed out, major social media platforms have had to develop their own policies on how to respond to content removal requests from foreign governments (Gillespie, 2017).

Against this background, this chapter delves into the regulation practices of platforms, exploring how various driving factors influence these regulatory models. Through scholarly discussions and policy case studies, the chapter further investigates the impact of these practices of social media on free speech and other core values. Additionally, it also addresses the challenges identified within these regulatory frameworks and proposes solutions to mitigate or overcome them.

5.2 Factors Shaping Platforms' Regulatory Frameworks

Online platforms, as corporate entities, engage in regulatory measures against content on their platforms through a process of "self-regulation." However, it is an ongoing process that is influenced by various stakeholders, such as external moderators, user communities, governments, advertisers, media organizations, civil society groups, and academic experts. Few scholars argued that the social media firm's content moderation strategy is primarily shaped by its revenue model (Yildirim & Zhang, 2022). However, beyond the revenue, few other factors influence the platform moderation policies and practices in the current era. Sander identified four distinct factors that influence the process of content moderation: corporate philosophy, regulatory compliance, profit maximization, and public outcry (Sander, 2020), which will be explored in this section.

5.2.1 Corporate Philosophy

Corporate policy influences the content shared and permitted across their sites. Therefore, the platforms shape their architecture in accordance with their policies and user experiences. Based on the environments, where the social media sites are willing to nurture, these platforms enforce their moderation policies underlying various degrees (Sander, 2020). These philosophies often affect the free speech rights on their platforms. For example, during the Black Lives Matter protest, Facebook adopted many discriminatory measures towards content moderation—placing additional restrictions labeling the content violating privacy, community standards, and policy.

Also, these policies and philosophies often emerge and change over time. In December 2023, Elon Musk, the founder of Twitter and SpaceX, reinstated the Twitter account of conspiracy theorist Alex Jones in 2018 after users on the platform voted in favor of his return. Jones had been blocked on several platforms, including Twitter, due to abusive behavior in 2018. Musk, considering the possibility of allowing Jones back on Twitter, conducted a poll on the platform, invoking the Latin phrase *"Vox Populi, Vox Dei,"* which means "the voice of the people is the voice of God." Following the poll results, Musk restored Jones' Twitter account. It is an example of the rapid changes in the corporate philosophy that would affect the platforms' moderation decisions.

5.2.2 Regulatory Compliance

The self-regulation of platforms has also been significantly influenced by the regulatory measures, from time to time introduced by the authorities at the national and regional levels. Particularly, after the prolonged debates on regulating social media, many jurisprudence are involved in law-making in this context. In 2017, Germany passed its social media act—the Network Enforcement Act (NetzDG) six months later.

Facebook allocated significant resources to comply with legal requirements, specifically related to NetzDG. The platform has dedicated 65 staff members to process NetzDG complaints, even though the total number of complaints amounted to 1704 pieces of content. On average, each designated employee deals with fewer than five complaints per month. The staffing approach is flexible to accommodate fluctuations in the volume of complaints (Meta, 2018).

Beyond that, regional institutions such as the European Union (EU), from time to time also refine the regulatory models. For example, the new Digital Service Act (DSA) of the EU affects social media platforms related to Artificial Intelligence moderation, transparency requirements, imposing additional responsibilities to the platforms, and a few more which came into full force in 2024 February. In December 2023, the European Commission initiated formal proceedings to investigate whether company X may have violated the provisions of DSA. The areas under scrutiny include risk management, content moderation, dark patterns, advertising transparency, and data access for researchers. The decision to open formal infringement proceedings is based on a preliminary investigation, which involved analyzing X's risk assessment report, transparency report, and responses to information requests. The focus includes the dissemination of illegal content related to Hamas' terrorist attacks against Israel (European Commission, 2023).

A key observation is that regulatory compliance among platforms is predominantly enforced in more powerful states, such as Western democracies, and within American legal systems. Conversely, regulatory frameworks from the Global South often lack the authority to regulate these platforms effectively, and the platforms themselves do not always comply with the laws of these countries. However, there has been a shift recently, with many countries from the Global South beginning to establish regulatory models for these private platforms. For instance, India passed legislation in 2021[1] that subjects these platforms to specific regulatory scrutiny.

5.2.3 *Profit Maximization*

Platforms from the bottom, as corporates earn billions of revenues from advertising. The data leverage of the users is indispensable for the platforms, to strike down highly targeted advertising that caters specifically to individual user characteristics (Ghosh & Scott, 2018). The data collected also empowers platforms to customize and present content in ways that enhance user engagement. The financial benefit for online platforms lies in increased user engagement, as more time and attention spent on their sites allow for the continual accumulation of behavioral data. This, in turn, enhances the platforms' capabilities in targeted advertising and user engagement, ultimately contributing to the growth of advertising revenue (Balkin, 2018a, b).

At present, most of the popular platforms employ algorithms for content moderation. These algorithms are designed to learn from user behavior and preferences, contributing to the profile maximization goal. They may prioritize content that aligns with users' interests and engagement patterns. However, on very limited occasions, profit-maximizing social media companies often choose to ban certain users or restrict content as a strategic move in simple economics. The rationale behind this decision is to boost the willingness of marginal users to pay. In an advertising-centric business model, platforms opt to remove content only if it contributes to increased user engagement, leading to more time spent consuming content and interacting with advertisements. Ultimately, these actions are geared toward optimizing revenue generation in the context of the platform's business model (Jiménez-Durán, 2023).

[1] The Information Technology (Intermediary Guidelines and Digital Media Ethics Code) Rules (2021).

5.2.4 *Public Outcry*

Although the social media platforms' regulatory practices are predominantly shaped by the above factors, in a few exceptional circumstances, regulations by platforms is susceptible to influence from public outcry, especially when collective action by users, civil society groups, or the general public is combined with extensive media coverage or legal action (Klonick, 2018).

In July 2019, Facebook censored numerous posts and user accounts following the death of a prominent Kashmiri separatist militant killed by the Indian army. Academics, journalists, and local newspaper pages had content deleted when discussing recent events in the disputed region. Facebook stated that content supporting or praising Hizbul Mujahideen and Burhan Wani is removed, but acknowledged some removals were in error and have been restored. The platform maintains a stance against content that praises or supports terrorism but emphasizes the importance of contextualizing discussions on the subject (Doshi, 2016).

Amnesty International's study revealed that content inciting violence and discrimination reached the highest levels of Myanmar's military and civilian leadership (Amnesty International, 2022). Senior General Min Aung Hlaing, Myanmar's military leader, posted discriminatory content on Facebook in 2017, and later orchestrated a coup in February 2021. Facebook faced criticism for its failure to act, leading to social outcries. Meta, Facebook's parent company, is now facing three active complaints for remediation related to the Rohingya crisis. Civil legal proceedings were initiated against Meta in the UK and the USA in December 2021. In response to the criticism, Meta has implemented improvements, including hiring more content reviewers proficient in Myanmar's languages, enhancing Artificial Intelligence to detect hate speech, especially in Burmese, and establishing a dedicated team for the country (Global Witness, 2022).

5.3 Platforms' Content Moderation

Beyond creating self-regulatory frameworks such as guidelines, policies, and standards, SMPs enforce their policies and regulations primarily in the form of content moderation. This process involves monitoring, reviewing, and managing user-generated content to ensure it adheres to the platform's established guidelines and policies. However, the shift of content moderation to platform companies should be regulated with the utmost caution in the Internet era, as it frequently intersects with free speech and other relative constitutional values.

Kyle Langvardt pointed out that:

> Such a system, whether it is condemned as "censorship" or accepted as "content moderation," sits in tension with an American free speech tradition... (Langvardt, 2018).

Although all the SMPs engage in content moderation to prevent issues like spam, it was historically suggested that platforms were reluctant to invest in comprehensive moderation until they faced public pressure or scandals. Most platforms publish rules or community standards against content such as hate speech and harassment, which tend to be similar across platforms. Over the past decade, content moderation policies have become more complex, likely due to increased global reach, diverse content, and mounting pressure to justify decisions.

The process of content moderation is evolving and ongoing, as Gillespie points out that:

> At the top, most platforms have an internal policy team charged with overseeing moderation. They set the rules, oversee their enforcement, adjudicate the particularly hard cases, and craft new policies going forward in response (Gillespie, 2017).

Platform liability regimes make content moderation more effective by holding platforms accountable for hate speech shared by users. Generally, platforms are not liable for user-generated content unless they have knowledge of it. However, once they receive a notice, platforms are compelled to proactively moderate the content to avoid being held liable for users' speech (Fagan, 2020).

Platforms carry out their content moderation primarily in two ways: manual (human) and automated. Human moderation involves individuals (moderators) manually reviewing and assessing content. On the other hand, algorithmic moderation utilizes algorithms and machine learning to automatically analyze and filter content across social media platforms. The latter is an emerging model due to the reason it can process large volumes of content quickly and consistently, yet it is intrigued with many challenges as the regulatory model approaches predominantly through AI. Therefore, this model is backed up with the participation of human moderators.

5.3.1 Moderation by Human

Human moderation, or manual moderation, involves individuals actively reviewing and assessing user-generated content on online platforms. This practice plays a crucial role in ensuring that content aligns with community guidelines, legal standards, and ethical norms. While the contemporary regulatory framework for social media increasingly favors AI-based content moderation—primarily due to the vast volume of content generated across these platforms—human moderation remains indispensable. It is particularly vital in handling complex cases where a nuanced understanding of the context in which content is created is required. This is especially true in a global context, where content is shared across diverse linguistic, cultural, and normative backgrounds.

For example, during the Senate hearing on child safety issues in January 2024,[2] the CEOs of prominent social media platforms, including Meta (formerly Facebook), X, TikTok, Snapchat, and Discord, acknowledged the imperative of incorporating human moderators to address challenges associated with algorithmic content moderation. The executives provided insights into the extent of their workforce dedicated to Trust and Safety Personnel, also known as human moderators, tasked with managing content-related issues. According to disclosures made during the hearing, Meta and TikTok reported a combined workforce of 40,000 Trust and Safety Personnel operating globally. Snapchat indicated that they employ 2000 professionals in this capacity. X revealed that their workforce includes 2300 professionals specializing in Trust and Safety, while Discord conveyed that they have *"100s of people"* dedicated to these responsibilities.[3] This information underscores the commitment of these platforms to supplement algorithmic moderation with human expertise to ensure a more comprehensive and nuanced approach to content moderation and user safety.

However, there are numerous challenges and backlogs associated with human moderation in the current digital landscape. Gosztonyi criticizes the commitment and the role of human moderators in content moderation:

> As moderators are not experts in a particular area, Facebook provides them with a guide, with yes/no answers to a series of questions, at the end of which they can decide whether or not to remove content. Context, languages, dialects and user intent can further complicate the issue (Gosztonyi, 2021).

Galli et al. also point out that given the sheer volume of information shared online, human moderation alone is insufficient to manage content effectively and automated filters are essential for monitoring and detecting potentially unlawful or abusive content on digital platforms (Galli et al., 2022). Also, in sensitive areas like content moderation, where users with low dispositional trust may doubt that human moderators can make *unbiased* and accurate decisions about classifying user-generated content (Ruckenstein & Turunen, 2020). Molina and Sundar point out that in such contexts, users' skepticism about the fairness and correctness of human judgment can undermine the effectiveness and credibility of the moderation process (Molina & Sundar, 2024).

5.3.2 Algorithmic Content Moderation

Automated content moderation practices of the platforms are facilitated through Artificial Intelligence in the contemporary world. Due to higher content shared

---

[2] See https://www.theguardian.com/us-news/2024/jan/31/tiktok-meta-x-congress-hearing-child-sexual-exploitation.

[3] Transcript available at: https://www.rev.com/blog/transcripts/senate-hearing-with-ceos-of-meta-tiktok-x-snap-and-discord-about-child-safety-1-31-24-transcript.

across the platforms, automated content moderation become more prominent in social media platforms. Social media platforms are significantly expanding their utilization of Artificial Intelligence, employing computer-coded algorithms to moderate user-generated content (Cobbe, 2021).

Long back, Grimmelmann defined content moderation as:

> *governance mechanisms that structure participation in a community to facilitate cooperation and prevent abuse* (Grimmelmann, 2015).

The contemporary scholars Gorwa, Binns, and Katzenbach defined algorithmic content moderation in their scholarly work as:

> systems that classify user-generated content based on either matching or prediction, leading to a decision and governance outcome such as. removal, geo-blocking, account takedown (Gorwa et al., 2020).

Algorithms automatically analyze user-collected data to deliver content tailored to their interests and anticipated engagement. This process operates without regular human intervention or oversight (Dias Oliva, 2020).

Balkin pointed out that:

> algorithmic employees cost even less than human employees: they do not have families, they do not take coffee breaks, and they can do some—but by no means all—of the work of discovery and selection that human employees can do (Balkin, 2018a, b).

Big tech companies support algorithmic interventions because they bolster operational efficiency and enable the delivery of more tailored and responsive services to users.

In 2018, the CEO of Facebook, Mark Zuckerberg, addressed that:

> these are not problems you fix, but issues where you continually improve. Just as a free society will always have crime and our expectation of government is not to eliminate all crime but to effectively manage and reduce it, our community will also always face its share of abuse. Our job is to keep the misuse low, consistently improve over time, and stay ahead of new threats.[4]

Simply, Algorithmic content moderation encompasses a variety of techniques rooted in statistics and computer science, with differing levels of complexity and efficacy. The common objective across these methods is to analyze and assess content, whether it be text, audio, image, or video, by identifying, matching, predicting, or classifying it based on specific properties or general features. Algorithmic content moderation is usually carried out online, particularly on intellectual property rights and free speech—such as prohibited degree of content including, harassment, terrorist content, hate speech, pornography, defamation, and a few more.

---

[4]Transcript from a leaked discussion between Mark Zuckerberg and Facebook employees, Oct 1, available at: https://www.theverge.com/2019/10/1/20892354/mark-zuckerberg-full-transcript-leaked-facebook-meetings.

5.4 Challenges of Algorithmic Content Moderation

The assertion that recent automated content moderation on platforms, particularly by Facebook, involves substantial AI capabilities is deemed overstated. While platforms claim high success rates, such as Facebook's report that *"65.4% of hate speech content actioned was found and flagged"* before user reports, it is clarified that the majority of automated identifications pertain to duplicates of content already reviewed by human moderators (Gillespie, 2020).

Gillespie further argued that:

> Perhaps, automated tools are best used to identify the bulk of the cases, leaving the less obvious or more controversial identifications to human reviewers (Gillespie, 2020).

However, the growing algorithmic content moderations face a lot of challenges which are underscored in many scholarly works. More specifically, there are also concerns about the democratic legitimacy of speech rules being determined by a relatively homogenous group of Silicon Valley elites. Additionally, there are process-related concerns on the overall lack of transparency and accountability in content moderation practices.

The decisions are not correct all the time, since the AI creates massive disparity when it fails to understand the context in which the content is generated. Moderation, particularly when perceived as unjust, can evoke a sense that the platform did not comprehend the legitimacy of the user's post and failed to uphold their right to free expression (Gosztonyi, 2023; Matsakis, 2018). Moreover, the use of automated systems can lead to feelings of absurdity, especially when these systems make significant errors or misjudgments based on the previous data sets generated or inserted by the AI.

There is the ongoing challenge of *"deepfakes"* which uses deep-learning algorithms to create realistic simulations of a person's face, voice, or body. Major social media platforms have specific policies for deceptively manipulated media as well as synthetic audio and video. A number of platforms are revising their rules and protocols for these areas. Although their policies are comprehensive in many aspects of the challenge, the use of automated systems for content identification is mentioned as a source of potential errors, as they may generate false positives or overlook nuanced contextual differences that determine whether a piece of media violates platform policies (Ajder & Glick, 2022).

For example, during the 2020 presidential election in the United States, a viral deep-fake video featuring Joe Biden saying "*We can only re-elect Donald Trump*" has been flagged as manipulated, misleading, and partly false by the major SMPs such as Twitter, TikTok, and Facebook. Despite violating TikTok's community guidelines, the video remained accessible on multiple accounts, including one named *@therepublicanhypehouse*, as noted by the watchdog organization Media Matters. The incident highlights the challenges platforms face in effectively enforcing content moderation policies and removing deep-fake content (Tenbarge, 2020).

Gosztonyi and Lendvai argue with the example of Twitter during the 2020 election that, although there are a number of prevalent policies, numerous content were flagged, but could not potentially find the deepfakes—portraying the challenges in combatting deepfakes across the social media platforms despite the existence of the policies (Gosztonyi & Lendvai, 2023). To address this challenge, the authors propose the *"platform regulation triangle,"* a concept introduced by Gorwa (2019). This model integrates state and international legislation with the internal monitoring efforts of online platforms, creating a comprehensive approach to platform regulation.

In the decision-making of "*online speech*," the primary challenge lies in the intricate, personal, and context-dependent nature of language. Even widely recognized slurs may be reclaimed by certain groups. Inadequate context awareness can result in crude classification, leading to content being flagged for review by moderators who often lack the necessary context to determine whether the speaker belongs to the group targeted by the "hate speech" (Gorwa et al., 2020). Challenges are more complex when the content fits into the borderline category—the platforms from time to time grapple with developing a policy to govern the content that falls into the category (Gillespie, 2022).

As a global operation, automated content review processes on platforms involve choices that may jeopardize speech from marginalized communities due to over-removal risks. This system may overlook situations where content is shared for purposes like criticism, art, satire, or news reporting (Díaz & Hecht-Felella, 2021). Roberts pointed out that platforms' content moderation mechanisms, whether operated by humans or machines, often struggle to comprehend political developments, language shifts, or emerging trends crucial for proper moderation, particularly regarding speech from marginalized groups (Roberts, 2019).

The primary challenge in algorithmic platform moderation lies in incorporating general human rights principles into specific rules and procedures suitable for the unique context of online platforms (Laidlaw, 2015). This difficulty is exacerbated by the distinct and variable capacities of platforms, as well as the diverse range of features and services offered by major online platforms.

Due to factors such as cultural diversity, contextual nuances, varied content types, and language variations, the task of algorithmic content moderation becomes increasingly complex and nuanced. This complexity often results in rapid, discriminatory content moderation practices worldwide. Treating perspectives from the Western world and the Global South with a one-size-fits-all approach is hardly feasible. Consequently, decisions made by algorithms frequently exhibit bias, leading to contrasting and often discriminatory outcomes. Beyond these, policy research indicates that platforms deliberately employ their tools and algorithms to suppress marginalized voices worldwide, especially when these platforms serve as forums for discussing international issues.

There are many instances where algorithmic content moderation—deployed by the platforms— discriminately affected free speech in the global online speech arena. Simultaneously, recent studies clearly identify that SMPs—predominantly Meta—occasionally systematically silence marginalized voices across their platforms. In a report published in February 2024, Access Now found that during the Israeli-Palestinian conflict, SMPs—Instagram and Facebook—suppressed online content that supported the Palestinian cause (Access Now, 2024). Palestinian journalists and activists, both within and outside of Gaza, faced account suspensions or restrictions on various platforms. For example, journalist Leila Warah's Instagram account was suspended during this timeline.[5] Also, a significant amount of content, including documentation of atrocities and human rights abuses, was arbitrarily deleted.

However, from Meta's end, it is argued that the restrictions and the reduced engagement of the pro-Palestinian content across their platform are due to a technical glitch.[6] Access Now points out in its report that the platforms' policy, aimed at addressing online incitement to violence, faces criticism for its vague and overly broad interpretation of *"glorification"* or *"support"* of certain individuals and groups. This broad interpretation results in a sweeping net that inadvertently captures legitimate content, potentially infringing on the right to freedom of expression and opinion.

Human Rights Watch also found in their study about the discriminatory content moderation by the Meta and their impacts on free speech and expression. However, they also noted that *"shadow banning"*—the practice of blocking or partially blocking a user or the user's content from some areas of an online community in such a way that the ban is not readily apparent to the user—is challenging to verify due to the lack of platform notifications. However, some users presented compelling evidence supporting their claims. This evidence includes *"before"* and *"after"* screenshots showing a significant decrease in views when posting content about Palestine, decreased engagement metrics (likes, comments, shares) on such content, screenshots indicating the account or content is not searchable, a slowdown in new followers, and demonstrations that the content is not visible to others (Human Rights Watch, 2023).

A study by Jaidka et al. on Twitter's shadow-banning algorithms within the United States identified two key challenges: (a) Temporal instability – fluctuations over time in how shadow-bans are applied to tweets addressing political or social issues; and (b) Systematic biases – the presence of biases in shadow-ban applications, particularly targeting new users or those with low social influence (Jaidka et al., 2023). The issue of systematic bias is also raised by Ranttila stating that:

> Additionally, Republican politicians have claimed they have been victims of shadow bans when their accounts did not populate in search results on Twitter (Ranttila, 2023).

These challenges have led to serious repercussions, affecting both the enjoyment of human rights and the preservation of the rule of law and democratic values online. I have identified six key recent case studies from around the world, where the

[5] See https://twitter.com/Mondoweiss/status/1711706749294526682.

[6] See https://www.cbc.ca/news/canada/toronto/palestinian-facebook-posts-1.6052322.

algorithmic content moderation by platforms has proliferated challenges to these values.

The cases identified in this study are not an exhaustive list of all incidents that have occurred over time. However, they have been selected for their significance in capturing a diverse range of global contexts, from Western nations to the Global South, and for highlighting distinct issues within this domain. By conducting an in-depth analysis of these key case studies, this research aims to provide a deeper understanding of the complex challenges surrounding this topic.

5.4.1 Gamergate (Harassment Campaign)

The *GamerGate* controversy, which arose in 2014, drew global attention to concerns surrounding sexism and misogyny within gaming communities (Ferguson & Glasgow, 2021). The movement was difficult to define since *Gamergaters*—the proponents of the movement failed to define its goals (Jesse Singal, 2014). The #GamerGate movement was born with a blog post by Eron Gjoni about the corruption in the gaming industry. It was ostensibly sparked by allegations of unethical behavior by game developers and journalists, but it quickly became entangled with broader issues related to gender, sexism, and diversity in the gaming industry. However, critics argued that Gamergate was a platform for harassment and that it highlighted broader issues of misogyny within gaming culture.

The movement was organized through social media platforms and anonymous message boards such as 4chan and Reddit. However, Twitter was used as a prominent industry in taking this movement.[7] The hashtag #Gamergate was widely used to spread tweets across the platform. Many women who were vocal about issues related to gender representation in video games, as well as those critical of the Gamergate movement, became targets of harassment on Twitter.

Amnesty International pointed out that:

> The very nature of the Internet allows content posted on social media platforms to 'go viral' and be shared across platforms almost instantly - which means that violent and abusive content can be easy to share or repeat and difficult to contain (Amnesty International, 2018).

Twitter's algorithms were not efficient since Twitter has prioritized free speech over community since its conception, it has created a platform without addressing the socio-psychological principles that lead to intergroup conflict (Conbere, 2019). A study proves that Twitter accounts which are more than 75% of Gamergate posts that spread violence are still active, and neither deleted nor suspended (Chatzakou et al., 2017). On occasions, Twitter became the avenue for an amplified mix of voices within GamerGate, which has blended into a stew of anti-feminism, hatred, and violent threats (Hahn, 2014).

---

[7] See https://wikious.com/en/Gamergate_(harassment_campaign).

Twitter was criticized for its inability to respond quickly and prevent harassment over the service. Within the United States, Twitter and other social media sites are not liable for content posted by third parties of their service under Section 230 of the Communications Decency Act (1996), and so have no legal obligation to police malicious content such as harassment and threats.

The events surrounding *Gamergate* continue to be referenced in discussions about online toxicity, digital harassment, and the need for improved moderation and safety measures on social media platforms. Also, it revisits the urge to reform the existing laws related to the content moderation framework of the social media platforms from the government end as well.

5.4.2 DE Platforming Alex Jones Issue

Alexander Jones is an American radio show host associated with the far-right and alt-right movements, known for his prominent role as a *conspiracy* theorist. Broadcasting The Alex Jones Show from Austin, Texas, he reaches a nationwide audience through syndicated and Internet radio on the Genesis Communications Network. Jones's various websites, including InfoWars, NewsWars, and PrisonPlanet, actively promote conspiracy theories and disseminate misinformation.

Alex Jones's conspiracy theory spewing over numerous historical and tragical incidents of the United States (Killelea, 2017) includes his controversial opinions on the September 11 Attack, the Sandy Hook Elementary School shooting, the Khan Shaykhun chemical attack, the Pizzagate conspiracy theory, and many more.

After the prolonged criticism against the platforms not restricting the content shared by Jones—which violates certain policies—he was banned in 2018 for promoting hate speech and antisemitic conspiracy theories across the Internet and social media platforms including YouTube, Facebook, and Twitter (currently X) (Coaston, 2018). In September 2018, Jones faced a permanent suspension from Twitter and Periscope due to his verbal attacks on CNN journalist Oliver Darcy (Conger & Nicas, 2018). In 2019, YouTube alleged that Jones repeatedly engaged in the violation of the contents which are *"removable"* such as harassment and bullying—which led to the ban of all channels and videos related to him (Alexander, 2019).

Facebook stating that:

> We've always banned individuals or organizations that promote or engage in violence and hate, regardless of ideology

banned Jones on their platforms (Schwartz, 2019).

Jones's banning was almost welcomed by the majority opinion within and beyond the US. However, Jones described himself as the victim of a *war on free speech*—enshrined in the First Amendment (Coll, 2018). Jones and his supporters argued that it was not legal censorship.[8] However, in December 2023, after circulating the poll of "*Vox Populi, Vox Dei*"—most people voted in favor of the restoration of the Jones's account—Elon Musk restored the account in X (formerly Twitter) (Jones, 2023). However, the bans on other platforms such as Facebook, YouTube, and others, are still in force.

Terry et al. argued that the vast online communication landscape, including political speech, is subject to the discretion of social media and other providers. Despite permitting a considerable amount of speech, these platforms can act as gatekeepers without legal consequences, potentially threatening free expression. It is essential to clarify what content platforms allow or remove, considering whether removed speech would have been protected by the government (Terry et al., 2020).

Underlying the private and governmental regulations, they commented on Section 230 of the Communication Decency Act:

> Put simply, in an environment where private platforms are already deciding what speech is to be included or not, to add government oversight and regulation would only complicate the issue (Terry et al., 2020).

5.4.3 *Christchurch Mosque Shootings*

On June 13, 2019, Tarrant, who currently faces 51 counts of murder, 40 counts of attempted murder, and one count of engaging in a terrorist act, entered a plea of not guilty to all charges related to the Christchurch Mosque shootings (Macklin, 2019).

The assault was broadcast live on Facebook. Following the report on this video, Facebook removed this video sooner, particularly within 24 h, and it blocked 1.2 million copies of the video. Still, Facebook revealed that the video was viewed at least 4000 times before its removal—thus *replica* copies could not be spotted easily.[9]

Christchurch's attack and live streaming on Facebook provoked the debate about using the social media space as a tool of terrorism. In recent years, terrorists have increasingly utilized social media. For instance, in 2013, Al-Shabaab militants live-tweeted the attack on the Westgate shopping mall in Nairobi, Kenya. Additionally, in January 2015, a terrorist who perpetrated a shooting at a kosher market in eastern Paris recorded the incident using a GoPro camera (Marsh & Mulholland, 2019).

Following the Christchurch incident, Facebook placed certain restrictions on Live and invested $7.5 million in research and development of this issue (Meta, 2019). The platform introduced a "one-strike" policy, which temporarily restricts access for users that break Facebook rules.

Underlying this incident, Hattotuwa noted that:

---

[8]Transcript available at: https://www.pbs.org/newshour/show/why-kicking-alex-jones-off-social-media-is-not-legally-censorship.

[9]See https://www.bbc.com/news/business-47620519.

> American corporate entities are now required to oversee to a degree technically infeasible and humanly impossible, information produced on or spread through their services. This risks the imposition of draconian controls over what's produced, judged by hidden indicators, with little independent oversight and limited avenues for appeal (Hattotuwa, 2021).

It clearly portrays whether algorithmic and automated decision-making by social media platforms would not be effective when it deals with a wide array of contents from different cultural norms and languages. Rauf agonized that engaging in negative behaviors on social media has the potential to exacerbate real-world inequalities rooted in the structures and institutions of a techno-capitalistic society (Rauf, 2021).

Addressing the unequal or discriminatory content moderation, he further asserted that:

> In an era of free speech, censorship is carried out by algorithms as some news items get aired and others not. However, by giving air to terror, media play into the terrorists' hands as it helps spread fear and extremist ideology (Rauf, 2021).

Conway deliberately claimed that the predominant social media platforms adopt a right-based approach in governing their content, adopting the US approach (Conway, 2020). However, the approach would not fit all jurisdictions—as I argue throughout this book from distinct perspectives.

During the time of the attack, New Zealand had no legislation to deal with online hate speech—thus was compelled to be governed by the policies of the Facebook platforms. It created redundance and this massacre insisted on the global call for the regulatory aspects of online hate. Still, it should be dealt with carefully since the content shared across online spaces may carry certain values such as commentary, news, and genuine criticism (Lowe, 2019).

In this context, the significance of the ruling in *Glawischnig-Piesczek v. Facebook Ireland Limited*[10] by the Court of Justice of the European Union (CJEU) cannot be understated. The ruling set a precedent for how social media platforms operating within the European Union must manage content. The court affirmed that authorities could issue global injunctions against platforms when content shared is *manifestly illegal.* This case arose from a situation involving a former Austrian politician and member of the Green Party. In 2016, a Facebook user shared an article about her, accompanied by comments that referred to her as a *"corrupt oaf"* and a *"lousy traitor,"* among other insults. The CJEU's decision underscores the obligations of platforms to act against illegal content, extending the scope of such actions beyond national borders—particularly setting the precedent for incidents like Christchurch.

[10] Glawischnig-Piesczek v. Facebook Ireland Limited Case C-18/18 (2019).

5.4.4 Brexit Referendum

The Brexit referendum took place in the United Kingdom to decide whether the UK should remain a member of the European Union (EU) or leave—held on June 23, 2016. Finally, the referendum resulted in 51.9% of the votes cast in favor of leaving the EU—subsequently, the UK left the EU.[11]

The Digital News Report from the Reuters Institute revealed that in 2016, the ascendancy of social media as a news source paralleled the decline of print media. Both mediums played a role in providing information to approximately 35% of the UK's population. Following dedicated news websites, social media stands as the second most crucial platform for individuals to come across news on the Internet (Newman et al., 2021). Critics allege that the Brexit referendum has been heavily influenced by the content shared across social media platforms. Also, the social media platforms failed to take adequate measures where the content shared mis/disinformation, hatred content, and use of digital technologies such as "bots" that targeted advertisements (Brändle et al., 2022).

Marshall and Drieschova pointed out that social media influenced the Brexit referendum from two distinct perspectives: First, in contrast to the traditional media which has the content *gatekeepers,* social media reached a wide array of audiences; and second, the rising political distrust and trust in traditional or conventional media turned around the public towards the social media (Marshall & Drieschova, 2018).

Few other studies argued, together with the print media, that the social media platforms including Facebook, YouTube, and Twitter users supported leaving the EU with the slogans of *"vote Leave,"* *"take control,"* and *"Brexit"* (Hänska & Bauchowitz, 2017). While these platforms play a significant role in the digital democracy era, as the ambassadors' platforms, the misinformation and fake news on the issues related to immigration, Islam, and foreign policy heavily influenced the decision of the referendum (Yan, 2019).

Jaishankar expressed the endangered risks associated with the amplification of the content across social media as follows:

> The unintended consequences of digital democracy — misinformation and discontent, polarization and gridlock — mean that the boundary between politician and troll is blurring (Jaishankar, 2016).

He further argued that representative democracy is under serious threat and *Brexit* is its first causality.

Brexit reminds us of how social media content may influence the decision of a political sovereign. It should be addressed since the social media platforms are inadequate during the incidents in identifying and taking down the content which were serious threats such as information manipulation and polarization.

[11] See https://www.bbc.com/news/uk-politics-36616028.

5.4.5 2016 US Presidential Election

The 2016 US presidential election was similar to the incident of Brexit. As one of the world's superpowers, the United States' politics impacts the globe. The backdrop and campaigns of the election were largely shaped by the Internet, and predominantly by social media platforms such as Facebook, Twitter, and YouTube. Beyond conventional media, social media platforms allow individuals to interact with the content shared by the contents, such as comments, and retweets. Therefore, the candidates are involved with numerous strategies through social media campaigns. Marks pointed out that Clinton's campaign strategy was laid under the traditional media, while Trump had a much looser style—particularly focusing on social media outlets predominantly (Marx, 2017).

However, during the post-elections, numerous controversies were revealed around the social media campaigns used in the elections. The *Cambridge Analytica* data breach was made to create psychological profiles of millions of Facebook users without their consent. These profiles were then allegedly used to target and influence voters with personalized political advertisements during the 2016 United States presidential election. It was nearly more than 50 million profiles which is a third of active North American Facebook users, and nearly a quarter of potential US voters.[12] Further, it was found that Russian influence made Donald Trump president through fake profiles on social media and targeted advertising (Special Counsel Robert S. Mueller, III, 2019). Also, the proliferation of fake news across the platforms, especially on topics such as gun rights, race relations, and immigration issues affected the election results (Lee, 2020).

In his study, Carlson highlighted a moral panic over fake news following the 2016 US presidential election, depicting it as contaminating the information space, confusing, and discrediting legitimate news (Carlson, 2020). However, he further asserted that a deeper look shows varied opinions on the nature of the problem, who is responsible, and the appropriate actions to take.

While the traditional media were immediately held liable for contents shared across their handles, although the platforms acknowledged the problem, social media platforms took a longer time to address and resolve this issue. For example, Twitter responded in 2018, after two years stating that they are notifying the users of Twitter about the interactions connected to the accounts potentially connected to a propaganda effort by the Russian government (Twitter, 2018). Yet, studies show that the lesson of the 2016 election taught the platforms to address the issue, and there was a gradual improvement in the 2020 election campaign (Fung, 2020).

[12] See https://www.theguardian.com/news/2018/mar/17/cambridge-analytica-facebook-influence-us-election.

5.4.6 Violence in Myanmar

The Rohingya genocide refers to a continuing pattern of persecution and violence against the Muslim Rohingya population carried out by the Myanmar military. This tragic event can be divided into two distinct phases: the initial military crackdown spanning from October 2016 to January 2017, and an ongoing second phase that began in August 2017. Against this backdrop, the role of the social media platforms—predominantly Facebook—became controversial as a tool for the spread of the incitement of violence against the Rohingya people. A fact-finding mission supported by the United Nations identified more than 150 public social media accounts, pages, and groups on Facebook that consistently disseminated messages constituting hate speech against Muslims in general or specifically targeting the Rohingya community (Amnesty International, 2022).

Scholars further argued that Facebook should be held responsible for the content shared across the platforms and the failure to moderate the content (Domino, 2020). Amnesty International reported that the platforms that profit through the content shared across must be held responsible for their recklessness in moderating harmful content (Amnesty International, 2022).

Few other studies noted the negligence and reluctance on the part of Facebook during the Rohingya massacre, as Facebook neglected calls from Myanmar's civil society to address hate speech on its platform before the violence outbreaks in 2016 and 2017. It only conducted a human rights impact assessment in 2018, years after entering the market and after significant damage had been done in the country (Domino, 2020).

Nourooz Pour pointed out that Facebook's inability to fulfill its *ante-factum* responsibilities in addressing hate speech in Myanmar can be traced back to deficiencies in both operational and policy aspects of the platform (Nourooz Pour, 2023). The algorithms and other methods such as *"multi-step reporting"* encountered many challenges in identifying and taking down the content which are harmful in nature. The crisis sparked the discussion around a regulatory regime of the social media platforms, with the tensions between private actors and public authorities—both domestic and international (Rapp, 2021).

However, this massacre portrayed the inability of Facebook's internal regulations such as algorithms, community standards, and others. Arguing that Facebook's algorithms amplified the anti-Rohingya propaganda-related contents online, in 2021, in the United Kingdom and the United States, Rohingya members sued Facebook for £150bn over the Myanmar genocide (Aziz, 2022).

5.5 Coming Over the Challenges

Although these complex challenges associated with the platforms' moderation are often acknowledged, the existing overseeing models such as appeals, oversight boards, and transparency reports have become redundant so far as they are purely *voluntary.*

Gorwa et al. pointed out the necessity of transparency in decision-making, stating that:

> As algorithmic moderation becomes more seamlessly integrated into user's day-to-day online experience, human rights advocates and researchers must continue to challenge both the discourse and reality of the use of automated decision making in moderation, and not let firms hide behind the veil of black-boxed complexity as they seek to disengage from important content policy discussions (Gorwa et al., 2020).

Contemporary efforts are shifting from a *"self-governance"* model to a *"co-governance"* model, as outlined in the previous chapter. This approach includes regulatory measures to oversee or directly regulate platforms, enacted by authorities across various countries and regions, such as the European Union.

For example, the Digital Service Act of the EU mandates the intermediaries to prepare an annual report that is publicly available, in accordance with the requirements of the Act, which should include the content they engage in moderation, measures taken, and terms and conditions of the enforcement outcomes.[13] Also, the Member States of the European Union, such as Germany, France, and the UK (previously member) are devising themselves into the new content regulation governance (Helberger, 2020). The new Online Safety Act (OSA) of the United Kingdom (UK) prescribes the transparency requirements of the intermediaries in Chapter 3 of Part 4 of the Act. The OSA imposes obligations on social media companies to disclose their safety measures to the public. However, the requirement for transparency reports is limited to providing them only to Ofcom—the UK's communications regulator. Consequently, the potentially harmful decisions and actions of private technology companies will remain concealed from the public, limiting transparency and accountability (Fowler-Mason, 2023). It is suggested that the mandatory transparency requirement of reports of platforms including reported content, moderation decisions, flagged content, removals, and appeal disclosures would enable certain policy-level decision-making of the private platforms. The recommendations initially intended for platforms meeting specific threshold requirements, should serve as guidance for transparency reporting across all platforms, irrespective of their size.

Further, regardless of their size, all platforms should prioritize substantial investment in creating transparent, consistent, and publicly available content moderation policies. This is emphasized over resorting to reactive and ad hoc decisions triggered

[13] Article 49 of DSA.

by scandals, especially when such decisions result in harm to marginalized communities being considered an acceptable trade-off for growth.

The content moderation policy of social media platforms needs a comprehensive overhaul to consider power dynamics among various groups and address structural inequalities that hinder equal access to these platforms. Gillespie wrote about *"reduction"* techniques as an alternative to the *"take down"* of contents that could address structural inequities in online visibility by countering the marginalization faced by certain communities amid claims of platform evenhandedness and bad faith tactics. However, he expressed *skepticism*, noting that unless reduction techniques are grounded in a different theory of participation and equity, guided by an ethic of care, and subject to accountable oversight and public debate, they may exacerbate the marginalization of communities (Gillespie, 2022). Therefore, the present inequalities rendered by the platforms affect the marginalized people across the global south—the platforms use this discretion in a manner that effectively balances free expression with equity, prioritizing user safety and ensuring due process (Díaz & Hecht-Felella, 2021). This includes the transparency requirements related to the keywords for hate speech, harassments, and terrorist contents.

Further, purely relying on algorithmic decisions may lead to discrepancies often. Meta, in its recent explanation on handling satire and humor, emphasizes the subjective nature of these elements across people and cultures. Meta highlighted the importance of human review by individuals with cultural context due to the subjective nature of humor and satire (Gillespie, 2020). As Gillespie suggested, there are two potential ways to approach the partnership between human and automated moderation. First, machine learning tools could be optimized to identify the most severe and harmful content, protecting human moderators from exposure to such distressing material. Second, machine learning and algorithm tools could support human moderation teams by providing contextual data about specific violations, helping moderators understand diverse norms across subcommunities (Gillespie, 2020). Incorporate the *human-in-the-loop* principle to ensure meaningful oversight of decisions made by AI tools (Lai et al., 2022; Molina & Sundar, 2024; Ruckenstein & Turunen, 2020). This aligns with the UN Guiding Principles on Business and Human Rights, emphasizing the need for companies to establish internal accountability mechanisms to implement policies and support the right to remedy (Human Rights Watch, 2023).

The diversity of services, spaces, and operating societies further complicates the task of content moderation. Even if a balanced approach is effectively implemented with the suggestions discussed in the preceding paragraphs, the complexity of content moderation ensures that there will always be trade-offs that some users find disagreeable, and a certain level of human or algorithmic error is inevitable. Yet, I believe these recommendations will assist in reducing the challenges posed by platform moderation.

References

Access Now. (2024, Feb 19). It's not a glitch: How meta systematically censors Palestinian voices. Retrieved from Access Now: https://www.accessnow.org/publication/how-meta-censors-palestinian-voices/

Ajder, H., & Glick, J. (2022). *Just joking - deepfakes, satire, and the politics of synthetic media.* MIT Open Documentary Lab.

Alexander, J. (2019, March 19). *YouTube terminates channel dedicated to circumventing Alex Jones ban.* Retrieved from The Verge: https://www.theverge.com/2019/3/19/18272690/alex-jones-youtube-ban-info-wars-resistance-news

Amnesty International. (2018). *#toxic twitter: Violence and abuse against women online.* Amnesty International.

Amnesty International. (2022). *The social atrocity meta and the right to remedy for the Rohingya.* Amnesty International.

Aziz, A. (2022). *Rohingya diaspora online: Mapping the spaces of visibility, resistance and transnational identity on social media.* New media & Society.

Balkin, J. M. (2018a). Fixing social media's grand bargain. *Hoover Working Group on National Security, Technology, and Law, Aegis Series Paper, (1814).*

Balkin, J. M. (2018b). Free speech is triangle. *Columbia Law Review, 118*(7), 2011–2056.

Brändle, V. K., Galpin, C., & Trenz, H. J. (2022). Brexit as 'politics of division': Social media campaigning after the referendum. *Social Movement Studies, 21*(1–2), 234–253.

Carlson, M. (2020). Fake news as an informational moral panic: The symbolic deviancy of social media during the 2016 US presidential election. *Information, Communication & Society, 23*(3), 374–388.

Chatzakou, D., Kourtellis, N., Blackburn, J., De Cristofaro, E., Stringhini, G., & Vakali, A. (2017). Hate is not binary: Studying abusive behavior of# gamergate on twitter. In *Proceedings of the 28th ACM conference on hypertext and social media*, (pp. 65–74).

Coaston, J. (2018, Aug 6). *YouTube, Facebook, and Apple's ban on Alex Jones, explained.* Retrieved from Vox: https://www.vox.com/2018/8/6/17655658/alex-jones-facebook-youtube-conspiracy-theories

Cobbe, J. (2021). Algorithmic censorship by social platforms: Power and resistance. *Philosophy & Technology, 34*(4), 739–766.

Coll, S. (2018, Aug 12). *Alex Jones, the First Amendment, and the Digital Public Square.* Retrieved from The New Yorker: https://www.newyorker.com/magazine/2018/08/20/alex-jones-the-first-amendment-and-the-digital-public-square

Conbere, T. (2019, 6). A wretched hive of scum and villainy: How Twitter encourages harassment (and how to fix it). *A Thesis Presented to the Conflict and Dispute Resolution Program and the Graduate School of the University of Oregon in partial fulfillment of the requirements for the degree of Master of Science.* University of Oregon.

Conger, K., & Nicas, J. (2018, Sept 6). *Twitter bars Alex Jones and Infowars, citing harassing messages.* Retrieved from The New York Times.: https://www.nytimes.com/2018/09/06/technology/twitter-alex-jones-infowars.html

Conway, M. (2020). Routing the extreme right: Challenges for social media platforms. *The RUSI Journal, 165*(1), 108–113.

Dias Oliva, T. (2020). Content moderation technologies: Applying human rights standards to protect freedom of expression. *Human Rights Law Review, 20*(4), 607–640.

Díaz, Á., & Hecht-Felella, L. (2021). *Double standards in social media content moderation.* Brennan Center for Justice at New York University School of Law.

Domino, J. (2020). Crime as cognitive constraint: Facebook's role in Myanmar's incitement landscape and the promise of international tort liability. *Case Western Reserve Journal of International Law, 52*, 143–198.

Doshi, V. (2016, July 19). *Facebook under fire for 'censoring' Kashmir-related posts and accounts.* Retrieved from The Guardian: https://www.theguardian.com/technology/2016/jul/19/facebook-under-fire-censoring-kashmir-posts-accounts

European Commission. (2023, December 18). *Commission opens formal proceedings against X under the Digital Services Act.* Retrieved from European Commission: https://ec.europa.eu/commission/presscorner/detail/en/IP_23_6709

Fagan, F. (2020). Optimal social media content moderation and platform immunities. *European Journal of Law and Economics, 50*(3), 437–449.

Ferguson, C. J., & Glasgow, B. (2021). Who are GamerGate? A descriptive study of individuals involved in the GamerGate controversy. *Psychology of Popular Media, 10*(2), 243–247.

Fontaine, R., & Rogers, W. (2011). *Internet freedom: A foreign policy imperative in the digital age.* Center for a New American Security.

Fowler-Mason, E. (2023, Feb 8). *The Online Safety Bill needs more algorithmic accountability to make social media safe.* Retrieved from LSE Blog: https://blogs.lse.ac.uk/medialse/2023/02/08/the-online-safety-bill-needs-more-algorithmic-accountability-to-make-social-media-safe/

Fung, B. (2020, Aug 14). *Facebook, Twitter and Google failed to protect the 2016 election. Now they want to prove they've learned their lesson.* Retrieved from CNN: https://www.cnn.com/2020/08/14/tech/tech-elections-2020/index.html

Galli, F., Loreggia, A., & Sartor, G. (2022). The regulation of content moderation. In S. D. D. M. Vicente (Ed.), *The legal challenges of the fourth industrial revolution: The European Union's digital strategy* (pp. 63–87). Springer International Publishing.

Ghosh, D., & Scott, B. (2018). *Digital deceit: The technologies behind precision propaganda on the internet.* New America.

Gillespie, T. (2017). Governance of and by platforms. SAGE handbook of social media, pp. 254–278.

Gillespie, T. (2020). Content moderation, AI, and the question of scale. *Big Data & Society, 7*(2).

Gillespie, T. (2022). Do not recommend? Reduction as a form of content moderation. *Social Media + Society, 8*(3).

Global Witness. (2022, Mar 20). *Facebook approves adverts containing hate speech inciting violence and genocide against the Rohingya.* Retrieved from Global Witness: https://www.globalwitness.org/en/campaigns/digital-threats/rohingya-facebook-hate-speech/

Gorwa, R. (2019). The platform governance triangle: Conceptualising the informal regulation of online content. *Internet Policy Review, 8*(2), 1–22.

Gorwa, R., Binns, R., & Katzenbach, C. (2020). Algorithmic content moderation: Technical and political challenges in the automation of platform governance. *Big Data & Society, 7*(1).

Gosztonyi, G. (2021). Some human and technical aspects of online content regulation. *Journal of Liberty and International Affairs, 7*, 149–159.

Gosztonyi, G. (2023). *Censorship from Plato to social media: The complexity of social Media's content regulation and moderation practices* (Vol. 61). Springer Nature.

Gosztonyi, G., & Lendvai, G. F. (2023). Deepfake: A multifaceted dilemma in ethics and law. *Journal of Information Ethics, 32*(2), 109–121.

Grimmelmann, J. (2015). The virtues of moderation. *Yale Journal of Law and Technology, 17*, 42–109.

Hahn, J. D. (2014, Oct 17). The hashtags and death threats behind #GamerGate, gaming's latest controversy. Retrieved from Complex: https://www.complex.com/pop-culture/a/jason-duaine-hahn/gamergate-sexism-identity-twitter

Hänska, M., & Bauchowitz, S. (2017). Tweeting for Brexit: How social media influenced the referendum. In J. A. Mair (Ed.), *Brexit, Trump and the media* (pp. 31–35). Abramis Academic Publishing.

Hattotuwa, S. (2021). *The nature of disinformation and nurture of democratic responses: Reflections, research, and writing on Aotearoa New Zealand's Christchurch massacre.* ICT4Peace Foundation.

Helberger, N. (2020). The political power of platforms: How current attempts to regulate misinformation amplify opinion power. *Digital Journalism, 8*(6), 842–854.

Human Rights Watch. (2023). *Meta's broken promises systemic censorship of Palestine content on Instagram and Facebook.* Human Rights Watch.

Jaidka, K., Mukerjee, S., & Lelkes, Y. (2023). Silenced on social media: The gatekeeping functions of shadowbans in the American Twitterverse. *Journal of Communication, 73*(2), 163–178.

Jaishankar, D. (2016, June 29). *Brexit: The first major casualty of digital democracy.* Retrieved from Brookings: https://www.brookings.edu/articles/brexit-the-first-major-casualty-of-digital-democracy/

Jesse Singal. (2014, Oct 20). *Gamergate Should Stop Lying to Journalists — and Itself.* Retrieved from Science of Us: https://web.archive.org/web/20141023061146/http://nymag.com/scienceofus/2014/10/gamergate-should-stop-lying-to-itself.html

Jiménez-Durán, R. (2023). The economics of content moderation: Theory and experimental evidence from hate speech on Twitter. *George J. Stigler Center for the Study of the Economy & the State Working Paper, (324).*

Jones, T. (2023, Dec 11). *Elon Musk and X welcome back conspiracy theorist Alex Jones.* Retrieved from Poynter: https://www.poynter.org/commentary/2023/realalexjones-alex-jones-back-on-x-twitter/

Jougleux, P. (2022). *Facebook and the (EU) law. How the social network reshaped the legal framework.* Springer Nature AG.

Killelea, E. (2017, Feb 21). *Alex Jones' Mis-Infowars: 7 Bat-Sh*t Conspiracy Theories.* Retrieved from Rolling Stone: https://www.rollingstone.com/culture/culture-lists/alex-jones-mis-infowars-7-bat-sht-conspiracy-theories-195468/satanists-are-taking-over-america-116484/

Klonick, K. (2018). The new governors: The people, rules, and processes governing online speech. *Harvard Law Review, 131*(6), 1598–1670.

Kretschmer, M., Furgal, U., & Schlesinger, P. (2022). The emergence of platform regulation in the UK: an empirical-legal study. *Weizenbaum Journal of the Digital Society–special issue: Democracy in Flux–Order, Dynamics and Voices in Digital Public Sphere.*

Lai, V., Carton, S., Bhatnagar, R., Liao, Q. V., Zhang, Y., & Tan, C. (2022). Human-ai collaboration via conditional delegation: A case study of content moderation. In *Proceedings of the 2022 CHI Conference on Human Factors in Computing Systems*, (pp. 1–18).

Laidlaw, E. B. (2015). *Regulating speech in cyberspace: Gatekeepers, human rights and corporate responsibility.* Cambridge University Press.

Langvardt, K. (2018). Regulating online content moderation. *Georgetown Law Journal, 106*(5), 1353–1388.

Lee, J. M. (2020, Oct 16). How fake news affects U.S. elections. Retrieved from UCF Today: https://www.ucf.edu/news/how-fake-news-affects-u-s-elections/

Lowe, D. (2019). Christchurch terrorist attack, the far-right and social media: What can we learn? *The New Jurist.*

Macklin, G. (2019). The Christchurch attacks: Livestream terror in the viral video age. *CtC Sentinel, 12*(6), 18–29.

Marsh, J., & Mulholland, T. (2019, Mar 15). *How the Christchurch terrorist attack was made for social media.* Retrieved from CNN: https://www.cnn.com/2019/03/15/tech/christchurch-internet-radicalization-intl/index.html

Marshall, H., & Drieschova, A. (2018). Post-truth politics in the UK's Brexit referendum. *New Perspectives, 26*(3), 89–105.

Marx, J. (2017). Twitter and the 2016 presidential election. *Critique: A Worldwide*, 17–37.

Matsakis, L. (2018, Dec 5). *Tumblr's Porn-Detecting AI Has One Job—and It's Bad at It.* Retrieved from Wired: https://www.wired.com/story/tumblr-porn-ai-adult-content/

Meta. (2018). *NetzDG transparency report.* Meta.

Meta. (2019, May 14). *Protecting Facebook live from abuse and investing in manipulated media research.* Retrieved from Meta: https://about.fb.com/news/2019/05/protecting-live-from-abuse/

Molina, M. D., & Sundar, S. S. (2024). Does distrust in humans predict greater trust in AI? Role of individual differences in user responses to content moderation. *New Media & Society, 26*(6), 3638–3656.

Newman, N., Fletcher, R., Schulz, A., Andi, S., Robertson, C. T., & Nielsen, R. K. (2021). *Reuters institute digital news report 2021*. Reuters Institute for the study of Journalism.

Nourooz Pour, H. (2023). Transitional justice and online social platforms: Facebook and the Rohingya genocide. *International Journal of Law and Information Technology, 31*(2), 95–113.

Popiel, P. (2022). Digital platforms as policy actors. In T. Flew (Ed.), *Digital platform regulation: Global perspectives on internet governance* (pp. 131–150). Springer International Publishing.

Ranttila, K. (2023). Social media and monopoly. *Ohio Northern University Law Review, 46*(1), 161–179.

Rapp, K. (2021). Social media and genocide: The case for home state responsibility. *Journal of Human Rights, 20*(4), 486–502.

Rauf, A. A. (2021). New moralities for new media? Assessing the role of social media in acts of terror and providing points of deliberation for business ethics. *Journal of Business Ethics, 170*(2), 229–251.

Roberts, S. T. (2019). *Behind the screen: Content moderation in the shadows of social media*. Yale University Press.

Ruckenstein, M., & Turunen, L. L. M. (2020). Re-humanizing the platform: Content moderators and the logic of care. *New Media & Society, 22*(6), 1026–1042.

Sander, B. (2020). Freedom of expression in the age of online platforms: The promise and pitfalls of human rights-based approach to content moderation. *Fordham International Law Journal, 43*(4), 939–1006.

Schneier, B. (2015). *Data and goliath: The hidden battles to collect your data and control your world*. WW Norton & Company.

Schwartz, M. S. (2019, May 03). *Facebook Bans Alex Jones, Louis Farrakhan And Other 'Dangerous' Individuals*. Retrieved from NPR: https://www.npr.org/2019/05/03/719897599/facebook-bans-alex-jones-louis-farrakhan-and-other-dangerous-individuals

Special Counsel Robert S. Mueller, III. (2019). *Report on the investigation into Russian interference in the 2016 presidential election*. U.S. Department of Justice.

Tenbarge, K. (2020, May 13). *TikTok decided this deceptively edited Joe Biden clip broke its rules, but the app only punished some of the users who posted it Kat Tenbarge*. Retrieved from Business Insider: https://www.businessinsider.com/tiktok-remove-joe-biden-clip-content-moderation-misleading-elect-trump-2020-3

Terry, C., Anderson, J., Wiley, S. K., & Memmel, S. (2020). Free expression or protected speech? Looking for the concept of state action in news. *University of Baltimore Journal of Media Law & Ethics, 8*(2), 102–116.

Twitter. (2018, Jan 19). *Update on Twitter's review of the 2016 US election*. Retrieved from Twitter: https://blog.twitter.com/en_us/topics/company/2018/2016-election-update

Yan, S. (2019). Social Media & Brexit: The Role of Social Media in the Outcome of the UK's EU Referendum. *Presented at the Debating Communities and Networks conference*.

Yildirim, P., & Zhang, Z. J. (2022, Jan 24). *How Social Media Firms Moderate Their Content*. Retrieved from Knowledge at Wharton: https://knowledge.wharton.upenn.edu/article/social-media-firms-moderate-content/#:~:text=John%20Zhang%2C%20and%20Wharton%20doctoral,the%20latter%20when%20it%20does

Chapter 6
Digital Authoritarianism: The Chinese Model and Beyond

6.1 Introduction

Highly centralized power, characterized by political repression and the exclusion of dissent and challenges, leads to authoritarianism in public society. In *Totalitarian and Authoritarian Regimes*, political scientist Juan Linz defined authoritarianism as:

> Political systems with limited, not responsible, political pluralism, without elaborate and guiding ideology, but with distinctive mentalities, without extensive nor intensive political mobilization, except at some points in their development, and in which a leader or occasionally a small group exercises power within formally ill-defined limits but quite predictable ones (Linz, 2000).

Henderson contends that authoritarianism transcends specific political ideologies, focusing instead on the nature of authority itself—how it is exercised and obeyed, which includes blind obedience to oppressive rule, all of which can pose significant threats to human freedom and dignity (Henderson, 1991). On a few occasions, the label "false populism" has been used to describe instances where populism is exploited as a rhetorical tool to advance authoritarian objectives, all while maintaining democratic institutions like competitive elections and avoiding overt violence against opponents (Halmai, 2019).

Authoritarianism generally carries four characteristics: a lack of political diversity, oppressive measures to address societal problems, limited political engagement, and broad executive powers with ambiguous boundaries (Moustafa & Ginsburg, 2008).

Meloen points out that authoritarian organizations have increasingly adopted a key organizational principle known as the authoritarian hierarchy, exemplified in fascism by the "*fuehrer principle,*" which emphasizes centralized, unquestioned leadership (Meloen, 2000). The authoritarian regimes of governments have been threats to democracy, the majority form of self-government that recognizes and prima facie places priorities on recognizing human rights and fundamental freedoms. Although many scholars around the globe claim that authoritarian approaches to

S. Balendra, *Free Speech in the Puzzle of Content Regulation*, Law, Governance and Technology Series 70, https://doi.org/10.1007/978-3-031-75813-3_6

pervert franchise or electoral forms put significant strain on the democratic process, it expands the attacks on fundamental rights, such as free expression, a free press, freedom of association, religious freedom, and Internet freedom, among others (Berthin, 2023).

A study of Freedom House identified modern approaches of authoritarianism reflected in undermining the rule of law, attacking media freedoms, and discriminating against and mistreating different public groups, including minorities, refugees, and migrants (Repucci & Slipowitz, 2022). Many policy studies identified that global freedom has drastically declined in the recent past. The report published by Freedom House in 2022 pointed out that, compared to 25 countries that improved global freedom, 60 countries dwindled their index (Berthin, 2023). The study further identified that around 38% of the global population lives in countries without freedom.

Against this backdrop, a debate about regulating Social Media Platforms (SMPs), vesting control and authority with a government authority, would potentially add *icing on the cake* for the authoritarian regimes to extend their agendas across the digital space. In many countries, such as China, Russia, Sri Lanka, and Myanmar, the digital space is the only avenue left to accommodate advocacy and free speech in challenging jurisdictions.

As private content moderation presents unique challenges to free speech, as discussed in the preceding chapter (Chap. 5), the argument is quite lean about *external regulations* that empower the government authorities to interfere in content moderation governance. On this backdrop, this chapter attempts to dive into the discussion on the implications around the external regulations that could potentially harm free speech, and information flow across the SMPs. Particularly, this chapter dives into the discussion on the rise of digital authoritarianism in cyberspace, predominantly carried out by governmental authorities. While identifying and analyzing the key methods by which these authorities engage in authoritarian practices, the chapter attempts to alarm out the danger of vesting absolute authority to a governmental body—such as a model of external regulation. By doing this, I attempt to address, though the platform moderation by the SMPs (self-regulation) carries certain setbacks, as discussed in the previous chapter, shifting of the authority to governments, will end up as an extension of digital authoritarianism across the global social media users.

6.2 The Rise of Digital Authoritarianism

As technology evolves rapidly, the form of authoritarianism has also shifted from the traditional form into the digital paradigm with numerous approaches. In identifying features of a free Internet, Morgus and Sherman argued that "*The U.S. and other liberal-democratic nation-states make reference to an internet that is, in some combination, free, open, interoperable, secure, and resilient*" (Morgus & Sherman,

2018). However, these ideal standards are not observed in the Internet reciprocity of authoritarian regimes.

Digital authoritarianism can be understood as the operation of digital information technology infrastructures by authoritarian governments to surveil, repress, and manipulate domestic and foreign populations (Polyakova & Meserole, 2019a, 2019b). The tools empowered by technology and Artificial Intelligence (AI), including bots, lead to the strengthening of these authoritarian regimes (Akın Ünver, 2018). Brandt argues that the digital authoritarian approach is generally carried out through four pathways: mass surveillance, cyber-operations, censorship, and information operations (Brandt, 2022). Preventive repression is often the first and most important line of defense for authoritarians; however, it has multiple effects on dissenting groups in a democratic society. More specifically, it is identified in the mobilization of a larger group of the public, such as disrupting the dissenting group, cutting off their communication, making gathering more complicated, and restricting access to resources (Dragu & Lupu, 2021).

Civic digital space is shrinking since authoritarian governments are using technology as a pillar of restriction through repressive laws to control activism in cyberspace. Dragu and Lupu further argue that while physical integrity rights have improved, the advancement of technology enables governments to employ non-violent forms of repression to pre-empt dissent, posing risks to other human rights and democratization efforts, as stronger legal constraints may increase the costs of such repression, potentially reducing its occurrence but also leading to greater public dissent. (Dragu & Lupu, 2021).

In the social media era, China and Russia have emerged as leading jurisdictions in deploying authoritarian measures within the digital sphere, often referred to collectively as the "*Chinese Model*" due to their broad, sweeping approaches to Internet control and censorship. Scholars write that China has become the exemplar of this new form of "authoritarian legality" (Gosztonyi, 2023; Hendley, 2022; Lilkov, 2020; Zhang, 2024). It is criticized as a *nationalist-isolationist* policy as this approach stifles the free speech, expression, and information flow across the digital space—as *the governments decide what the people want to see* (Robles-Carrillo, 2022). But from the government's perspective, the issue centers on cyber sovereignty, a topic explored in detail in Chap. 3 of this book. China adopts the view that nations have the sovereign right to independently develop and regulate their Internet, while rejecting the notion of any single country, particularly the United States, achieving dominance in the unregulated realm of cyberspace.[1]

The chapter leads the discussion on how different methods are employed by authoritarian regimes in extending their agendas in the demographics both locally and internationally, and how they invade free speech and other human rights along with democratic values.

[1] See https://www.bbc.com/news/world-asia-china-35109453.

6.2.1 *Mass Surveillance*

When private companies or authorities watch and analyze what people do online, it can make things more convenient for users, like giving them targeted advertisements or personalized content that match their interests. But collecting extensive data about what people do online has become a major challenge for digital citizenship in the digital world (Hintz et al., 2017).

The digitalization of services, particularly after the COVID-19 pandemic outbreak, has transformed the governance structure in numerous countries. Digital adoption has taken a quantum leap at various levels. However, the advanced governance model occasionally led to challenges in monitoring and surveillance.

Authoritarian states including Russia and China, using cameras, facial recognition, drones, GPS tracking, and other digital technologies, carry out mass surveillance and monitoring. This fundamentally detaches expectations of privacy. On facilitating surveillance tools, China is aggressively pursuing global technological dominance. The COVID-19 pandemic and the response measures have emboldened the usage, access, and manufacture of technology for surveillance in China (Khalil, 2020). It has been criticized that Chinese authorities are sweeping authoritarian controls with technologies such as phone scanners, facial-recognition cameras, face and fingerprint databases, and many others (Mozur & Krolik, 2019). With local networks of nearly 200 million closed-circuit televisions (CCTV), China has the world's largest surveillance network (Khalil, 2020). Following China, other countries such as the United States, Russia, India, the United Kingdom, and Singapore have configured high-level digital surveillance societies. Studies show that over 80 countries now apply some form of digital surveillance (Finkel, 2015). Although limited surveillance is necessary for the security of states, modern surveillance activities extend beyond legitimate goals other than were originally intended (OHCHR, 2022a, 2022b). Authoritarian states extend their application to the targeted monitoring and persecution of dissenting political opinions—opposition parties, minorities, and human rights defenders (Bellasio et al., 2021). While the open and free Internet is considered a predominant feature of cyberspace, surveillance operations, particularly from fragile democratic states, harm the principle of Internet freedom (Morgus & Sherman, 2018).

6.2.2 *Cyberattacks*

The primary victims of cyber operations are civil society activists, human rights defenders, and the public who raise their voices in cyberspaces—social media handles, emails, web portals, etc. The government's repressive movements in the form of cyberattacks target accounts to block access, seek confidential information, or make contact (Michaelsen, 2020).

Casey pointed out that cyberattacks launched by electoral autocracies (governments that hold elections but lack true democratic practices, such as fair and free voting processes, protection of civil liberties, and checks and balances on government power) are primarily focused on achieving two broad objectives:

1. Weakening True Democracies: This involves actions designed to undermine the institutions, public trust, and processes that are fundamental to democratic governance. For example, cyberattacks may target electoral systems to manipulate outcomes, steal sensitive information to discredit political figures or parties, or spread disinformation to polarize public opinion and erode trust in democratic institutions.
2. Limiting Political Opposition, Dissent, and Exposure to Liberal Democracies: Autocratic regimes use cyberattacks to suppress internal opposition and prevent the spread of democratic ideals within their borders. This can involve censoring online content, surveilling and harassing political activists, and launching cyberattacks against independent media outlets to prevent them from reporting on government abuses or promoting democratic values (Babb, 2022).

Considering the suppression of dissenting opinions, many authoritarian states approach Distributed Denial of Service (DDoS) attacks with the assistance of regime-backed hacking groups. Decades ago, the primary targets of cyber operations were the information systems of a military adversary directed at its population and other states (Burton, 2019).

The *Sony Hack*, involving the United States-based Sony Pictures, was executed by a group of hackers called "*Guardians of Peace,*" allegedly from North Korea, on 24 November 2014. The hack was in retaliation for the previous demand to halt the Sony Pictures movie, "The Interview," a CIA assassination attempt against Kim Jong-un, the North Korean leader (Burton, 2019). This hack made it clear that the United States is a country where political speech and freedom are well recognized under the First Amendment and valued as the lifeblood of democracy (Wilton, 2017). As Obama criticized, this hack was a severe infringement on free speech and expression (Howard, 2014). Although Russia and China have become major jurisdictions involved in cyberattacks and manipulation of information (Christopher & Matthews, 2016; Schneider, 2023), currently, cyberattacks are not only carried out by dominant powers but also by emerging powers as well.

Recently, actors from Iran escalated attacks beyond jurisdictional limitations, including the United States and the European Union (Burt, 2022). Michaelsen's statement highlighted Iran as a target of cyberattacks and espionage activities conducted by a diverse group of countries, including France, Russia, Canada, the United Kingdom, and Saudi Arabia. This situation sheds light on the complex web of international relations and the strategic use of cyber operations in pursuing national interests, intelligence gathering, and geopolitical maneuvering (Michaelsen, 2018).

As the Internet has become a new avenue for the enjoyment of human rights and democratic values, it is necessary to protect democratic institutions from cyberattacks to maintain not only security but also public trust in democracy

(Dales, 2021). However, regulatory frameworks without corresponding definitions of cyberattacks could suppress free speech and democratic political organization in digital spaces (Hathaway et al., 2012). Scholars also identified that to overcome the challenge of cyberattacks, democracies should be more cohesive and strategic in assessing the economic, political, information, and cyber tools of authoritarian regimes such as Russia and China (Brandt & Taussig, 2019).

One of the major challenges in addressing cyberattacks is the lack of regulatory frameworks, both substantive and procedural. Additionally, due to the nature of the attacks, such as technological advancements and the cross-border nature, cyberattacks have become one of the most complex challenges to address in cyberspace.

6.2.3 Censorship

Censorship—that too in the extreme of *blanket* censorship is another form of authoritarian approach carried out by states under the guise of regulating the content circulating in the cyber paradigm.

Deibert defined censorship as:

> The act or system of practice suppressing, limiting, or deleting objectionable or any other kind of speech (Deibert, 2008).

While censorship is an essential tool in both online and offline contexts to restrict prohibited or dangerous speech, authoritarian regimes like China employ a comprehensive and indiscriminate approach known as blanket censorship. The Chinese government controls the country's gateways to the global Internet, enabling authorities to restrict connectivity and access to content hosted abroad, which underpins the "Great Firewall"—the informal term for its extensive Internet censorship system. King et al. identify three ways of censorship deployed by the Chinese authorities: the Great Firewall, keyword blocking, and hand censoring—which suppress online free speech with these three layers (King et al., 2013).

This extreme form of censorship impacts free speech and expression and, more prominently, erodes democratic values by providing the public with incomplete information (Gosztonyi, 2023; King et al., 2013; Qiu, 1999). As this book discussed in Chap. 2, digital squares have become the new avenues for political debates and discussions in the era of digital democracy. These extreme censorship measures often invade the public participation and interactions in the digital spaces (Weidmann & Rød, 2019; Wong & Liang, 2021).

This point is also raised by Kyriakopoulou:

> The online dialogue and interaction—if sustained—can produce the need for collective action or become the starting point of smooth political participation depending on the circumstances under which further organised action may emerge. The creation of a 'public sphere', an online space of deliberation, may be the hope for the online activists who use online tools to fight for democracy (Kyriakopoulou, 2011).

These measures curtail free speech and expression—essential human rights—by implementing extensive censorship and banning numerous websites and social media platforms (Gosztonyi, 2023; Polyakova & Meserole, 2019a, 2019b; Zhuravskaya et al., 2020). As a dangerous trend, many emerging countries such as Myanmar, Vietnam, and Sri Lanka—particularly from the majority world—are leaning approach towards this model of regulations and censorship, which is an alarm for free speech and other democratic values online.

Moynihan and Patel point out:

> Nonetheless, some countries have sought to emulate the Chinese government's draconian approach to the online space. Vietnam's cybersecurity law draws directly from the Chinese model in stifling any form of political speech that the state deems undesirable rather than simply minimizing cybersecurity threats (Moynihan & Patel, 2021).

6.2.4 *Internet Disruptions*

Internet disruptions, such as shutdowns or restrictions, are tools that can be used by authorities to intentionally block or hinder access to information and restrict freedom of speech and expression. In the digital age, where much of the media and public discourse occurs online, such shutdowns can severely impact press freedom by limiting the ability of journalists to report and of citizens to access news and share information (Jain & Variath, 2020).

Authoritarian governments adopt shutting down Internet services or blocking applications to control the information available or communicated to various stakeholders within their jurisdiction. Though owing to the emerging issue of the information era, Internet censorship has become prevalent across the world, the lack of knowledge, accountability, and transparency of these practices often tends to have deleterious consequences against human rights and democratic values (Deibert, 2008). Therefore, it raises serious concerns in jurisprudences with authoritarian nature and fragile democracies. Especially, Internet censorship has been fragmented as a tool to suppress free speech and political participation online.

A study conducted by The Berkman Klein Center Study identified that:

> Filtering directed at political opposition to the ruling government is a common type of blocking in many countries across the world (Zittrain et al., 2017)

.

The United Nations revealed that 931 shutdowns between 2016 and 2021 in 74 countries were recorded, highlighting a severe deterioration of human rights, specifically free speech (OHCHR, 2022a, 2022b). A study of the Freedom House also warns about this trend as it is on the high rise, pointing out that in 20 countries, Internet access was suspended, and in 21 countries, social media access was blocked in 2021 (Repucci, 2019).

However, scholarly debates clearly differentiated the Internet censorship issues in authoritarian regimes from the rest. While all political regimes may practice censorship to varying degrees, established democracies are characterized by their efforts to minimize censorship and enhance freedom of expression. This is rooted in democratic principles that value and protect individual rights and the free flow of information as essential to the functioning of a healthy society and the democratic process. In contrast, authoritarian states often impose strict censorship to control information, suppress dissent, and maintain power, limiting the public's ability to access diverse viewpoints and participate fully in civic life (Dick et al., 2019).

This authoritarian approach is frequently witnessed during the time of elections and protests to restrict the free flow of information and communication. Particularly during elections, it seriously harms the exchange of ideas and political campaigns predominantly done through social media platforms in the digital era. Freedom House identified in a study that during 2018–2019, nearly 14 countries including Cambodia, Egypt, Bangladesh, Zimbabwe, and Mexico censored certain websites during the electoral duration (Shahbaz & Funk, 2019). It contradicts certain human rights and democratic values, including the 2014 Report of the Special Rapporteur on the promotion and protection of the right to freedom of opinion and expression mandates:

> Providing the conditions for free and open political communication is an essential element of ensuring fair and democratic electoral processes (UN Human Rights Council, 2014).

Jain and Variath argue that the Internet shutdowns and disruptions have evolved as a new law enforcement measure but have a significant arbitral approach, particularly during the elections, pointing out that:

> During elections, the suspension of services reduced the visibility of the opposition. Governments typically justify elections-related disruptions as retaliation to national security threats or concern for the fairness of the electoral process. Considering how powerful a tool internet has tuned into, digital disruptions enables to wither away powerful movements (Jain & Variath, 2020).

Authoritarian governments further suppress the content shared by users in cyberspace through "*throttling*" measures in which Internet service providers intentionally slow down customers' service to limit the total bandwidth consumed. Indeed, "throttling" measures are an absolute violation of net neutrality rules which mandate that all corporations, including Internet service providers (ISPs), should treat Internet data and users equally. They should not restrict access, slow down access speeds, or block content for some users to serve their interests (Vigliarolo, 2018).

6.2.5 Information Warfare

Information warfare is generally identified as the collection, distribution, modification, and disruption of information to gain an advantage over an adversary party. As an authoritarian movement, information warfare disrupts information and influences people while diminishing trust in the government (Prier, 2017).

Russia, China, and Iran are considered significant states involved in information operations from an authoritarian narrative. Information warfare helps manipulate and spread information worldwide with high-technology features such as bots, also known as information operations. Although the narratives may not be shared daily, they intensify during crises such as the COVID-19 pandemic, human rights abuses of Uighurs in Xinjiang, the invasion of Ukraine, etc. (Brandt, 2022).

These information operations manipulate information and data from cyber access, including social media platforms, search engines, and other web portals. Regimes carry out these operations with different narratives such as geopolitics, power thirst, etc. For example, the alleged Russian involvement in the United States election of 2016 had a lasting impact on democracy.

A study by Nye criticized that:

> During the election period, Russian operatives used Facebook to publicize 129 staged events, drawing the attention of 340,000 users; 10 million people saw ads paid for by Russian accounts; and 126 million Americans saw posts by 470 accounts affiliated with the Russian Internet Research Agency (Nye, 2019).

Recently during the invasion of Ukraine, Russia adopted a similar strategy of information warfare, as Lokot pointed out:

> Destroying connectivity in Ukraine has further isolated vulnerable communities in Russia-occupied areas. It has cut them off from trusted news sources and left them unable to report on instances of torture, hostage-taking, murders, and other war crimes (Lokot, 2023).

Information warfare is also considered a serious form of the authoritarian regime since it results in severe violations of human rights, free speech, expression, and reliable information. The use of bots, AI, and advanced technologies are used as tools to spread false information; Prier alleged these online weapons should frighten every leader in a democracy (Prier, 2017).

Due to the paradoxical nature of the Internet as a tool for both freedom and control, while technology has vastly expanded access to information and opportunities for expression, it also presents a relatively easier means for authoritarian states to exert control over information. Unlike television and radio, which can broadcast over wide areas and sometimes across borders with less direct control, Internet data primarily travels through fiber optic cables. These cables are physically located within countries or under their territorial waters, giving states the capability to monitor, intercept, or even completely shut down Internet traffic. Despite the Internet's potential to democratize information, its infrastructure allows authoritarian regimes to exert a high degree of control and surveillance over online content and communication (Wolterman, 2018).

However, as a recommendation, scholars Rosenberger and Gorman suggested building information resilience in society and seizing the information initiative in accordance with principles would enable democracies to overcome the challenges of information warfare (Rosenberger & Gorman, 2020). To get rid of political information warfare, developing a strategy of deterrence would help governments sustainably deal with this issue (Erixon & Lee-Makiyama, 2011).

As democratic jurisprudences grapple with interventions of authoritarian controls by governmental authorities in the digital space that contest the enjoyment and realization of human rights and political participation, cyber governance should be rerouted to finding an appropriate track to control information warfare and regulate the digital space. Contemporary authoritarian regimes often employ various measures to extend their agendas, importantly eroding free speech and democratic values. Vesting powers in governments without proper checks and balances can stifle human rights discourses worldwide, potentially leading to a miscarriage of justice and undermining the rule of law. Therefore, relying on external regulations as an alternative to address the challenges posed by platform moderation could become a serious threat to free speech online.

References

Akın Ünver, H. (2018). *Artificial intelligence, authoritarianism, and the future of political systems.* Centre for Economics and Foreign Policy Studies.

Babb, C. E. (2022). *Digital dictators: How different types of authoritarian regimes use cyber attacks to legitimize their rule?* Carleton University Ottawa.

Bellasio, J., Slapakova, L., Quimbre, F., Stockwell, S., & Silfversten, E. (2021). *Human rights in the digital age.*

Berthin, G. (2023). *Fighting corruption is key to countering authoritarianism, and protecting human rights.* Retrieved January 11, from https://freedomhouse.org/article/fighting-corruption-key-countering-authoritarianism-and-protecting-human-rights

Brandt, J. (2022). *Digital authoritarianism: Pathways, trends, solutions.* Montreal Institute for Genocide and Human Rights Studies.

Brandt, J., & Taussig, T. (2019). Europe's authoritarian challenge. *The Washington Quarterly, 42*(4), 133–153.

Burt, T. (2022). *Nation-state cyberattacks become more brazen as authoritarian leaders ramp up aggression.* Retrieved November 4, from https://blogs.microsoft.com/on-the-issues/2022/11/04/microsoft-digital-defense-report-2022-ukraine

Burton, J. (2019). Cyber-attacks and freedom of expression: Coercion, intimidation and virtual occupation. *TalTech Journal of European Studies, 9*(3), 116–133.

Christopher, P., & Matthews, M. (2016). *The Russian "Firehose of Falsehood" propaganda model: Why it might work and options to counter it.* RAND Corporation.

Dales, S. (2021). *Digital authoritarian threats to United States' democracy.* Digital Democracy Research Hub.

Deibert, R. (2008). Black code Redux: Censorship, surveillance, and the militarization of cyberspace. In M. Boler (Ed.), *Digital media and democracy: Tactics in hard times* (pp. 137-). MIT Press.

Dick, A. L., Oyieke, L. I., & Bothma, T. J. D. (2019). *Are established democracies less vulnerable to Internet censorship than authoritarian regimes? The social media test.* International Federation of Library Associations and Institutions.

Dragu, T., & Lupu, Y. (2021). Digital authoritarianism and the future of human rights. *International Organization, 75*(4), 991–1017.

Erixon, F., & Lee-Makiyama, H. (2011). Digital authoritarianism: Human rights, geopolitics and commerce. *(No. 5/2011). ECIPE Occasional Paper.*

Finkel, E. (2015). The phoenix effect of state repression: Jewish resistance during the Holocaust. *American Political Science Review, 109*(2), 339–353.

Gosztonyi, G. (2023). *Censorship from Plato to social media: The complexity of social media's content regulation and moderation practices* (Vol. 61). Springer Nature.

Halmai, G. (2019). Populism, authoritarianism and constitutionalism. *German Law Journal, 20*(3), 296–313.

Hathaway, O. A., Crootof, R., Levitz, P., Nix, H., Nowlan, A., Perdue, W., & Spiegel, J. (2012). The law of cyber-attack. *California Law Review, 100*, 817–886.

Henderson, L. (1991). Authoritarianism and the rule of law. *Indiana Law Journal, 66*(2), 379–456.

Hendley, K. (2022). Legal dualism as a framework for analyzing the role of law under authoritarianism. *Annual Review of Law and Social Science, 18*(1), 211–226.

Hintz, A., Dencik, L., & Wahl-Jorgensen, K. (2017). Digital citizenship and surveillance society – Introduction. *International Journal of Communication, 11*, 731–739.

Howard, A. (2014). *Obama White House stands by free speech in Sony hacking scandal*. Retrieved December 18, from https://www.msnbc.com/msnbc/obama-white-house-stands-free-speech-sony-hacking-fight-msna489106

Jain, S., & Variath, A. A. (2020). Internet shutdowns and virtual curfews: Searching for rights in digital darkness. *CASIHR Journal on Human Rights Practice, 4*(2), 35–48.

Khalil, L. (2020). *Digital authoritarianism, China and COVID*. Retrieved November 2, from https://www.lowyinstitute.org/publications/digital-authoritarianism-china-covid

King, G., Pan, J., & Roberts, M. E. (2013). How censorship in China allows government criticism but silences collective expression. *American Political Science Review, 107*(2), 326–343.

Kyriakopoulou, K. (2011). Authoritarian states and internet social media: Instruments of democratisation or instruments of control? *Human Affairs, 21*(1), 18–26.

Lilkov, D. (2020). Made in China: Tackling digital authoritarianism. *European View, 19*(1), 110–110.

Linz, J. J. (2000). *Totalitarian and authoritarian regimes*. Lynne Rienner Publishers.

Lokot, T. (2023). Russia's networked authoritarianism in Ukraine's occupied territories during the full-scale invasion: Control and resilience. *LSE Public Policy Review, 3*(1), 145–162.

Meloen, J. D. (2000). The political culture of state authoritarianism. In S. A. Renshon (Ed.), *Political psychology: Cultural and crosscultural foundations* (pp. 108–127). Palgrave Macmillan UK.

Michaelsen, M. (2018). Transforming threats to power: The international politics of authoritarian Internet control in Iran. *International Journal of Communication, 12*, 3856.

Michaelsen, M. (2020). *The digital transnational repression toolkit, and its silencing effects*. https://freedomhouse.org/report/special-report/2020/digital-transnational-repression-toolkit-and-its-silencing-effects

Morgus, R., & Sherman, J. (2018). *The idealized Internet vs. Internet realities (Version 1.0)*. Cybersecurity Initiative.

Moustafa, T., & Ginsburg, T. (2008). The functions of courts in authoritarian politics. In T. Ginsburg & T. Moustafa (Eds.), *Rule by law* (pp. 1–22). Cambridge University Press.

Moynihan, H., & Patel, C. (2021). *Restrictions on online freedom of expression in China*. Chatham House.

Mozur, P., & Krolik, A. (2019). *A surveillance net blankets China's cities, giving police vast powers*. Retrieved December 17, from https://www.nytimes.com/2019/12/17/technology/china-surveillance.html

Nye, J. S. (2019). *Protecting democracy in an era of cyber information war*. Belfer Center for Science and International Affairs.

OHCHR. (2022a, June 23). *Internet shutdowns: UN report details 'dramatic' impact on people's lives and human rights*.

OHCHR. (2022b). *Spyware and surveillance: Threats to privacy and human rights growing, UN report warns*. Office of the United Nations High Commissioner for Human Rights.

Polyakova, A., & Meserole, C. (2019a). *Exporting digital authoritarianism: The Russian and Chinese models*. Brookings.

Polyakova, A., & Meserole, C. (2019b). Exporting digital authoritarianism: The Russian and Chinese models. *Policy brief, democracy and disorder series*, 1–22.
Prier, J. (2017). Commanding the trend: Social media as information warfare. *Strategic Studies Quarterly, 11*(4), 88–113.
Qiu, J. L. (1999). Virtual censorship in China: Keeping the gate between the cyberspaces. *International Journal of Communications Law and Policy, 4*(1), 25.
Repucci, S. (2019). *Media freedom: A downward spiral.* https://freedomhouse.org/report/freedom-and-media/2019/media-freedom-downward-spiral
Repucci, S., & Slipowitz, A. (2022). *The global expansion of authoritarian rule.* Freedom House.
Robles-Carrillo, M. (2022). The European Union strategy for cybersecurity. In D. M. Vicente, S. de Vasconcelos Casimiro, & C. Chen (Eds.), *The legal challenges of the fourth industrial revolution: The European Union's digital strategy* (pp. 173–192). Springer International Publishing.
Rosenberger, L., & Gorman, L. (2020). How democracies can win the information contest. *The Washington Quarterly, 43*(2), 75–96.
Schneider, N. (2023). *China and Russia are pushing the boundaries of cyber-attacks to harm other states.* Retrieved September 4, from https://www.cityam.com/china-and-russia-are-pushing-the-boundaries-of-cyber-attacks-to-harm-other-states
Shahbaz, A., & Funk, A. (2019). *Digital election interference - Freedom on the net 2019 key finding: Politicians and hyper partisans use digital means to manipulate elections.* Freedom House.
UN Human Rights Council. (2014). *Report of the Special Rapporteur on the promotion and protection of the right to freedom of opinion and expression, Addendum: Mission to Montenegro.* United Nations.
Vigliarolo, B. (2018). *Net neutrality: A cheat sheet.* Retrieved June 11, from https://www.techrepublic.com/article/net-neutrality-the-smart-persons-guide/
Weidmann, N. B., & Rød, E. G. (2019). *The Internet and political protest in autocracies.* Oxford University Press.
Wilton, C. (2017). Sony, cyber security, and free speech: Preserving the first amendment in the modern world. *Pace Intellectual Property, Sports & Entertainment Law Forum, 7*(1), 1–43.
Wolterman, J. (2018). Democracy, authoritarianism, and psychological warfare: Why illiberal states have an advantage in the information age. *Paper delivered at the SA ISSS-IS West Lafayette 2018 Conference, Indiana November 2018) [unpublished].* Unpublished.
Wong, S. H. W., & Liang, J. (2021). Dubious until officially censored: Effects of online censorship exposure on viewers' attitudes in authoritarian regimes. *Journal of Information Technology & Politics, 18*(3), 310–323.
Zhang, T. (2024). Authoritarianism and legality. *Asia Pacific Law Review, 32*(2), 311–321.
Zhuravskaya, E., Petrova, M., & Enikolopov, R. (2020). Political effects of the internet and social media. *Annual Review of Economics, 12*(1), 415–438.
Zittrain, J. L., Faris, R., Noman, H., Clark, J., Tilton, C., & Morrison-Westphal, R. (2017). *The shifting landscape of global internet censorship.* Berkman Klein Center Research Publication.

Chapter 7
Section 230: Ongoing Debates on the "Safe Harbor" Provision

7.1 Introduction

The United States (US), a global powerhouse and technological leader, plays a pivotal role in shaping the landscape of modern technology. Renowned for its spirit of innovation and a history deeply rooted in technological advancements, the United States has consistently been at the forefront of driving progress across various industries. From the invention of the personal computer to the development of the Internet, Silicon Valley has emerged as a symbol of innovation and entrepreneurship, fostering the growth of countless tech giants. Key social media platforms (SMPs) like Facebook, headquartered in Menlo Park, California, and YouTube, part of Google's parent company, Alphabet, have become global giants with billions of users. These platforms have not only connected people on a personal level but also transformed the landscape of news dissemination, advertising, and cultural trends.

More prominently, the electoral landscape of the United States is largely shaped by the norms, trends, and values across SMPs, significantly after the 2016 presidential election. As a jurisprudence largely influenced by the *First Amendment*, the United States has become one of the few jurisdictions that prominently protects free speech, expression, and other civil liberties, both offline and online. Therefore, Internet intermediaries, including SMPs, have minimal-level regulations protected by the *safe harbor* provision.

In 2023, the United States was identified by Freedom House as the jurisdiction with an open Internet, free from any restrictions on networks, social media bans, and progovernment commentators (Freedom House, 2023). The Internet in the United States is characterized as vibrant, diverse, and largely free from government censorship. The legal framework in the country offers robust protections for free expression online, making it one of the world's strongest safeguards for Internet freedom. However, the contemporary policy and regulatory debate revolve around the broader immunity model enshrined by the *safe harbor* provision, in the social media era, prompting a need to revisit them according to the needs of reforms.

S. Balendra, *Free Speech in the Puzzle of Content Regulation*, Law, Governance and Technology Series 70, https://doi.org/10.1007/978-3-031-75813-3_7

On one hand, the United States provides broader immunities to SMPs, while on the other, it is deeply concerned about various contemporary issues across the platforms. As part of a series of efforts, recently in January 2024, the CEOs of SMPs, including Facebook, X, Snapchat, TikTok, and Discord, testified before the Senate about child exploitation.[1] During this meeting, Mark Zuckerberg, the CEO of Meta, issued a public apology to parents of victims who experienced sexual exploitation or harassment on social media platforms. Snap Inc., accused of facilitating their children's access to illegal drugs on Snapchat, had CEO Evan Spiegel expressing condolences to the parents of over sixty (60) teenagers involved. He apologized for not being able to prevent the tragedies and mentioned the company's efforts to block search terms related to drugs on the platform.[2] This is one example of how the United States is vigilant about SMPs, particularly concerning online child safety. It is expected that federal-level legislation addressing this issue and imposing responsibilities may be passed in the near future.[3]

Several US states have enacted laws to protect the trust and safety of the digital sphere over time. This includes addressing cybercrimes, online privacy, and AI-related issues such as deepfakes, with exemptions for satire (Ajder & Glick, 2021). However, a common feature across these frameworks is the shield of protections provided to technology platforms. For example, in New York, the new law[4] passed in December 2020 protects performers' likenesses from unauthorized commercial use postmortem but includes broad fair-use exceptions for parody, criticism, and educational or newsworthy content. The law offers a *safe harbor* if a deepfake carries a conspicuous disclaimer stating unauthorized use. Similarly, California's law[5] prohibits distributing materially deceptive audio or visual media of election candidates with actual malice but exempts satire and parody, as determined by the courts. Exemptions are also provided for labeled altered media and deceptive political advertisements.

A common feature of the US technology regulatory framework is the *safe harbor* arrangements, which shield technologies from civil and/or criminal liabilities. This arrangement leans toward the "self-regulation" model as it provides platforms with the autonomy to regulate content across their spaces. Therefore, exploring Section 230 of the Communications Decency Act (CDA) will significantly contribute to the scholarly discussion as a case study of the self-regulation model. It goes without saying that any discussion on technology platform policy would be incomplete without considering US jurisdiction, given that the major platforms are

---

[1] See https://ny1.com/nyc/all-boroughs/politics/2024/01/31/social-media-ceos-testify-senate-committee-child-exploitation.

[2] See https://www.theguardian.com/us-news/2024/jan/31/tiktok-meta-x-congress-hearing-child-sexual-exploitation.

[3] See https://www.ctvnews.ca/business/meta-tiktok-and-other-social-media-ceos-testify-in-heated-u-s-senate-hearing-on-child-exploitation-1.6749729.

[4] Bill S1042A.

[5] Bill AB-730.

headquartered in the United States. Accordingly, this chapter delves into Section 230 of the CDA, exploring the broad immunity it provides and its impact on free speech and other competing values across social media platforms.

7.2 Regulating Social Media Contents in the United States

Private platforms, along with the government, play a pivotal role in overseeing and regulating content within the social media landscape of the United States. However, this chapter aims to undertake a comparative analysis of the broader immunity framework established by the government, prominently underlaid by Section 230 of the CDA. With the objective of regulating the Internet, in the backdrop of the CDA, President Clinton believed that regulating the Internet was extremely difficult, much like "trying to nail Jello to the wall" (Kapur, 2024). Although parts of the CDA were struck down by the Supreme Court for violating free speech rights, one part of the Act, Section 230, became very important in the Internet governance of US jurisprudence. Currently, Section 230 serves as the primary regulatory framework governing the responsibilities and immunities of Internet intermediaries, including major technology platforms.

In the United States, freedom of speech and expression is robustly safeguarded against government constraints, enshrined by the *First Amendment* to the US Constitution and protected by various state constitutions and laws at both state and federal levels. This commitment has influenced the metaphor of the United States into the invasion of social media content regulations, prominently concerning free speech and expression in the contemporary information technology era.

In answering the question of whether certain provisions of the CDA violated the First and Fifth Amendments due to their overly broad and vague nature, the court, in *Reno v. ACLU*,[6] emphasized that the Act violated the First Amendment by imposing a blanket restriction on content that infringed upon free speech. Specifically, the definitions of "indecent" and "offensive" were contested, with the court criticizing the Act for its lack of clear definitions, pointing out:

> The interest in encouraging freedom of expression in a democratic society outweighs any theoretical but unproven benefit of censorship.

This judgment not only remains a significant precedent in the US perspective but is also globally cited in many cases.

Jakubcin argues that the court has extended equal protection to internet content, similar to the protections granted to print media and telephone dial-a-porn messages, pointing out:

> For instance, in the past, the availability of many large newspapers, small town newspapers, and pamphlets gave a potential speaker a choice of many forums, with relatively easy access,

[6] *Reno v. American Civil Liberties Union*, 521 US 844 (1997).

> for expression through the print media. Similarly, the Internet gives a potential speaker easy access to a variety of means for expression such as e-mail, bulletin boards, and web-sites (Jakubcin, 1998).

Section 230 of the CDA underscores the Internet as a primary platform for expansive speech, opportunity, and intellectual progress. Congress, through Section 230, protects free speech by granting immunity to Internet users from liability for content distribution, excluding intellectual property violations. Notably, major platforms like Facebook, Google, and X are *not obliged* to censor user content to avoid legal repercussions. The purpose of Section 230 is to prevent censorship on privately owned websites, fostering an environment of free speech without the threat of prosecution or lawsuits. The US government, both the judicial and administrative branches, largely supports users' free speech rights on the Internet, emphasizing the importance of preserving an open and expressive online space (Everett, 2018).

7.2.1 Background of Section 230

In 1991, a landmark legal case, *Cubby, Inc. v. CompuServe, Inc*,[7] unfolded, with Cubby accusing CompuServe and Don Fitzpatrick of libel, business disparagement, and unfair competition. CompuServe, an online general information service during that era, successfully defended itself against liability. The court ruled that CompuServe, functioning as the distributor of a columnist's content, could not be held accountable since it did not review the material before publication. Four years later, in 1995, in the case of *Stratton Oakmont, Inc. v. Prodigy Servs. Co.*,[8] Prodigy, a web service company hosting online bulletin boards, engaged in the moderation of its online message boards, deleting certain messages deemed offensive or in bad taste. In October 1994, a user posted a statement on the platform, accusing Stratton Oakmont, Inc., a Long Island securities brokerage firm, and its president, Daniel Porush, of criminal and fraudulent acts. In response, Stratton and Porush filed a defamation lawsuit against both the user and the platform. In this case, the court differentiated Prodigy from *CompuServe* and affirmed Prodigy's status as a publisher, citing its established policies and representations as sufficient grounds. These legal proceedings highlighted the necessity for clear-cut legislation to regulate the digital sphere shaped by the intervention of the Internet.

Against this backdrop, the United States introduced the *broader immunity* model in 1996 through the Communication Decency Act. The CDA represented the initial effort to regulate both cable television, primarily overseen by the Federal Communications Commission (FCC) at the time, and the Internet, which had been opened to commercial use by the National Science Foundation Act in 1992. President Bill Clinton signed the CDA into law on February 8, 1996. Section 230 of the CDA, also

[7] *Cubby, Inc. v. CompuServe Inc.*, 776 F.Supp. 135 (S.D.N.Y. 1991).

[8] *Oakmont, Inc. v. Prodigy Services Co.*, 1995 WL 323710.

known as the *safe harbor* provision, mirrors the concept of providing a degree of immunity for Internet intermediaries, including Internet service providers (ISPs) and users, upon meeting specific criteria. Notably, this section was not part of the original act but was subsequently suggested and introduced by Representatives Christopher Cox and Ron Wyden.[9]

7.2.2 Section 230 Explained

Section 230, commonly known as the *safe harbor* provision, grants immunity to online intermediaries and service providers against content shared by third-party users on their platforms.

The provision states:

> No provider or user of an interactive computer service shall be treated as the publisher or speaker of any information provided by another information content provider.[10]

Furthermore, the provision ensures that service providers cannot be held liable for voluntarily taking action to restrict access to objectionable material on their platforms.

It specifies:

> No provider or user of an interactive computer service shall be held liable on account of—
> (A) any action voluntarily taken in good faith to restrict access to or availability of material that the provider or user considers to be obscene, lewd, lascivious, filthy, excessively violent, harassing, or otherwise objectionable, whether or not such material is constitutionally protected; or
>
> (B) any action taken to enable or make available to information content providers or others the technical means to restrict access to material described in [subparagraph (A)].[11]

However, it is important to note that the immunity provided by Section 230 has limitations. It does not extend to certain circumstances, including cases involving federal criminal law, intellectual property law, state laws deemed "consistent" with Section 230, certain electronic communication privacy laws, or specific federal and state laws related to sex trafficking.[12] In these situations, Section 230 does not provide protection against legal liability or immunity.

[9] See https://www.eff.org/issues/cda230/legislative-history.

[10] Community Decency Act 1996, s 230(c) (1).

[11] Community Decency Act 1996, s 230(c) (2).

[12] Community Decency Act 1996,s 230(e).

7.3 Social Media in the United States

Social media in the United States has received mixed reviews regarding its impact on the larger society. There is a common perspective that social media may contribute to "filter bubbles" (Pariser, 2011) or "echo chambers (Sunstein, 2018)", fostering one-sided information due to algorithms or user self-selection. Yet, from another end, social media exposes individuals to a diverse range of political opinions, potentially even more than traditional media or personal interactions.

7.3.1 Emergence and Evolution

Like many other jurisprudence, the United States also witnessed numerous significant social media movements calling for changes in democratic and human rights. For example, after the shooting death of Michael Brown on August 9, 2014, social media, particularly hashtags like #Ferguson and #MikeBrown, played a crucial role in shaping the narrative. DeRay Mckesson, deeply affected by posts depicting the incident, traveled from Minneapolis to Missouri to join protests. The hashtags became symbolic of racial inequality, police misconduct, and the value of black life in America. Beyond the specific incident, people used the hashtags to highlight broader issues of police misconduct and racial double standards across the country. Social media, especially X, helped amplify the conversation and turned Ferguson into a national symbol for justice and broader discussions about inequality in the criminal justice system. The hashtags became a way for people to call out instances of injustice and sparked a larger dialogue about the persistent problem of police misconduct in Ferguson and nationwide.[13]

Bonilla, Y., and Rosa, J., pointed out in their studies that the #Ferguson movement allowed global attention to be brought to local issues and promoted visibility and accountability. The unique aspect of X, compared to earlier technologies, lies in its multivocality and dialogical nature. Unlike traditional media, X enables users to engage with diverse perspectives simultaneously, offering real-time updates through live streams; tweets from protestors, journalists, and police; and reactions from thousands of users (Bonilla & Rosa, 2015).

Other than this, various impactful social media movements have originated in the United States, exemplifying the intersection of online platforms and societal change. The ALS Ice Bucket Challenge, initiated by the ALS Association in 2014, achieved widespread success by combining simplicity, entertainment value through self-made videos, and a nomination system. Participants, including celebrities, engaged in the challenge by pouring ice water on themselves or others, prompting donations totaling $115 million for ALS research. The campaign's triumph significantly influenced the ALS Association, enabling investments in research, assistive

[13] See https://www.cnn.com/2014/11/19/us/ferguson-social-media-injustice/index.html.

technologies, and enhanced healthcare services for individuals affected by amyotrophic lateral sclerosis.[14]

The Arab Spring, emerging in the early 2010s, marked a series of protests and uprisings in Tunisia that rapidly spread across North Africa and the Middle East. Led by young activists, the movement aimed to challenge oppressive regimes and address issues such as low living standards. Social media played a pivotal role in organizing protests, raising political awareness, and documenting events. Citizen journalism, empowered by social media, became a vital tool for shaping narratives during political upheavals, emphasizing its role in promoting freedom of speech and civic engagement. The Black Lives Matter (BLM) movement originated as an online community addressing antiblack racism and police violence, particularly against African Americans. Utilizing the hashtag #BlackLivesMatter on social media, the movement gained momentum and visibility, evolving into an organization with over 40 chapters. Cofounder Patrisse Khan-Cullors created the hashtag, which was used extensively on X, reaching nearly 30 million mentions from July 2013 to May 1, 2018. Inspired by a love letter to black people by cofounder Alicia Garza, the movement emerged as a potent force for advocacy and social change.

The *me too. Movement*, symbolized by the hashtag #MeToo, serves as a platform for women to express solidarity and share experiences of sexual harassment. Originating in 2006, the movement gained widespread attention in 2017 when high-profile actresses disclosed their experiences in the film industry. The increased visibility broadened understanding of the movement's goals, raising awareness about sexual harassment and assault. Ultimately, the me too. Movement seeks to diminish tolerance for abusive behavior and enhance support for victims.

The advanced features of SMPs amplified many movements, as discussed above, as they facilitate rapid organization without formal structures, enabling quick mobilization and reaching large audiences in short periods. The benefits include accelerated mobilization, global reach, and creative communication strategies, all of which have contributed to the success of social movements. Yet the study conducted by Auxier, B., and McClain, C., revealed *a nuanced public perception* of social media within the American populace. Approximately two-thirds of Americans acknowledge the positive dimensions of social media platforms, attributing them to their role in bringing attention to crucial issues that might otherwise be overlooked (65%) and providing a platform for underrepresented groups to voice their perspectives (64%). Furthermore, half of the surveyed individuals believe that social media facilitates the accountability of powerful figures. However, a notable segment of the population expresses a more critical view, with 79% of respondents feeling that social media serves as a distraction from genuinely important matters. Additionally, a substantial 76% of participants perceive these platforms as fostering a sense of making a difference through *slacktivism*—online activism characterized by a perceived lack of meaningful impact. The overall public perception of social media thus encompasses a duality, acknowledging its positive contributions in highlighting vital issues

[14] See https://hbswk.hbs.edu/item/why-the-als-ice-bucket-challenge-is-a-social-media-blockbuster.

and amplifying marginalized voices while harboring concerns about potential distractions and the superficial nature of online activism (Auxier & McClain, 2020).

7.3.2 The Impact on Electoral Campaign Strategies

Beyond social media movements, the significant role of the platforms in the United States includes electoral canvassing and information flow across various platforms during the electoral timelines. Though it predominantly played a significant role after 2016, before 2010 as well, the role of these platforms during the electoral regime existed at a minimal level. SMPs offer a cost-effective avenue for political candidates to compete and communicate, as demonstrated by a study showing that politicians experienced increased campaign financing after setting up X accounts. Figures like Alexandria Ocasio-Cortez and Barack Obama, dubbed the *first social media president*, highlighted the impact of platforms like X on building electoral support.[15] In the 2008 campaign, social media played a crucial role, with three-quarters of Internet users engaging with election material. This influence has only grown, with an upsurge in political ads on platforms like Google and Facebook. For instance, in the 2020 election, Joe Biden's campaign spent $191,922,173, and Donald Trump's spent $268,473,419 on political ads on these platforms (Hastuti et al., 2023).

The content and information circulating on SMPs in the United States have significantly influenced various elections over time. Thomas et al. find that during the 2016 and 2020 elections, X served as a channel for the dissemination of opinions, particularly those from Democratic-leaning users, regarding Trump. This influence may have swayed voters with weaker prior affiliations, such as independents and possibly moderate Republicans, to vote against Trump. Factors contributing to this effect include the demographic characteristics of X users—typically young, well educated, residing in urban areas, and favoring the Democratic party. Additionally, Trump's active presence on the platform may have directly influenced moderate voters, leading to a "backlash" against the content of his tweets (Thomas et al., 2023).

Particularly during the 2016 elections, social media caused a major upheaval in traditional campaign norms, marking a shift characterized by unprecedented unpredictability. Michael Slaby, chief integration and innovation officer for President Obama's campaigns, noted that the change was not merely technological but also a complete transformation in the norms of campaign communications. Long-standing norms, controlled by political and media elites, were significantly damaged or even entirely erased.

[15] See https://www.newyorker.com/news/our-columnists/the-distinct-political-paths-of-barack-obama-and-alexandria-ocasio-cortez.

Jim Ruttenberg, a media columnist for The New York Times, highlighted the impact of various digital platforms, like email, websites, Facebook, X, text messaging, Instagram, Periscope, and Snapchat, creating a media hurricane. This disrupted the election plans of experienced strategists and candidates who were accustomed to methodical campaigning, forcing them to adapt to the new and unpredictable terrain shaped by social media (Hendricks & Dan, 2017).

In a democratic society, citizens, news media, and elected officials collaborate to shape and uphold a public sphere, and the nature of public discourse on social media during 2016 emerged as a response to the strategic needs of various actors within these groups. Studies showcased that during the 2016 election, Facebook became the predominant platform tool for digital campaigns, reaching nearly 80% of the adult population in the United States (Madrigal, 2017). From another perspective, scholars have opined about the influence of SMPs in the 2016 election, debating whether the trends observed will persist or if they were unique to the Trump-Clinton race and the specific characteristics of that electorate (Madrigal, 2017).

While the 2016 presidential election set up a unique trend in electoral campaigns and communication through the evolution of SMPs, on the flip side, political polarization was caused due to the content shared across the platforms—particularly X. This content has impacted and influenced public opinions, potentially swaying electoral outcomes.

A study conducted by Philip N. Howard et al. identifies two significant features of social media content during the 2016 election. Firstly, SMPs exhibited a higher prevalence of links to polarizing and conspiratorial content, including Russian news stories, unverified or irrelevant WikiLeaks pages, and junk news, compared to professionally produced content. The proportion of misinformation was found to be twice as much as content from experts and candidates. Secondly, a significant portion of the studied political content on social media platforms during the 2016 presidential election directed users to polarizing material from Russian sources, WikiLeaks, and junk news. This content employed divisive rhetoric, faulty reasoning, or misleading information to manipulate public understanding and promote conspiracy theories (Horward et al., 2018). Swing states like North Carolina, Arizona, Nevada, and others, including those with significant Electoral College votes, received concentrated doses of polarizing content (Horward et al., 2018).

As another challenge, due to the open nature of SMPs, they often contribute to information chaos during election times in the United States. Despite procedural efforts to secure elections, social media platforms are criticized for allowing the spread of disinformation and undermining accurate public perception and trust in the democratic process. Additionally, the increasing threats and harassment faced by election workers, with a focus on online platforms (SMPs) being a significant channel for such intimidation, raise concerns. There are also worries about the potential for misinformation and attempts to delegitimize elections in the postelection period (Erin et al., 2022).

Beyond this, in the 2016 US presidential election, social bots were utilized on social media, particularly X, to reinforce existing beliefs and facilitate the rapid dissemination of information within online communities. A study by Bessi, A., and

Ferrara, E., suggested that humans are more inclined to engage in online political discussions during specific events, such as debates or news releases, and sophisticated bots systematically push their agenda regardless of circumstances (Bessi & Ferrara, 2016).

This study further highlighted three potential issues associated with the presence of social bots in online political discussions:

1. The redistribution of influence to suspicious accounts with potentially malicious intent,
2. An increase in political polarization, and
3. The amplification of misinformation and unverified information (Bessi & Ferrara, 2016).

In 2018, it was revealed that *Cambridge Analytica*, involved in Donald Trump's presidential campaign of 2016, had improperly utilized the personal data of more than 50 million Facebook users.[16] This major data scandal was exposed, leading to Cambridge Analytica's liquidation and Facebook CEO Mark Zuckerberg testifying before the US Congress in 2018. The *Cambridge Analytica* scandal played a pivotal role in Donald Trump's presidential campaign (2016) by employing sophisticated data analytics and psychographic profiling to tailor political messages and advertisements, aiming to sway voters in favor of Trump. The Facebook tools were weaponized, particularly through effective data analytics, empowering politicians to influence specific voter groups significantly. This outcome resulted from social media polarization within the existing dataset (Redoano, 2019). Later in 2022, Meta Platforms, the owner of Facebook, agreed to a $725-million settlement in a class-action lawsuit.[17] The lawsuit claimed that Facebook improperly shared users' information with Cambridge Analytica. The settlement reflects a resolution to the legal dispute over privacy violations related to the misuse of user data by Cambridge Analytica, marking a significant financial repercussion for Meta Platforms.

Although the 2016 election and the role of social media created many controversies, as discussed above, the trend continued during the 2020 election. Joe Biden, the Democratic nominee, although not known for heavy use of social media in the past, allocated portions of his campaign budget for advertising on platforms like Facebook. He spent an estimated $1.6 million leading up to the California Democratic primary, surpassing Trump's spending.[18] It is noteworthy that in both the 2016 and 2020 presidential elections, there was a 10% increase in the number of X users in the United States (Thomas et al., 2023).

This election (2020) was also influenced by SMPs largely, from preparation to protests against the results, demonstrating their influential power in connecting

[16] See https://www.timesofisrael.com/trump-campaign-mined-facebook-user-data-using-israeli-intelligence-gathering/.

[17] See https://www.reuters.com/legal/facebook-parent-meta-pay-725-mln-settle-lawsuit-relating-cambridge-analytica-2022-12-23/.

[18] See https://www.nytimes.com/2020/06/08/us/politics/biden-trump-facebook-ads.html.

people across political beliefs. After the experiences of the 2016 elections, large Internet companies, including SMPs, implemented measures to label false information during the 2020 US elections (Andika et al., 2022). The election concluded with Biden's victory, celebrated on social media platforms like TikTok and Instagram. This dynamic interaction on social media marked a monumental experience for candidates, their teams, and the electorate during the 2020 US elections.

Currently, the United States is anticipating its upcoming election in 2024. Studies reveal potential digital risks that need to be addressed to safeguard democracy and electoral integrity during the elections. Social media platforms and generative artificial intelligence (AI) remain significant digital challenges in the new paradigm of the social media era (Barrett et al., 2024).

7.3.3 The Constitutional Status and State Action Doctrine

Current debates at both scholarly and policy levels in the U.S. focus on whether private tech platforms should be subject to the state action doctrine. Due to the massive transformation into this technology, as discussed in the earlier chapters, such private platforms have been confronted with an unprecedented amount of speech, some of which include content related to hate speech, harassment, pornography, and misinformation campaigns. However, these platforms embody a range of mechanisms and content regulation policies to filter speech on their platforms. In the recent past, the social media platforms faced a number of lawsuits, including several high-profile cases, challenging their content regulation policies and decisions.

For example, in *Trump v. X*,[19] the question of violation of the right to free speech under the First Amendment to the United States Constitution was examined in the backdrop of the *state action doctrine*. However, the court found that the First Amendment protects against government actions that restrict speech, not private actions by companies like X. This is based on the *state action doctrine*, which stipulates that constitutional protections apply primarily to government conduct, not to private entities. In this case, the plaintiffs needed to provide sufficient factual allegations in their complaint to support their claim that X's actions amounted to state action. Since the plaintiffs did not meet this burden, their First Amendment claim was dismissed.

In some limited cases, courts have indeed subjected private actors to constitutional scrutiny. An example of this is the case of *Brentwood Academy v. Tennessee Secondary School Athletic Association*,[20] where the court ruled that because state school officials were deeply involved in the operations of the ostensibly private organization regulating school sports and the state education board recognized this organization, it should be considered a state actor.

[19] Case No. 21-cv-08378-JD.

[20] *Brentwood Academy v. Tennessee Secondary School Athletic Association*, 531 U.S. 288 (2001).

However, in social media lawsuits where plaintiffs claim constitutional violations, particularly under the First Amendment, they might find some limited support for their argument. However, the prevailing legal perspective is that social media companies are not considered state actors and therefore cannot be held liable for constitutional violations. It has been a heavy hurdle in moving with these suits in advocating for free speech.

Proponents of social media lawsuits primarily invoke two exceptions to apply the state action doctrine: (1) the public function exception and (2) the entwinement exception. The public function exception draws its origin from *Marsh v. Alabama*,[21] where the Supreme Court determined that a privately owned, company-run town was considered a state actor after it arrested and punished a Jehovah's Witness for distributing religious literature. The court reasoned that despite being privately owned, the town was operated in a manner similar to any other municipality, primarily for the benefit of the public. As such, its activities were deemed to perform an essentially public function, thereby subjecting it to constitutional scrutiny.

Although the public function exception has been interpreted narrowly in subsequent cases, some scholars contend that social media companies should still be considered state actors. They argue that these platforms function as modern-day "public squares and meeting places," serving as the "town squares of the twenty-first century" (Jackson, 2014; Patty, 2019).

Under the entwinement exemption, in the social media lawsuits, plaintiffs argue that social media companies are closely linked to government actions because of the government's role in developing the Internet and the legal protections provided under Section 230(c) of the Communications Decency Act. Specifically, in the *Trump* case, the plaintiffs alleged that Congress "coerced" and "threatened" X and other platforms, pressuring them to ban former President Trump. This argument is used to support the claim that these companies should be considered state actors, subject to constitutional constraints.

Though these exemptions are contested, the current precedent is that the First Amendment applies to governmental restrictions on speech, not to actions taken by private companies to manage content on their platforms. Consequently, individuals who had been banned or censored or had their content removed by social media companies have not been successful in arguing that such actions violate their First Amendment rights because the courts do not view these platforms as state actors.

For example, in *Prager University v. Google LLC*,[22] the Ninth Circuit Court of Appeals reaffirmed that social media platforms like YouTube (owned by Google) do not become state actors merely because they provide a space for public discourse through user-generated content. The court pointed out that even though these platforms may play a significant role in facilitating communication and information exchange, this does not equate to them performing a traditional, exclusive public function like the government.

[21] *Marsh v. Alabama*, 326 U.S. 501 (1946).

[22] *Prager University v. Google LLC*, 951 F.3d 991, 997 (9th Cir. 2020).

7.4 Application and Analysis of Section 230

The Act has been in force for almost three decades in the United States, and currently, there are proposals suggesting amending or removing Section 230. However, given the US legal tradition that predominantly prioritizes free speech rights, the provision is considered a pivotal effort to protect online free speech. It plays a crucial role on the Internet in the United States, shielding online service providers from lockdowns and heavy censorship. While arguments in favor of Section 230 emphasize its role in combating digital authoritarianism and providing protections for Internet intermediaries and service providers, opponents argue that this shield of immunity renders defamation suits across the Internet ineffective.

In the landmark case of *Zeran v. America Online, Inc*,[23] Zeran sued the AOL platform for publishing an inappropriate advertisement using his name. He claimed that AOL failed to remove the posts within a reasonable time and asserted that Section 230 of the CDA did not preclude the imposition of distributor liability. Zeran argued that AOL had a duty to remove the defamatory posts after being given sufficient notice. However, on appeal,[24] the Fourth Circuit confirmed that AOL was eligible for immunity under Section 230 and rejected Zeran's argument. The court asserted that AOL should be treated as a distributor rather than a publisher.

Yaffa A. Meeran argued that the post-Zeran legal framework has extended the protection provided by Section 230, which originally shielded Internet service providers like AOL, Verizon, or Comcast as interactive computer services (Meeran, 2018). According to Meeran, subsequent court decisions have broadened the Section 230 immunity to cover a broader array of online services. Additionally, some rulings have narrowed the criteria for defining a website as an information content provider, thereby expanding the scope of the Section 230 immunity in the process. Meeran cited keynote cases, including *Blumenthal v. Drudge*[25] and *Jones v. Dirty World Entertainment Recordings LLC*,[26] to support the argument on how the Zeran decision influenced courts in hearing suits (Meeran, 2018).

In addition, numerous cases have upheld the shield offered by virtue of Section 230 to Internet intermediaries. In *Gentry v. eBay*,[27] the platform, serving as the meeting point of sellers and buyers, faced allegations regarding *fake sports memorabilia* sold by its users. Section 230 shielded eBay from liability in this case, suggesting that the platform is not held responsible for the actions of its users, specifically the sale of fraudulent sports memorabilia. Similarly, in a case brought against Google,[28] one of the popular search engines on the Internet, accusing it of creating snippets with defamatory implications due to an automated process, the

[23] *Zeran v. America Online, Inc.*, 129 F.3d 327 (4th Cir. 1997).

[24] *David L. Hudson Jr., Zeran v. America Online, Inc.* (4th Cir.) (1997).

[25] *Blumenthal v. Drudge*, 992 F.Supp. 44 (D.C.D.C., 1998).

[26] *Jones v. Dirty World Entertainment Recordings LLC*, 755 F.3d 398 (6th Cir. 2014).

[27] *Gentry v. eBay, Inc.*, 121 Cal. Rptr. 2d 703 (Cal. Ct. App. 2002).

[28] *Maughan v. Google Tech., Inc.*, 49 Cal. Rptr. 3d 861 (Cal. Ct. App. 2006).

court upheld the protection provided to the search engine in that scenario. In *Doe v. MySpace*,[29] Section 230 shielded MySpace with immunity from liability for user-to-user communications leading to a criminal assault.

Scholars argued that while Section 230 does not offer "complete" immunity, its protections have been significantly broadened by the judiciary beyond what is explicitly stated in the statute since its enactment. In contemporary legal interpretations, Section 230 is now perceived as an extensive legal safeguard for SMPs (Kosseff, 2017). For instance, under the current understanding of Section 230, SMPs are granted civil immunity for various actions, including hosting illegal child pornography with knowledge, racially discriminating in content removal, and facing a wide range of traditional product-defect claims (Kosseff, 2019; Rucker, 2023).

Bloomberg Law, in a study, found a general increase in the annual number of complaints and motions to dismiss citing Section 230 (Karalis & Golriz, 2023).[30] The key factor contributing to this increase is the judicial approach toward the application of Section 230 in protecting the platforms, with parties contesting matters in the courts. Courts have adopted a robust approach in defending online platforms broadly, shielding them from accountability for illegal activities on their systems, even in cases where they actively promote or ignore such activities. While the Supreme Court has not clarified the interpretation of Section 230, state and lower federal courts generally agree on its broad application (Peter & Golriz, 2018).

In Chap. 4, I discussed how the immunity model supports the amplification of free speech online, without the intervention of state machinery and administrative authorities, which are predominantly controlling speech and discussion across online platforms. However, Section 230 and the immunity protection end up presenting a unique challenge across the SMPs from another end.

The policy, scholarly discussions, and case analyses expressed the challenges of upholding immunity when it comes to the conflicting rights of free speech and defamation within the same paradigm. While the reputation of individuals and institutions is also recognized as a significant right under the First Amendment to the Constitution, due to the arrangement of Section 230, courts are compelled to give greater weight to Internet service providers (ISPs) over the victims of defamatory publications. For Example, O'Donnell pointed out that due to the broader immunity granted to these intermediaries, some platforms, despite having the capability to address deepfake issues, have been slow in developing responses, possibly due to the legal protection they enjoy (O'Donnell, 2021).

Collateral censorship, as coined by Professor Jack Balkin, occurs when A restricts B's speech not due to A's fear of personal liability but out of concern that the government might hold A accountable for the consequences of B's speech (Balkin, 1999). It involves preemptive censorship by one party to avoid potential

[29] *Doe v. MySpace, Inc.*, 528 F.3d 413 (5th Cir. 2008).

[30] See https://news.bloomberglaw.com/bloomberg-law-analysis/analysis-product-claims-spike-as-scotus-ponders-section-230-fix.

legal repercussions from the government based on the speech or actions of another party. However, Section 230 has become a huge hindrance in excelling at collateral censorship—which would easily address online safety and trust issues.

The legislative history and court interpretations of the CDA suggest a prioritization of the interests of anonymous posters and ISPs over those of victims. Currently, ISPs enjoy significant immunity from legal action for actions taken by third parties on their platforms, regardless of the editing and publishing decisions made by the ISPs. This situation leaves victims with limited and often ineffective remedies for addressing harmful content or actions online (Spiccia, 2013). Spiccia suggested, beyond the "immunity" provision, that the section should be amended to protect the interests of multiple stakeholders across the Internet, including victims, Internet Service Providers, and publishers.

From a free speech advocacy, the entrenched immunity granted to Internet intermediaries stands as a crucial element in the evolving information era. It indirectly reinforces the protection of free speech online for users (Balkin, 2014), ensuring that their content is shielded from arbitrary removal or takedowns by platforms. However, from the other end, as immunity should not be granted freely, many critics argue that the existing immunity arrangement under Section 230 prevents platforms from acting responsibly toward cyber defamation, hate speech, and online misinformation (Goodman & Whittington, 2019; Kosseff, 2017, 2019).

However, I argue that the unrestricted or broader immunity, as offered by the Communications Decency Act, Section 230, though it ultimately protects free speech online, often leads to consequences that undermine defamation proceedings, potentially infringing upon other fundamental human rights such as "Reputation" and "Dignity." It poses a significant threat to Internet platforms, challenging the resilience of the Internet in the contemporary era.

A more nuanced situation arises where the platform's immunity is delegated, even for issues related to highly sensitive content under anti-terrorism laws. In a recent case, *Force v. Facebook, Inc.*,[31] the plaintiffs, the families of the victims of Hamas terrorism, claimed that pro-Hamas content appeared on terrorists' Facebook newsfeeds, and the "suggested friends" feature recommended Hamas supporters to each other. The plaintiff argued that Section 230 would not be applicable since Facebook is deemed as the developer of the content, not merely a publisher. Despite Section 230's protection against liability for third-party content, the court ruled that Facebook should not be held liable for its newsfeed content and friend suggestions. The court determined that decisions regarding content display, including the use of algorithms to recommend content based on users' interactions, are considered traditional editorial functions protected by Section 230. The court concluded that Facebook's algorithmic processing of third-party speech does not make the platform the author of that speech. This reflects how the provision broadly protects a wide array of content, which can sometimes act as a shield for harmful material, potentially impacting the broader community negatively. The case formed the realization

[31] *Force v. Facebook, Inc.*, 934 F.3d 53 (2nd Cir. 2019).

that holding Facebook accountable for users' actions linked by its algorithm would force the platform to limit suggestions based on a broad range of user signals. If Section 230 is altered to make platforms susceptible to lawsuits for users' actions connected by algorithms, it would compel them to avoid matching users or recommending groups and pages when there are concerns about the shared interests being inappropriate or problematic.

Similarly, in *Fields v. X*,[32] two government contractors of the United States were killed in Jordan by Abu Zaid in 2015. Later, through X, The Islamic State (IS) group claimed responsibility. Subsequently, the families of the deceased filed a suit against X, alleging that it is responsible for the online content shared across its platform. However, the court dismissed the plaintiff's claim, pointing out that X is protected under Section 230 of the Communications Decency Act since it meets the three requirements: the defendant must be an interactive computer service, the cause of action asserted by the plaintiff must treat the defendant as the "publisher or speaker" of the harmful information at issue, and the information must be "provided by another information content provider."

As technology continues to advance, the advanced features of the Internet, information, and technology face several challenges due to the existence of Section 230, which was introduced nearly three decades ago (Kosseff, 2019). The procedural application of Section 230 also becomes crucial in cases involving complaints that raise concerns about the use of machine-learning algorithms. The lack of access to discovery makes it nearly impossible to establish whether these algorithms influenced the capacity of specific terrorists to organize successful attacks. This difficulty arises because information related to user accounts, including the operation of algorithms, is likely proprietary (Tremble, 2017).

The context of Section 230, which grants liability protection to online sources, is that this protection is viewed as a benefit, not a penalty. Unlike real-world newspapers and bulletin boards, online sources enjoy this legal privilege. Therefore, the immunity is a privilege to be earned through compliance with conditions, and failure to comply does not constitute a denial of a right or punishment but a forfeiture of the granted privilege (Klon Kitchen, 2020).

As the broad immunity granted to ISPs creates certain repercussions in the flow of online content, there is significant opposition to affording this immunity freely. The question arises: *If the immunity to Internet service providers and platforms is not free, then at what price?*

Recent debates have centered around the *duty of care* as a basis for claiming immunity under Section 230. From a corporate social responsibility (CSR) perspective, the duty toward customers or users plays an integral role in corporate responsibility. Indeed, where harmful content may also provide financial incentives to these platforms, exercising caution becomes essential to secure protection under the provision (Smith & Van Alstyne, 2021).

[32] *Fields v. X*, 16-cv-00213-WHO.

The concern was that Section 230, initially intended to support the growth of the Internet, might now be contributing to problems like the spread of harmful content or misinformation. Kosseff argues that the statute might be too broad and that the legal protections originally designed for smaller platforms or early Internet start-ups might no longer be appropriate for massive, profit-driven corporations (Kosseff, 2019).

Also, Gosztonyi adds up this point, criticizing:

> Even though these companies have grown to have unimaginable economic power, CDA230 gives them almost unlimited immunity—whether they restrict content or users upload unacceptable content (Gosztonyi, 2023).

Beyond this, scholars and policymakers argue that Section 230 has led to a lack of accountability and transparency requirements for Internet service providers. In 2020, discussions with the CEOs of X, Google, and Facebook were significant regarding Section 230. Among them, Mark Zuckerberg, the CEO of Facebook, claimed that he advocates for the amendment of the provision, particularly enhancing the transparency of content moderation decisions.[33]

Few other scholars propose that for the best reform of Section 230, Internet service providers and social media platforms should take on a role similar to a publisher. This approach would empower platforms to exercise caution over the content disseminated and make efforts to remove, restrict, or flag dangerous or suspicious content, either manually or through artificial intelligence, such as algorithms. Additionally, platforms may provide users with an opportunity to review these actions (Cheng & Norcross, 2021).

However, even with Section 230 in force, major Internet platforms have chosen to establish community guidelines that limit certain speech, even if it is legally permissible in the United States. They often remove content that is deemed *lawful but awful*. This decision is influenced by factors such as a sense of social responsibility, a wish to avoid negative publicity, and the requirements of advertisers. Section 230 plays a role in promoting free speech while allowing platforms to conduct content moderation, contributing to an overall improvement in public discourse (Chander, 2022b).

The SMPs exhibit transparency in certain aspects, such as publishing content rules and community standards, as well as disclosing interactions with government entities. However, there is a lack of transparency in the consistent application of these rules, leaving users uncertain about decision-making processes. It is emphasized that intermediaries must prioritize openness to uphold the robustness of the public discourse they facilitate. Given the significant influence and importance of digital intermediaries in the Internet era, their actions warrant scrutiny, considering their amplified role in shaping public discourse (Gosztonyi, 2023; Peters & Johnson, 2016).

[33] See https://www.theguardian.com/technology/live/2020/oct/28/section-230-hearings-live-twitter-facebook-google-congress-mark-zuckerberg-jack-dorsey-sundar-pichai.

7.4.1 Why Section 230 Is a "Global Problem"

Section 230 was enacted by Congress to provide immunity to Internet providers from specific lawsuits. However, a significant problem arises due to the lack of explicit definition regarding its geographical scope. The current legal debate revolves around whether this immunity shields a platform from lawsuits globally or only in cases where the underlying conduct occurred within the United States. Despite the crucial question of the geographical extent of Section 230, courts have thus far avoided addressing it directly. Instead, their focus has been on determining where the immunity applies, and the prevailing answer is "in US court." This approach has led to a paradoxical situation wherein the Section 230 immunity is extended to conduct taking place anywhere in the world. Courts mistakenly interpret this as a domestic application of the statute, inadvertently broadening its scope globally. The absence of a clear delineation of the geographical boundaries has created ambiguity, allowing for an unintended expansion of Section 230's reach beyond its originally intended jurisdiction.

Beyond considering the *safe harbor* provision within the US landscape, Anupam Chander highlighted an intriguing issue in his recent scholarly piece regarding Section 230—that it plays a vital role in cultivating a culture of free speech by empowering US-based technology companies to host speech by political dissidents on a global scale. The openness permitted in the United States contributes significantly to maintaining a diverse range of speech on the global Internet, even encompassing content that may be deemed illegal in other parts of the world. Section 230 serves as a lifeline for dissidents by preventing or complicating attempts by foreign governments to censor marginalized voices. This is achieved through methods such as Internet service provider (ISP) filters and Domain Name System (DNS) blocks. By providing immunity to online platforms, Section 230 becomes a crucial safeguard against external efforts to stifle free expression, ensuring that a wide array of voices, including those challenging political norms, can continue to be heard and disseminated globally (Chander, 2022a).

In hearing *X, Inc. v. Taamneh*,[34] The Supreme Court of the United States has ruled that Facebook, Google, and X cannot be held liable for "aiding and abetting" the Reina nightclub terrorist attack in Istanbul, Turkey, perpetrated by the Islamic State of Iraq and Syria (ISIS) under Section 2333 of the US Code. The court determined that the mere failure to remove content does not amount to "substantial assistance" unless an independent duty to act is identified. In this case, the appellants were found not liable for "aid and abetment" as the respondents failed to establish active involvement, such as providing special treatment to terrorist organizations. The ruling clarifies that platforms are not automatically responsible for the content posted on their platforms unless there is evidence of direct involvement or support for terrorist activities, emphasizing the need for an identified independent duty to trigger liability.

[34] *X, Inc. v. Taamneh*, 598 U.S. 471 (2023).

In *Gonzalez v. Google*,[35] the court avoided addressing the broader question of the immunity provided by Section 230 of the Communications Decency Act. The case involved Nohemi Gonzalez, a victim of the 2015 ISIS attack in Paris, whose family sued Google under the Anti-Terrorism Act. The Ninth Circuit dismissed the case, citing the Section 230 immunity and deeming it a domestic application, even though most relevant activities occurred extraterritorially. The Supreme Court did not delve into the territoriality issue, and the Ninth Circuit's ruling on Section 230's domestic application remains in effect. Currently, the case is on appeal and is waiting for a decision. Both of these cases challenged the broad immunity from liability that websites have enjoyed regarding hosting and recommending terrorist content.

The approaches taken in these two cases have sparked massive debates in the tech-legal field, with critics arguing that the Supreme Court issued narrowly focused rulings. These rulings, according to critics, avoided placing limitations on Section 230, a legal provision that protects social media platforms from lawsuits over user-posted content from anywhere in the world, extending beyond the United States. The criticism centers on the perception that the Supreme Court's decisions did not sufficiently address the broader implications of Section 230, which has significant consequences for the legal landscape surrounding social media platforms. Critics argue that a more comprehensive examination of the law and its potential limitations could have provided clearer guidance in navigating the complex intersection of technology, free speech, and legal liability.

In the *Equustek* suit,[36] the case originated from a 2011 patent dispute in Canada between Equustek Solutions Inc. and Datalink Technologies Gateway LLC. Datalink was falsely marketing its products as Equustek's and incorporating Equustek's trade secrets. The main individual defendant fled the country, defying Canadian court orders. In compliance with the court decision, Google blocked over 300 Datalink websites from its Canada-specific search results. However, these sites remained listed on search results for users outside Canada, such as those on Google US. In the Canadian Supreme Court case of *Google Inc. v. Equustek Solutions Inc.*,[37] the court upheld a decision requiring Google to globally delist Datalink search results. The District Court for the Northern District of California issued preliminary injunctive relief against the Canadian court order. The court argued that the Canadian order likely violates Section 230 of the Communication Decency Act, deprives Google of US federal law benefits, and undermines the public interest protected by Section 230, which aims to preserve free speech on the global Internet.

These rulings clearly portray the impact of Section 230 on a global scale, and the merits, demerits, and challenges associated with the provision will affect not only US jurisprudence but also beyond.

---

[35] *Gonzalez v. Google LLC*, 598 U.S. 617.

[36] *Google LLC v. Equustek Solutions Inc.*, 2017 WL 5000834 (N.D. Cal. Nov. 2, 2017).

[37] *Google Inc., v. Equustek Solutions Inc.* [2017] 1 S.C.R. 34 (Can.).

7.4.2 How Does Section 230 Affect Content Moderation and Free Speech?

Though free speech scholars argue that the *safe harbor* provision secures free speech online, from a content moderation perspective, Section 230 protects online platforms, whether they choose to moderate user content or not, as long as they did not create the content themselves.

On one hand, it serves as a shield for technology giants, particularly SMPs, in matters related to content moderation. On the other hand, the global landscape of social media content moderation is significantly impacted by the diverse standards implemented across different regions. Despite contemporary regulatory developments, such as the initiatives to enact new laws like the Network Enforcement Act (NetzDG) of Germany, the Intermediary Rules of India, and the Online Safety Act of the United Kingdom, there is an underscored attempt to conceptually address legislative validity by compelling platforms to take down or remove specific content. The proscribed content, even if originating from a specific jurisdiction, may have implications on a global scale in accordance with the platforms' values.

Consequently, where there is a need to contemplate the worldwide application of these standards, Section 230 remains a significant obstacle to the global application of content moderation. As highlighted in the opening paragraphs of this chapter, most SMPs are primarily headquartered in the United States. In instances where there is a need to ensure the worldwide application of these standards, a recourse can only be pursued in the courts of the United States. Section 230, with its *safe harbor* provision, becomes a crucial barrier in these instances by protecting SMPs, presenting a challenge to the global application of content moderation. Although Section 230 itself lacks direct global applicability, its implications pose significant challenges in legal proceedings against major tech platforms, particularly those within the realm of social media in these cases.

For example, a notable example in 2017 highlights the consequences of Facebook's irresponsible actions in Myanmar during the violence against the Rohingya community, underscoring the need for platforms to be held more responsible (Amnesty International, 2022).

In such a scenario where values are affected globally, the US courts are deemed the appropriate jurisdiction to hear a suit against Meta. In such cases, Section 230 would serve to safeguard the platforms, thereby eliminating opportunities for the redress of violations of free speech.

Hence, while the broader immunity model initially provides social media platforms (SMPs) with a content moderation approach centered around "free speech," it introduces a challenging dynamic. This challenge indirectly affects free speech online when the moderation policies of these platforms impact global free speech. In instances where the platforms' moderation policies have a widespread impact on free speech, Section 230 becomes a barrier to instituting action against them, consequently impeding the protection of free speech.

Then Should Section 230 Be Abolished, Reformed, Or…?

The removal of Section 230, despite acknowledged repercussions, could have both local and global consequences. Advocates for free speech argue that a ruling favoring the plaintiff in online speech-related cases may compel social media companies to suppress constitutionally protected speech, potentially advancing an authoritarian agenda by state or private entities. This could result in the adoption of overly broad content moderation tools, restricting discussions on vital subjects, including online political discourse.

Repealing Section 230 and holding platforms liable for user-generated content could lead to self-censorship by tech companies out of self-interest to avoid legal repercussions. This may extend beyond speech related to terrorism to include various forms of expression that might potentially lead to harm or challenge established norms. This places vulnerable individuals, particularly those with limited means to defend themselves online, at greater risk (Daphne et al., 2023).

Significant changes to Section 230 could have significant global impacts. Firstly, it might lead other countries to adopt policies restricting online content or holding platforms accountable for hosted content, undermining the existing global consensus supported by key regulatory frameworks such as Section 230 CDA and the E-Commerce Directive of the European Union (EU). This raises questions about how tech companies can comply with divergent legal frameworks across different jurisdictions. Additionally, it would create serious repercussions in the free speech spectrum in jurisdictions with fragile natures and heavy-handed regulations against human rights as well as vulnerable democratic countries like Sri Lanka, Myanmar, and many more.

Secondly, given the Internet's borderless nature and the global presence of American tech companies hosting a substantial portion of online content, changes in US regulations and the corresponding actions of these companies could have substantial extraterritorial ramifications. To manage liability in the United States, American platforms may implement new, automated content moderation tools. However, this approach could result in widespread content censorship globally, as companies are more likely to apply broad measures than attempt to tailor solutions to specific jurisdictions (General Politics, 2023). In such cases, from a *private governance* approach also, it would be challenging to manage free speech online.

A Way Forward

The current issues with the existing legal framework, particularly the Section 230 immunity, are evident and numerous. However, finding an appropriate and lasting solution poses a significant challenge. Completely abolishing the Section 230 immunity is deemed excessive and potentially counterproductive. Opening the floodgates to tort, defamation, and privacy claims could strain both the companies responsible for content policing and the judicial system handling the resulting disputes.

Some propose using antitrust laws as a remedy, suggesting breaking up technology giants that fail to reform. However, likening the issue to nineteenth-century antitrust solutions for railroads is seen as an ill-fitting approach. The complexity of dealing with modern Internet platforms, often serving as both publishers and distributors, requires new tools, and Congress must determine how to tailor them effectively to address contemporary challenges (Hawkins & Stanford, 2020).

While the problems associated with Section 230 mandate reforms to the existing provision, the removal of these provisions might result in certain repercussions within the free speech regime, both in the United States and globally, particularly when navigating through the AI regime.

The overarching question would be: *In measuring this double-edged sword, how can this issue be overcome?*

In exploring to what extent, the SMPs can be treated as "publishers," an interesting argument pointed out by Russell L is that, unlike mainstream broadcasters and publishers subject to the oversight of the US FCC, SMPs neither generate content nor exercise editorial authority over the content on their platforms. However, if they do exert editorial authority, it may be treated more like traditional media (Weaver, 2022). However, I argue that content moderation by platforms does not equate to exercising editorial authority over the content. While some contend that platform-driven content removal is akin to editorial decisions, SMPs face considerable challenges when treated as equivalent to traditional mainstream broadcasters.

I would suggest an interpretative shift of the provision as the best solution in this case scenario. Reflecting on the pre-CDA regime, the *safe harbor* provision was introduced into the CDA due to judicial challenges associated with identifying the *publisher* on Internet platforms. The *safe harbor* provision in Section 230, originating from the *Prodigy* defamation case, signifies a legislative focus on shielding online platforms from liability for content publication decisions.

Several scholars argue that Section 230 has been overly broadly interpreted by the courts in their applications. As Citron, D. K., and Wittes, B., argued, the original Section 230 was specifically intended to provide immunity to providers concerning decisions related to the publication of content and not a *broader* immunity. If broader immunity was intended, it would have been explicitly stated (Citron & Wittes, 2018).

It was also stressed in the judicial pronouncement of *Fair Housing Council of San Fernando Valley v. Roommates.com, LLC*:[38]

> When Congress passed Section 230 it didn't intend to prevent the enforcement of all laws online; rather, it sought to encourage interactive computer services that provide users neutral tools to post content online to police that content without fear that through their "good samaritan . . . screening of offensive material," 47 U.S.C. § 230(c), they would become liable for every single message posted by third parties on their website.

Candeub, A., pointed out that Section 230 of the Communications Decency Act does not "explicitly" cover platforms' protection for content moderation actions beyond the reasons specified in Section 230(c)(2), such as moderating disinformation, hate speech, misgendering, or religious hatred or prioritizing traffic for specific content. However, some courts have interpreted Section 230 more broadly, granting

[38] *Fair Housing Council of San Fernando Valley v. Roommates.com, LLC*, 521 F.3d 1157 (9th Cir. 2008).

platforms protection for a wider range of content moderation reasons (Candeub, 2021).

As the legal landscape and societal perceptions have evolved, there is a potential gap between the original legislative intent behind Section 230 and its contemporary interpretation and application in legal cases. The broader interpretations by the courts have led to a more expansive immunity regime. I would suggest that courts narrowly interpret these terms, limiting the statute's application to "Good Samaritans"—online service providers taking reasonable steps to address illegal activities or illicit content when alerted, even if inadvertent underscreening occurs. It would be feasible to adopt an interpretational shift of CDA Section 230 through upcoming judicial pronouncements, particularly in cases involving major tech platforms to overcome existing challenges across the big tech platforms.

Should We Amend Section 230? If Yes, How?

First, I am not in favor of amending the provision; instead, I believe that through judicial activism and an interpretational shift, settling precedents can help address the issues discussed in the previous section. However, there are many arguments in favor of amending or removing the provision.

If we choose to march toward amending the section, rather than delving into textual suggestions, I will propose incorporating certain standards into the new legislative provision. Over the past decade, the global regulatory regime has grappled with similar challenges. For example, the regulatory developments in the UK regarding intermediary liability for online platforms emphasize the *duty of care* principle overseen by an independent regulator. Similar approaches are being considered in the United States, with discussions around the establishment of new federal agencies and the application of a *duty of care* principle, akin to *Good Samaritans*, in regulating social media companies (Galli et al., 2022).

Considering the constraints of time and investment, the new provisions should be wide enough to address both human and AI moderators and establish clear attributability of AI responsibilities to the platforms themselves (Armijo, 2021). This approach would create a regulatory framework adaptable to the evolving landscape of content moderation on social media platforms while considering practical constraints. Unlike the existing Section 230, there would be no need for rushed amendments.

In the context of addressing the leeway granted to social networks under CDA Section 230, the possibility of increased regulation to mandate content moderation is considered. The NetzDG serves as a model, offering potential guiding principles and mechanisms for such regulation. First, statutory regulation modeled after the NetzDG aims to ensure a certain equality of treatment among platform users. Second, it provides a remedy in cases where platforms fail to enforce their self-imposed standards (Zurth, 2021). To safeguard start-ups, a minimum user threshold could be set for the application of such regulations.

The proposed framework, with the objective bad faith exception to Section 230, would introduce a more nuanced and fair approach to evaluating the conduct of social media platforms or websites. This ensures that their immunity is contingent on the justifiability and severity of any bad-faith actions they may undertake (Pagano, 2018). Instead of relying on a subjective test, which is complex in the AI regime, employing an objective standard allows the legal system to ensure a fair and consistent assessment of the platform's behavior. The scope of immunity provided by Section 230 could be either broadened or narrowed based on justifiability. The extent of immunity granted to the platform would be determined by the severity and justifiability of the bad faith conduct under the new framework.

The new framework should clarify the distinction between acceptable editing and becoming a publisher who no longer enjoys immunity protections. Several common practices, such as labeling, delisting, and context commentaries, may not be technically considered as content editing, yet they undeniably impact how content is accessed, understood, and shared. The reformed provision should specifically address this issue and establish a clearer line regarding these practices, delineating what does and does not violate the editorial preconditions of the immunity protections. Moreover, the amended provision should not adversely affect anti-terrorism, child sex abuse, and cyber-stalking laws. Given the critical and inherent nature of these areas to national security, morality, and public order, as discussed in a few cases above, reforms to Section 230 should be made without ambiguity to safeguard *cyber resilience*.

As a jurisdiction with a focus on strengthening state-private governance over social media platforms, the new framework of the United States should pave the way for the establishment of federally mandated social media oversight boards. This involves enacting standards that require large social media platforms to create and maintain independent oversight boards, similar to the structure and charter of the Facebook Oversight Board (FOB) (Scheurman, 2022). Establishing a *status quo* based on the global number of users or annual revenues for the mandatory implementation of oversight boards could be a feasible approach in the enduring free speech debate surrounding immunity.

References

Ajder, H., & Glick, J. (2021). *Just joking! Deepfakes, satire and the politics of synthetic media.* WITNESS and MIT Open Documentary Lab.

Amnesty International. (2022). *The social atrocity: Meta and the right to remedy for the Rohingya.* Amnesty International.

Andika, M., Halifa, H., & Satria, A. (2022). The role of social media and its implication for democracy in 2020 U.S. elections. *Ilomata International Journal of Social Science, 3*(3), 325–336.

Armijo, E. (2021). Reasonableness as censorship: Section 230 reform, content moderation, and the first amendment. *Florida Law Review, 73*(6), 1199–1243.

Auxier, B., & McClain, C. (2020). Americans think social media can help build movements, but can also be a distraction.

Balkin, J. M. (1999). Free speech and hostile environments. *Columbia Law Review, 99*(8), 2295–2320.

Balkin, J. M. (2014). Old-school/new-school speech regulation. *Harvard Law Review, 127*(8), 2296–2342.

Barrett, P., Hendrix, J., & Carvajal, C. R. (2024). *Digital risks to the 2024 elections: Safeguarding democracy in the era of disinformation.* NYU Stern Center for Business and Human Rights.

Bessi, A., & Ferrara, E. (2016). Social Bots Distort the 2016 US Presidential Election online discussion. *First Monday, 21*(11).

Bonilla, Y., & Rosa, J. (2015). # Ferguson: Digital protest, hashtag ethnography, and the racial politics of social media in the United States. *American Ethnologist*, 4–17.

Candeub, A. (2021). Reading Section 230 as written. *Journal of Free Speech Law, 1*(1), 139–174.

Chander, A. (2022a). Section 230 and the international law of Facebook. *Yale Law Journal of Law and Technology*, 394–420.

Chander, A. (2022b). Section 230 and the international law of Facebook. *Yale Journal of Law & Technology, 24*(1), 393–420.

Cheng, S., & Norcross, H. (2021). Internet censorship in the time of a global pandemic: A proposal for revisions to section 230 of the Communications Decency Act. *Brigham Young University Prelaw Review, 35*(11), 123–138.

Citron, D. K., & Wittes, B. (2018). The problem isn't just backpage: Revising Section 230 immunity. *Georgetown Law Technology Review, 2*(2), 453–473.

Daphne, K., Anupam, C., Mary, F. A., & Artur, L. P. (2023, May 18). Q&A: Section 230 is at the Supreme Court. Here's why that matters for free expression.

Erin, S., Adam, C., & Ashleigh, M. (2022). *Social media and the 2022 midterm elections: Anticipating online threats to democratic legitimacy*. Retrieved November 3, from https://www.americanprogress.org/article/social-media-and-the-2022-midterm-elections-anticipating-online-threats-to-democratic-legitimacy/

Everett, C. M. (2018). Free speech on privately-owned fora: A discussion on speech freedoms and policy for social media. *Kansas Journal of Law & Public Policy*, 113–145.

Freedom House. (2023). *Freedom on Internet 2023.*

Galli, F., Loreggia, A., & Sartor, G. (2022). The regulation of content moderation. In D. M. Vicente, S. de Vasconcelos Casimiro, & C. Chen (Eds.), *The legal challenges of the fourth industrial revolution: The European Union's digital strategy* (pp. 63–87). Springer International Publishing.

General Politics. (2023). *The Domino Effect: The global implications of changes to Section 230.* Retrieved May 19, from https://www.global-counsel.com/insights/blog/domino-effect-global-implications-changes-section-230

Goodman, E. P., & Whittington, R. (2019). *Section 230 of the Communications Decency Act and the future of online speech.* The German Marshall Fund of the United States.

Gosztonyi, G. (2023). *Censorship from Plato to social media: The complexity of social media's content regulation and moderation practices* (Vol. 61). Springer Nature.

Hastuti, H., Harry, M. F., Andi, T. P., & Zalfa, Z. F. (2023). Analysis of social media opinion on the representation of the 2024 presidential election on Twitter: A social network analysis. *Jurnal Studi Ilmu Pemerintahan, 4*(1), 117–128.

Hawkins, M. D., & Stanford, M. J. (2020). Uproot or upgrade? Revisiting Section 230 immunity in the digital age. *University of Chicago Law Review Online*, 1–6.

Hendricks, J. A., & Dan, S. (2017). The Social Media Election of 2016. In R. Denton Jr. (Ed.), *The 2016 US presidential campaign: Political communication and practice* (pp. 121–150). Palgrave Macmillan.

Horward, P. N., Bence, K., Samantha, B., & Neudert, L. M. (2018). Social media, news and political information during the US election: Was polarizing content concentrated in swing states? *arXiv preprint arXiv:1802.03573.*

Jackson, B. F. (2014). Censorship and freedom of expression in the age of Facebook. *New Mexico Law Review, 44*(1), 121–167.

Jakubcin, R. (1998). Reno v. aclu: Establishing first amendment level of protection for the internet. *University of Florida Journal of Law and Public Policy, 9*(2), 287–296.

Kapur, A. (2024). *Can the Internet be governed?* Retrieved February 05, from https://www.newyorker.com/magazine/2024/02/05/can-the-internet-be-governed

Karalis, P., & Golriz, C. (2023). *Analysis: Product claims spike as SCOTUS ponders Section 230 fix*. Retrieved March 2, from https://news.bloomberglaw.com/bloomberg-law-analysis/analysis-product-claims-spike-as-scotus-ponders-section-230-fix

Klon Kitchen. (2020). *Section 230—Mend it, don't end it.* https://www.heritage.org/

Kosseff, J. (2017). Twenty years of intermediary immunity: The US experience. *SCRIPTed, 14*, 5–35.

Kosseff, J. (2019). *The twenty-six words that created the Internet.* Cornell University Press.

Madrigal, A. C. (2017). *What Facebook did to American democracy*. The Atlantic.

Meeran, Y. A. (2018). As justice so requires: Making the case for a limited reading of Sec. 230 of the Communications Decency Act. *The George Washington Law Review, 86*(1), 257–286.

O'Donnell, N. (2021). Have we no decency? Section 230 and the liability of social media companies for deepfake videos. *University of Illinois Law Review*, 702–738.

Pagano, N. A. (2018). The indecency of the Communications Decency Act 230: Unjust immunity for monstrous social media platforms. *Pace Law Review, 39*(1), 511–538.

Pariser, E. (2011). *The filter bubble: What the Internet is hiding from you.* Penguin UK.

Patty, M. (2019). Social media and censorship: Rethinking state action once again. *Mitchell Hamline Law Journal of Public Policy and Practice, 40*(1), 100–135.

Peter, K., & Golriz, C. (2018). The problem isn't just Backpage: Revising Section 230 immunity. *Georgetown Law Technology Review, 453*(2).

Peters, J., & Johnson, B. (2016). Conceptualizing private governance in networked society. *North Carolina Journal of Law & Technology, 18*(1).

Redoano, M. (2019). *Politics in the Facebook era: Examining the effects of voter 'micro-targeting' in the 2016 US presidential election.* The University of Warwick.

Rucker, L. H. (2023). The end of an era: The uncertain future of Section 230 immunity for social media platforms. *Vanderbilt Journal of Entertainment and Technology Law, 26*(1), 242–272.

Scheurman, T. (2022). Comparing social media content regulation in the US and the EU: How the US can move forward with section 230 to bolster social media users' freedom of expression. *San Diego International Law Journal, 23*(2), 413–[xiv].

Smith, M. D., & Van Alstyne, M. (2021). *It's time to update Section 230.* Retrieved August 12, from https://hbr.org/2021/08/its-time-to-update-section-230

Spiccia, P. (2013). The best things in life are not free: Why immunity under Section 230 of the Communications Decency Act should be earned and not freely given. *Valparaiso University Law Review, 48*(1), 369–416.

Sunstein, C. (2018). *Republic: Divided democracy in the age of social media.* Princeton University Press.

Thomas, F., Karsten, M., & Carlo, S. (2023). The effect of social media on elections: Evidence from the United States. *Journal of the European Economic Association*, 1–45.

Tremble, C. (2017). Wild westworld: Section 230 of the CDA and social networks' use of machine-learning algorithms. *Fordham Law Review, 86*(2), 825–870.

Weaver, R. L. (2022). Social media, Section 230, and free expression. *Mercer Law Review, 73*(2), 615–633.

Zurth, P. (2021). The German NetzDg as role model or cautionary tale? Implications for the debate on social media liability. *Fordham Intellectual Property, Media & Entertainment Law Journal, 31*(4), 1084–1153.

Chapter 8
Unveiling NetzDG: *The Digital Berlin Wall*

8.1 Introduction

As a country of the European Union (EU), Germany has a robust system of addressing issues related to the Internet and free speech after passing the Network Enforcement Act (NetzDG), which came into force in January 2018. Since the early 2010s, Germany has witnessed so many social media movements across different cities, yet the urge to regulate social media platforms (SMPs) led to the legislative attempt to enact NetzDG. Though Germany was flexible about Internet speech in the very early days, the subsequent tensions created by the movements of the right-wing populist party as well as the COVID-19 pandemic tensions compelled the government to regulate content online, more specifically across the SMPs. It is noted that after the NetzDG came into force, Internet freedom has declined drastically and needs urgent attention (Freedom House, 2022). A few scholars noted that within a short span of time, various states around the world have been either directly or indirectly inspired by Germany's efforts to strengthen intermediary liability laws (Mchangama & Fiss, 2019). The NetzDG has faced criticism for various reasons, particularly for its potential chilling effect on free speech and its conflicts with standards set by the European Union, such as those outlined in the EU E-Commerce Directive.

Though Germany's framework has been superseded by the EU's Digital Services Act (DSA), which is now fully in force, this chapter still examines the provisions, applications, and impacts of the previous German regulations on free speech. This analysis is crucial, as the book aims to explore various regulatory frameworks under three broader models, with Germany's approach serving as an apt example for "external regulation." By providing an in-depth analysis of Germany's framework, the chapter contributes to a comprehensive examination that spans from Western contexts to the Majority World, offering valuable insights, particularly from the perspective of the Global South.

S. Balendra, *Free Speech in the Puzzle of Content Regulation*, Law, Governance and Technology Series 70, https://doi.org/10.1007/978-3-031-75813-3_8

Accordingly, this chapter examines the social media landscape in Germany, with a focus on the regulatory framework established by the NetzDG and its implications for the democratic fabric of the Internet, particularly within SMPs. Also, this study accordingly examines the implications and interplay between NetzDG and the EU's regulatory frameworks: E-Commerce Directive and Digital Service Act. As a member of the EU, Germany is subject to regulations, such as the Digital Services Act (DSA), which replaced the provisions of NetzDG. However, this book dedicates a chapter to the NetzDG framework, recognizing its prominence and controversy since its proposal and enactment in 2017. Despite Germany's struggle with extreme Internet censorship, the NetzDG has faced criticism for its severe penalties, stringent deadlines for platforms, delegation of significant decision-making power to private entities, and concerns over free speech and the lack of implementation safeguards. As the book explores various models of regulatory authorities through a comparative case study approach, this examination of the NetzDG adds depth to the study undertaken in this book.

8.2 The Evolution of Social Media

In January 2023, Germany reported having 70.90 million social media users, accounting for 85.1% of its total population (Freedom House, 2023). This figure underscores the country's high engagement with SMPs, a trend that is consistent with many other global jurisdictions. Particularly noteworthy is the access to these platforms during crises and significant political events, exemplified by two key instances: the 2013 European flood and the federal elections in the same year.

During the 2013 European flood, social media, especially Facebook, played a pivotal role in coordinating and organizing recovery efforts across Germany. The platform facilitated effective communication among volunteers, allowing for the efficient matching of the demand and supply of resources among citizens. This demonstrated the power of SMPs as critical tools for information dissemination and community mobilization during times of crisis (Kaufhold & Reuter, 2016). Similarly, the 2013 federal elections in Germany highlighted the significant impact of social media in the political domain. SMPs were instrumental in mobilizing and canvassing, particularly attracting young voters aged 18 to 29 (Zeh & Holtz-Bacha, 2015). The continuous stream of information on these platforms has transformed the way political parties and candidates present their views and respond to issues. Rather than offering fixed or comprehensive stances, politicians now engage more dynamically with the electorate, commenting on and responding to events as they unfold. This approach allows them to adjust swiftly to prevailing public discussions and topics emphasized by mass media and news platforms.

The role of social media in shaping public discourse and driving action in Germany has evolved significantly, proving highly effective in crisis response, political mobilization, and environmental activism. Social media platforms enable rapid adjustments to the topics that dominate public discussions, including those highlighted in mass-mediated debates and by news media platforms (Helbling & Tresch, 2011).

According to Freedom House, social media has been instrumental in advancing the climate protection movement, a notable example being the *Fridays for Future* student protests. Originating in Sweden, these protests have harnessed the power of social media for organization and mobilization, making a significant impact in Berlin in September 2018 (Freedom House, 2023). The movement swiftly brought the climate crisis to the forefront of the national political agenda in Germany. By 2023, the tradition of holding protests on Fridays continued in various cities across Germany, demonstrating the sustained influence and reach of social media in fostering environmental activism.[1]

The *Patriotic Europeans Against the Islamisation of the West (PEGIDA)* movement in Germany, representing far-right ideologies, effectively leveraged social media, particularly Facebook, to cultivate counterpublic presence. The movement gained momentum amidst the 2015 refugee crisis, driven by a conspiracy theory alleging a plot to Islamize Germany, with refugees purportedly serving as instruments for this purpose.

However, PEGIDA encountered a significant obstacle when its Facebook page was deleted in an early example of *deplatforming* efforts aimed at curtailing far-right groups' online reach. Despite this, the *deplatforming* led to unintended consequences as PEGIDA and similar entities sought refuge on alternative platforms like Telegram.

Since 2019, Telegram has emerged as a sanctuary for far-right groups that have been *deplatformed* from mainstream social media sites, facilitating the continuation of their activities and communication (Zehring & Domahidi, 2023). This migration underscores the adaptability of far-right movements in the face of attempts to silence them online. Nevertheless, research on social media's influence on right-wing movements reveals a complex picture. High levels of engagement with right-wing content on social media are frequently linked to emotionally charged, fear-inducing, and xenophobic material. However, the evidence remains inconclusive regarding whether platforms like Facebook, particularly during periods of waning public attention, consistently lead to right-wing movements adopting more radical mobilization strategies (Schwemmer, 2021).

During the COVID-19 pandemic, SMPs played a pivotal role in disseminating information and facilitating dialogue on a variety of crisis-related topics, including the virus, vaccination efforts, governmental policies, and health precautions. Research from this period identified six primary reasons for COVID-19 vaccine hesitancy shared on SMPs: perceived low benefits of vaccination, perceived low risk of contracting COVID-19, health concerns, insufficient information, systemic distrust, and spiritual or religious objections (Fieselmann et al., 2022).

---

[1] See https://www.aa.com.tr/en/environment/thousands-take-to-streets-in-germany-demanding-climate-action/2992959.

In Germany, the pandemic also sparked protests against COVID-19-related restrictions. The *Querdenken* movement emerged as a significant online force opposing these measures.[2] While protest movements are often judged by their impact on immediate policy changes, success can also be gauged by their ability to gain momentum, institutionalize, increase their supporter base, and attract media attention over time. By these measures, the Querdenken movement has achieved notable success (Plümper et al., 2021). However, the movement has faced criticism for potentially fostering public distrust in governmental and administrative bodies, suggesting an agenda that extends beyond mere protest (Pfaff et al., 2021).

Another significant movement, #IchBinHanna, emerged in 2021 and 2022, leveraging SMPs to challenge the prevalence of fixed-term employment contracts under the Temporary Employment Contract Act. This movement, primarily comprising researchers, brought national attention to the precarious working conditions in academia, sparking discussions in the Bundestag.[3]

Despite SMPs often highlighting major issues within and beyond Germany, the spread of hate speech—particularly against refugees and fake news—compelled regulatory actions toward platforms. Consequently, the government swiftly implemented measures, demonstrating its commitment to combat various online threats. This move aimed to preserve the integrity of public discourse, especially during critical electoral periods, through a regulatory framework.[4]

8.3 Regulating Social Media Platforms

Historically, Germany has been cautious about blocking or shutting down digital content. Prior to the introduction of NetzDG, there was no legislation granting the government broad authority to block Internet access or shut down websites. However, as a member of the EU, Germany adheres to EU regulations.[5] In March 2022, following the EU's directive in response to Russia's invasion of Ukraine, the German government blocked access to websites of Russian state-owned media outlets, such as RT and Sputnik, accusing them of spreading propaganda aimed at civil society (Freedom House, 2023).

Although the Digital Services Act (DSA) is set to supersede certain aspects of the NetzDG in Germany by February 2024 (Clasen, 2023), the NetzDG currently remains the cornerstone of social media platform regulation in the country. This

---

[2] See https://www.dw.com/en/meet-germanys-querdenker-covid-protest-movement/a-57049985.

[3] See https://www.uni-goettingen-unbefristet.de/en/i-am-hanna-ichbinhanna-shows-the-reality-of-working-in-research-in-germany/.

[4] See https://www.aljazeera.com/news/2017/4/5/germany-seeks-to-fine-social-media-over-hateful-posts.

[5] Regulation 2022/350.

discussion will delve into the regulatory details and implications of NetzDG within this context.

8.3.1 Background of NetzDG

After World War II, Germany implemented stringent laws to counteract hate speech, including making *Holocaust denial* punishable by imprisonment. This legal approach starkly contrasts with the United States, where the Constitution primarily safeguards free speech (Glaun, 2021). The emergence of hate speech and misinformation on online platforms highlighted the need for a regulatory framework for social media in Germany. Sandra Schmitz and Christian M. Berndt observe that the battle against so-called *fake news* gained momentum in Germany following the US election campaign, emphasizing the urgency of legislative action (Schmitz & Berndt, 2018).

The *influx of refugees* in 2015 saw a surge in racist and xenophobic content on social media, prompting discussions on the need for regulatory oversight. Despite efforts by Facebook, X (formerly Twitter), and Google to address these issues by recruiting more German-language moderators (Oltermann, 2018) and implementing other measures, Justice Minister Heiko Maas concluded that legislation was necessary to penalize users who breached these standards, advocating for the removal or flagging of controversial content (Knight, 2018).

The German government's legislative response to online discrimination and agitation against ethnic minorities was fueled by events like the significant increase in such incidents during the 2015–2016 refugee crisis. A growing awareness of aggressive online behavior and *skepticism* toward the content moderation policies of major tech companies led to the drafting of the NetzDG law. This law mandates social networks to review and, if necessary, remove content within 24 h of a complaint, aiming to curb the spread of hate speech. It was enacted in July 2017, following unsuccessful attempts at self-regulation by social network companies. This contrasts with the EU's 2016 self-regulatory Code of Conduct on Countering Illegal Hate Speech Online, developed in partnership with major platforms (Heldt, 2019).

However, the legislative journey of NetzDG was marked by internal debates and disagreements within the major political parties, leading to proposed amendments to address various concerns. Also, debates on the NetzDG revealed concerns about its compatibility with European law. A Commission official noted the law's legal challenges and the political decision required in response. The Commission had several options, including suggesting changes, demanding a response from Germany, or informal negotiations, with the law's timing critical to its potential impact (Gorwa, 2021).

Yet after the prolonged steps, back and forth, the NetzDG law was passed effective January 1, 2018, reflecting Germany's understanding that illegal content is more frequent online than in traditional media, attributed to the Internet's reach and speed. It acknowledges the significant effects of online defamation, amplified by anonymity and the Internet's inherent properties (Zurth, 2021).

Scholars argued that Germany's approach, influenced by its Nazi past and codified in the 1949 *Grundgesetz*, advocates for strict limits on fundamental freedoms to prevent their exploitation by extremists. Even before the NetzDG, the legal system included speech restrictions, such as the ban on *Holocaust denial*, viewed as lessons from history (Isabelle, 2022). Yet the NetzDG represents a bold move to hold social media platforms accountable for online speech, establishing a domestic agent as a contact point for authorities, marking a significant shift in the responsibility for monitoring online discourse (Kaesling, 2018).

8.3.2 NetzDG Within the Umbrella of the EU

The discussion of Germany's regulatory framework may create confusion for readers from the Majority World as Germany is a member state of the European Union (EU). This raises the question of whether the regulatory model being referenced is specific to Germany or reflective of the broader EU framework. It is important to note that during the background and enactment of NetzDG, the E-Commerce Directive[6] (ECD) was already in force. However, Germany took the initiative to pass a domestic law to regulate online content from a national perspective.

At the time of the introduction of the NetzDG, the European Union was governed by the E-Commerce Directive (Directive 2000/31/EC), which specifically addressed the limitations[7] on the liability of service providers for third-party content. Within this framework, the European Commission had thus far refrained from directly regulating intermediaries, instead opting to encourage self-regulatory measures. Schulz points out, similarly, that the German government initially adopted this approach, with the Ministry of Justice urging the industry to enhance their complaint mechanisms. However, by 2017, the government expressed dissatisfaction with the effectiveness of these self-regulatory efforts, ultimately leading to the enactment of the NetzDG in Germany (Schulz, 2022).

Under Article 14 of the EU E-Commerce Directive, platforms become liable for hosting unlawful content only after being notified and are required to remove it *expeditiously*. NetzDG was introduced to better enforce these existing obligations by mandating new internal procedures, which are enforced through administrative penalties, as Helberger has pointed out (Helberger, 2020). However, scholars note that the term *expeditiously* is not precisely defined within the ECD, leaving some ambiguity regarding the specific time frame within which the content must be removed, and this ambiguity has led to different interpretations among EU member

[6]Electronic Commerce Directive (2000/31/EC).

[7]Articles 12–14.

states—including Germany's model oversteps with the intention of EU, introduced by frameworks such as DSA (Schulz, 2022; Spindler, 2017; Moon, 2019).

Also, there has been criticism that NetzDG violates the country-of-origin principle underlined by the EU Directive—as the NetzDG imposes specific requirements on social media platforms, regardless of whether or not they are based in Germany. Article 3(2) of the EU Directive provides:

> Member States may not, for reasons falling within the coordinated field, restrict the freedom to provide information society services from another Member State.

However, lawmakers claimed that the NetzDG, aimed at combating hate speech and other illegal content, falls within this exemption. Yet it is argued that the exemption can be applied in individual cases to protect public safety and that it cannot be used as a blanket justification to bypass the "country of origin" principle established by the E-Commerce Directive (Haupt, 2024b).

Similarly, during the implementation of the NetzDG, the EU introduced the Digital Services Act (DSA) in 2022, which addresses issues such as illegal content, transparent advertising, and disinformation, thereby updating the E-Commerce Directive. Alongside the Digital Markets Act (DMA)—which aims to make digital sector markets fairer and more contestable by establishing clear criteria to identify large platforms as *gatekeepers* and imposing specific obligations and prohibitions on them—the DSA represents a significant shift in the regulatory landscape. On February 17, 2024, the DSA became fully applicable to all the platforms across the European region.

In essence, the DSA establishes a harmonized legal framework across the EU, ensuring consistent rules for online platforms and services. Consequently, national laws like the NetzDG, which were originally designed to regulate online content within individual member states, will be largely rendered obsolete or significantly modified to align with the DSA's provisions. As an EU member state, Germany has implemented the DSA through the *Digitale Dienste Gesetz* (DDG), which transposes the DSA into German national law. Although the DDG, effective from May 2024, has amended the NetzDG, it has not entirely repealed it (Haupt, 2024a). According to a few scholars, the DSA is also influenced by regulatory frameworks like the NetzDG (Eifert et al., 2021; Haupt, 2024a; Griffin, 2021), making it both viable and valuable to explore the processes, merits, and challenges of the NetzDG in capturing the ongoing debates around social media content governance across different models, as discussed in other chapters of this book.

8.3.3 Salient Features of the Act

The primary purpose of NetzDG—often referred to as the Facebook Act (*Facebook-Gesetz*)—is to address the challenges of fake news, hate speech, and misinformation on the Internet. The regulatory framework achieves this objective by mandating that social media platforms remove content that is clearly hateful or false within a specified time frame.

The Act defines "social networks" as

> telemedia service providers which, for profit-making purposes, operate Internet platforms which are designed to enable users to share any content with other users or to make such content available to the public.[8]

In this NetzDG, there is no definition of hate speech or fake news. However, it refers to the criminal offenses under the German Criminal Code. To ensure a strict interpretation, the Act elaborates "unlawful content" as content that contravenes with the provisions selected under the German Criminal Code.[9] It includes offenses such as public incitement of crimes,[10] threats to commit offenses,[11] incitement to hatred,[12] and defamation of religions[13] or people[14] as examples of illegal hate speech. Offenses that resemble the spreading of fake news are intentional defamation,[15] treasonous forgery,[16] and forgery of data.[17]

Further, the framework set out obligations under Sections 2 and 3 for social media platforms with registered users above *two million* within Germany.[18] Therefore, major platforms such as Facebook, Google, and Twitter are subject to the application of this Act.

Section 2 of the Act primarily imposes reporting obligations on social media platforms (SMPs). As part of the reporting requirement, the Act mandates that platforms report when they receive more than 100 complaints from users about the content per calendar month and provide quarterly reports on how these complaints are handled.[19] The report shall include information about the processes of content moderation, the number of complaints received, and the outcome of decisions. The NetzDG further stipulates that the failure to meet the reporting requirements is an administrative offense, punishable by a fine of up to 500,000 euros.

Section 3 lists down the obligations related to the complaint mechanisms under the NetzDG. Also, the Act mandates social media networks to appoint a person to receive services within Germany.[20] The Act empowers the Federal Ministry of

---

[8] NetzDG 2017, s 1(1).
[9] NetzDG 2017, s 1(3).
[10] German Criminal Code 1872, s 111.
[11] German Criminal Code 1872, s 126.
[12] German Criminal Code 1872, s 130.
[13] German Criminal Code 1872, s 166.
[14] German Criminal Code 1872, s 186.
[15] German Criminal Code 1872, s 187.
[16] German Criminal Code 1872, s 100(a).
[17] German Criminal Code 1872, s 269.
[18] NetzDG 2017, s 1(2).
[19] NetzDG 2017, s 2(1).
[20] NetzDG 2017, s 5.

Justice as the administrative authority of the statute and grants it extensive authority to sanction an offense even if it is not committed in the Federal Republic of Germany.[21] The Act requires[22] networks to remove or block access to "manifestly unlawful" content within 24 hours after receiving the complaint. Further, the networks are obliged to remove all other unlawful content within 7 days after receiving a complaint, with minimal exceptions.[23]

In the practical implementation of the NetzDG, content moderation involves a two-step process. Initially, platforms assess flagged content based on their own terms of service (TOS) and community standards. If the content does not meet these criteria, it is globally deleted. If the content passes this evaluation, platforms then proceed to evaluate it in accordance with the NetzDG. If the content is considered unlawful or manifestly unlawful, it is locally deleted and made unavailable for German consumption (Isabelle, 2022).

On June 28, 2021, Germany introduced an amendment to the NetzDG with the goal of enhancing the detail and comparability of transparency reports from social media companies. Furthermore, this amendment aims to streamline the process for users to report unlawful content, making it more accessible and user-friendly. Initially, Section 3, paragraph 1, of the NetzDG required that reporting procedures be easily identifiable, directly accessible, and constantly available. However, inconsistencies in how providers implemented these guidelines resulted in some reporting mechanisms being obscured or requiring multiple steps to access. The amendment addresses these issues by stipulating that the complaint process must also be straightforward to use, ensuring that users can report content with ease.

Also, the amendment to the Network Enforcement Act introduces a significant requirement for social media platforms: the establishment of an appeal mechanism. This system enables both complainants and users affected by content moderation decisions to request a review of the actions taken on flagged content. Specifically, Section 3b of the amendment provides that appeals must be lodged within 2 weeks following the initial moderation decision. Furthermore, the amendment empowers the Federal Office of Justice to authorize private law arbitration bodies to facilitate out-of-court resolutions in disputes between users/complainants and social media companies. Participation in such arbitration is voluntary. This provision aims to benefit users impacted by platform moderation actions, promoting the principle of *natural justice* by ensuring that they have the opportunity to be heard.

The amendment to the Network Enforcement Act also significantly updates the requirements for transparency reports by social media platforms. Under this amendment, social media networks that receive over 100 complaints about illegal content

---

[21] NetzDG 2017, s 4(3).

[22] NetzDG 2017, s 3(2) 2.

[23] a. Where the content is unlawful, depending on the factual allegation or circumstance, the user would afford an opportunity to respond to the complaint. b. The social media network refers the decision within the stipulated time according to the provisions of the act to a recognized self-regulation institution and agrees to accept the decision of the institution.

each year are required to publish, in German, detailed biannual reports on how they handle these complaints.[24] These reports must now include additional information, particularly on the usage and effectiveness of automated procedures for detecting illegal content. Platforms are required to disclose the training data utilized for these procedures and explain their quality assurance and evaluation methods. Additionally, the reports should categorize the number of complaints based on the response time to the flagged content—specifying whether actions were taken within 24 h, 48 h, within a week, or later. Moreover, the amendment mandates these transparency reports to cover the newly introduced appeal process, including data on the number of appeals filed and the instances in which the initial moderation decisions were revised.[25]

The amendment to the Network Enforcement Act significantly broadens the authority of the Federal Office of Justice in Germany. Initially, the Office's powers were limited to levying fines for noncompliance with the Act. However, with the new amendment, it now has the capacity to oversee adherence to the Act comprehensively. Upon identifying a violation, the Federal Office of Justice can require social media platforms to correct the issue. Furthermore, the Office has been granted the ability to demand details on how the Act is being implemented, the number of users registered in Germany, and the number of complaints received over the previous year. Additionally, in the administrative procedures outlined by the Act, witnesses are compelled to provide testimony, enhancing the Office's capability to enforce compliance effectively.[26]

8.3.4 Application of the NetzDG

Between July and December 2021, major social media platforms revealed that thousands of items were either removed or blocked in response to complaints originating from Germany. Specifically, Facebook reported 108,255 blocked or removed items; Twitter disclosed 75,822; Google mentioned 43,847 items removed on YouTube; and TikTok blocked or removed 27,436 items during this period. Notably, only Facebook and TikTok provided details on the number of items removed specifically due to compliance with the NetzDG law, while other platforms did not specify the impact of the NetzDG on their content removals in their reports (Freedom House, 2022).

According to research conducted by the Centre for European Policy Studies (CEPS), within the first 6 months, despite Facebook's vast user base, it received significantly fewer NetzDG reports than YouTube and Twitter, with the disparity exceeding 100 times (Echikson & Knodt, 2018). This difference is largely attributed

[24] NetzDG 2017, s 2, paragraph 1.

[25] NetzDG 2017, s 2, paragraph 2.

[26] NetzDG 2017, s 4a.

to the accessibility of Facebook's complaint submission process. In contrast to YouTube and Twitter, which seamlessly incorporated NetzDG complaint procedures into their standard content-flagging interfaces, Facebook positioned its NetzDG complaint form on a separate page, which was not prominently displayed, necessitating several clicks to reach. This design choice is believed to have had a considerable impact on the frequency of NetzDG complaint submissions on Facebook.

Although the Act has been in effect for over 5 years, there have been relatively few legal cases associated with it in Germany. In 2019, Facebook faced a 2 million euro fine for failing to accurately report the number of complaints it received about controversial content, a violation deemed a breach of Internet transparency regulations. While Twitter and YouTube disclosed receiving 260,000 and 215,000 complaints about content, respectively, Facebook reported only 1704 instances of problematic content (CMS Law Now, 2019). Given Facebook's extensive user base, this discrepancy was widely criticized as *underreporting*.

In June 2021, following the amendment to the NetzDG, Google initiated legal proceedings in a German administrative court challenging the Act's requirement for 24 h content removal, arguing that it infringes on user privacy rights as established under European Union law.[27] By March 2022, the court concluded that this specific requirement indeed partially contravened EU law, thereby granting temporary relief (Library of Congress, 2022). It was determined that Sections 3a, 3b, and 3e of the NetzDG violated Article 30 of the European Union Directive 2018/1808 and Directive 2000/31/EC concerning electronic commerce.

In April 2023, the German Federal Office of Justice announced that it had begun proceedings to impose a fine on X (formerly known as Twitter) for not adequately addressing complaints about controversial content, as required by the NetzDG. It is anticipated that X could be subject to a fine amounting to as much as $33 billion, given that the law permits fines of up to 50 million euros for each individual violation (Otten, 2023).

8.4 Unpacking the NetzDG: Regulating Online Speech

The European Union's Digital Services Act (DSA), adopted by the European Parliament in July 2022, aims to standardize legislation on hate speech across member states. However, Germany's NetzDG, with a broader definition of illegal content, requires online platforms to remove a wider range of content compared to the DSA. There is advocacy from politicians and children's rights groups to maintain the stricter measures of the NetzDG even after the implementation of the DSA.

[27] See https://www.counterextremism.com/blog/google-sues-germany-over-hate-speech-law.

8.4.1 Challenges to Free Speech

The main criticism of the NetzDG law revolves around concerns regarding potential violations of freedom of speech. Scholars argue that the law's requirement for social networks to remove unlawful content within 24 h may lead to *overblocking* and effectively privatize the judicial process. This combination could have chilling effects on the freedom of speech. While the legality of the content targeted by the NetzDG is not the primary concern, the delegation of responsibility to private companies is seen as problematic. Overall, scholars agree that the NetzDG is not an effective solution for combating online hate speech (Heldt, 2019). Claussen argued that as the NetzDG indirectly limits the spectrum of opinions, it imposes obligations that infringe upon the constitutionally protected freedom to express opinions outlined under Article 5 of the German Basic Law (Claussen, 2018).

Article 5 recognizes the freedom of expression, providing that:

> Every person shall have the right freely to express and disseminate his opinions in speech, writing and pictures, and to inform himself without hindrance from generally accessible sources.

In addition, Human Rights Watch and other human rights defenders also opposed the NetzDG, alleging that the framework sets parameters to limit and restrict free speech in cyberspace.

In a study, Human Rights Watch pointed out:

> Two key aspects of the law violate Germany's obligation to respect free speech, Human Rights Watch said. First, the law places the burden on companies that host third-party content to make difficult determinations of when user speech violates the law, under conditions that encourage suppression of arguably lawful speech ... Second, the law fails to provide either judicial oversight or a judicial remedy should a cautious corporate decision violate a person's right to speak or access information... (Human Rights Watch, 2018).

This was reinstated by the United National Human Rights Committee, saying: "The Committee is concerned that these provisions and their application could have a chilling effect on online expression" (Office of the United Nations High Commissioner for Human Rights, 2017). Also, the Committee warned about the danger of the absence of a court oversight content removal mechanism.

Scholar Diana Lee compared the scope of the NetzDG with the free speech rights protected under the First Amendment to the Constitution of the United States. Lee argued that the German defamation law consists of much broader categories than US law, which particularly encompasses two broader categories of speech: *defamation* and *insults* (Lee, 2017).

According to Wolfgang Schulz, human rights issues are more complex within the application of the NetzDG, including:

(i) The individual offended by the speech, possibly the complainant
(ii) The provider of the social media platform
(iii) The author of illegal content that has been removed

(iv) The author of legal content that has been incorrectly taken down
(v) The recipients of the content (Schulz, 2022)

8.4.2 Tight Deadlines

From another perspective, it is criticized that the NetzDG would encourage the "over-removal" of legal content across social media. Under Article 1, Section 3, of the NetzDG, platforms must remove or block access to content that is *manifestly unlawful* within 24 h of receiving the complaint and, furthermore, to *all unlawful content* within a 7-day period. Shifting this responsibility to the platforms requires more expertise in the German language; also, the tight deadlines and heavy fines would lead to the removal of content without a proper in-depth analysis of the merits of the case (Tworek & Leerssen, 2019). The inability of social media networks to do an in-depth assessment of the context of their content was raised in connection with the shortcomings of this framework (Echikson & Knodt, 2018). The shift from public actors to private platforms would lead to the inability to identify the complex actors within a short span of time (Zurth, 2021).

The amendment to the NetzDG induced changes in the following regulatory frameworks of Germany: the Criminal Code, the law on criminal procedure, the NetzDG, the Telecommunication Act, and the law on the Federal Criminal Police Authority. Particularly, the new Section 3(b)–(c) of the NetzDG introduced salient features of the complaint mechanism for content providers as well as an out-of-court resolution mechanism (Bayer, 2022). Still, it has been claimed that the Act's regulatory approach has not been amended due to the lack of evidence regarding *overblocking* (Schulz, 2022).

Though a few studies attempt to cover the impact of the NetzDG on content across SMPs, on many occasions, they have overlooked the concept of *overblocking* as a consequence of the NetzDG (Maaß et al., 2024). However, Pohlmann, J., et al. wrote a different perspective addressing both ends, saying that the dominant discourse surrounding the NetzDG on the *overblocking* thesis, which suggests that the law's short time limits for content removal decisions might result in excessive blocking by social media platforms. This perspective is widely referenced in blog posts and newspaper articles, persisting even after NetzDG's full implementation in January 2018 and the release of transparency reports by platforms. In contrast, the *anti-overblocking* thesis, proposing that platforms make nuanced decisions to avoid unjust content removal or account blocking due to their financial interests, receives minimal attention in public discourse. Despite early discussions by scholars and support from Germany's former Minister of Justice, Heiko Maas, the *anti-overblocking* thesis is not prominently featured in discussions by bloggers or newspapers (Pohlmann et al., 2023).

8.4.3 Empowering Private Platforms

The NetzDG law, aimed at addressing online content concerns, has faced criticism since its initial draft, primarily viewed as an *ad hoc* legislative reaction and criticized for transferring public responsibility to a private entity (Heldt, 2019). Privatization, as influenced by the NetzDG, impacts the behavior of online platforms. Advocates of the NetzDG contend that the law's primary purpose and advantage lie in pressuring platforms, which may consider themselves too "big to care," to adopt a more responsible and proactive approach in monitoring published content due to the threat of liability. Conversely, critics of the NetzDG argued that this may lead to detrimental shifts in platform behavior. To meet tighter timelines, platforms may increasingly rely on less refined, automated content moderation tools (Isabelle, 2022).

The NetzDG shifts the traditional responsibility of the state for criminal law and prosecution to private social network providers. While Article 74 of the German Basic Law designates these functions as state responsibilities, the NetzDG mandates social networks to determine the legality of content and decide on its removal. This parallels the *Google Spain* case,[28] where the Court of Justice of the European Union (CJEU) ruled that individuals have the right to request the removal of information from Google search results. However, critics, including the Advocate General in the *Google Spain* case and German constitutional judge Masing, expressed concerns about creating "private arbitration courts" and extending private entities' control over legal judgments. The NetzDG is criticized for privatizing law enforcement by obligating social networks to assess and remove content, thereby diminishing the state's judicial competence. Despite social networks already evaluating reported content based on their terms and conditions, regulatory fines further emphasize this shift in responsibility (Claussen, 2018).

8.4.4 Why Is the Idea Problematic?

Section 3 of the NetzDG is criticized for two critical shortcomings. Firstly, its exclusive focus on *postmoderation* is deemed ineffective. The approach of identifying and moderating hateful content after it has been posted is considered impractical. Instead, the efficacy of interventions is seen to be limited by not addressing factors such as algorithmic recommendations, platform architecture, and social/interactive features, which play a role in influencing the likelihood of users posting or viewing hate content. The critique emphasized the importance of intervening at these earlier stages to enhance the overall effectiveness of content moderation (Griffin, 2022).

[28] *Google Spain SL and Google Inc. v Agencia Española de Protección de Datos (AEPD) and Mario Costeja González* (2014) C-131/12.

Danya's study explored the role of the *Rechtsstaat* idea in the policy discourse surrounding the NetzDG, utilizing a discursive institutionalist framework. The NetzDG is characterized as an institution, while *Rechtsstaat* is identified as an idea. Through a textual analysis of policy documents, the study revealed how various policy actors, both explicitly and implicitly, articulate and apply the *Rechtsstaat* idea and its five facets to justify their perspectives on the NetzDG. One illustrative example involves the facet related to the existence, validity, and primacy of law. The government employs this facet to emphasize the necessity of the NetzDG as a state action ensuring the validity and primacy of law on the Internet. In contrast, critics argued that the NetzDG, by requiring online platforms to remove illegal content, privatizes law enforcement, undermining this facet of the *Rechtsstaat* idea (Danya, 2020).

It is suggested that to effectively prevent criminal hate speech, measures should go beyond condemning the content itself and consider broader factors such as ideologies, norms, and environmental influences that contribute to the sharing and visibility of such content. Griffin pointed out that the focus should extend to legal content that strategically encourages hate speech or boosts its visibility. Achieving the goals of the NetzDG, which aims to reduce illegal hate speech, necessitates interventions that address not only the illegal content but also the impact of legal speech, including posts designed to bait and encourage hate speech by others (Griffin, 2022).

However, few other scholars highlighted that the NetzDG was a response to the widespread presence of hateful messages on social media and the perceived inadequacy of platform efforts in content moderation. Utilizing the NetzDG as a *quasi-experiment*, content moderation, compelled by regulation, can effectively achieve its primary objective of reducing hateful sentiments online and subsequently decreasing hate crimes against minorities offline (Jiménez Durán et al., 2023).

8.4.5 Shortcomings in the Implementation Process

NetzDG reports are deemed insufficient for evaluating the prevalence and visibility of hate speech, as well as the effects of the NetzDG. The inadequacies include a lack of detail, standardization across companies, and independent oversight. It is a comprehensive transparency obligation that not only facilitates independent oversight but also encourages more effective measures by exposing platforms to evidence-based public criticism for inadequately addressing hate speech (Griffin, 2022).

The implementation of the complaint procedure, particularly as demonstrated by Facebook, raises questions about whether it aligns with the legislative goal of the NetzDG. While the primary purpose of the complaint procedure is to protect users, Facebook's approach may suggest a focus on reporting rather than user protection. The transparency reports mandated by the NetzDG, including those from Facebook, provide limited insights, and compliance alone does not offer meaningful data. The argument that Germany's market size does not justify expecting platforms to self-regulate is countered by the expectation that global companies adhere to each country's laws. Despite concerns about Facebook's failure to implement a user-friendly complaint procedure, it has, in essence, achieved the legislative goal of quicker removal of hate speech. The German government aimed to expedite responses to offenses on social networks, evident in the 24 h takedown limit and the severe fines for noncompliance. While Facebook's procedure may violate the legal provision, the overall objective of speedy hate speech removal has been met. The implementation of the NetzDG resulted in expanded and specialized reviewer teams across platforms, indicating a positive impact on the review process. Despite concerns about Facebook's approach, it does not explicitly undermine the primary legislative goal, but it does diminish the significance of transparency reports for advanced evaluation (Heldt, 2019).

Further, the implementation of the NetzDG is debated in terms of its alignment with international law principles. While the German legislator argues that the law is necessary to combat hate crimes and punishable content for maintaining a peaceful society, a recent case involving a Czech citizen uploading Nazi symbols raised concerns. The German Federal Supreme Court, although recognizing a violation of the relevant criminal law protected by the NetzDG, rejected the application of German law in this cross-border scenario. This suggests potential limitations in enforcing the NetzDG for offenses committed abroad, indicating that the cross-border sanctioning aspect of the law may face challenges. Overall, while the NetzDG is not inherently in violation of international law, the application of German criminal law for offenses outlined in the law requires scrutiny by the German Federal Supreme Court, and a general international application is deemed unjustifiable (Claussen, 2018).

As part of the NetzDG model, there is a lack of adequate safeguards, particularly regarding the *case-by-case* analysis of content. The enforcement of fines has been properly channeled through the Act.[29] Still, no provision talks about the protection for good faith decisions to not remove or block content (Article 19, 2017). Also, no process of redress is foreseen for users against the illegitimate removal of their content shared across social media. This would protect free speech online, as it prevents violations of a person's freedom of expression without giving them the opportunity to challenge the decision (Theveny & Phillips, 2018). Due to this complex shortcoming, few scholars argue, in the abstract, that the German model is regarded as closer to China's model (Pillalamarri & Stanley, 2021), which is extreme in terms of Internet censorship.

Other than these aspects, the NetzDG is also criticized for its *steep sanction* regime, with fines ranging from 500,000 euros to up to 50 million euros (Guerrinia, 2020). Several other studies have noted that the lack of public awareness of the NetzDG and hate speech laws, in general, is a significant drawback. A study by Griffin emphasized that many individuals are unaware of the reporting procedures;

[29] NetzDG 2017, s 4(4).

those posting hate speech often lack awareness of or show indifference to the potential consequences of their actions, which diminishes the practical relevance of the NetzDG (Griffin, 2022).

8.4.6 Recommendations

In analyzing the framework of the NetzDG, there are certain challenges identified both procedurally and substantially. The global nature of the Internet introduces complexities in resolving borderless disputes, paradoxically combining its worldwide reach with potent local influence (Isabelle, 2022). Addressing content moderation in this context is challenging due to its resource-intensive and relentless nature. The difficulties arise from the need to make intricate and sometimes impractical distinctions, uncertainty about the appropriate standards, and the potential for a single failure to overshadow numerous quiet successes, as highlighted by Tarleton Gillespie (Gillespie, 2018).

While empowering private platforms in decision-making, particularly in matters tied to human rights such as free speech, may lead to controversies and potential violations, I argue in favor of such an arrangement. This is supported by the theory proposed by Balkin J. M.—*the new school speech regulation* (NSSR), which extensively explores how platforms and states regulate user speech (Balkin, 2014). NSSR refers to state regulation that coerces intermediaries, such as large corporations controlling essential digital infrastructure, into restricting speakers instead of directly coercing the speakers. The significance of communication infrastructure for meaningful free speech is highlighted, and the power of these corporations to control speech at a scale through technological measures makes them attractive targets for regulation. This trend extends beyond speech regulation, representing a broader pattern of designating "gatekeeper" companies as regulators. Balkin later described a shift from dyadic to triadic regulation, involving speakers, intermediaries, and governments at three crucial points in the regulatory process (Balkin, 2018).

I believe the shift towards regulatory measures is essential to distinguish the private from the public sector in a paradigm significantly shaped by technological evolution. However, this should be managed or overseen with the appropriate mechanisms at the government level.

The authority's primary objective with the NetzDG is to establish state oversight over digital platforms and mitigate hate speech by enforcing specific criminal law provisions via mandatory moderation of content. This approach, which relies heavily on censorship, does not align well with the nuanced dynamics of social media, which shape user behavior through algorithms and various interactive features. On the other hand, legal content potentially leading to hate speech often falls under the broad umbrella of platform governance, including design choices and content recommendation algorithms, where platforms already exercise considerable discretion. Therefore, the imposition of a criminal regime with steep penalties should be reconsidered.

While changes in platform regulation are necessary, online hate speech should not be isolated from broader societal factors. While on-platform solutions are crucial, they should complement rather than replace law enforcement, social work, and education programs that target underlying discrimination and prejudice. The suggested regulatory strategies would be most effective as part of a comprehensive antidiscrimination program that incorporates various policy fields beyond platform regulation (Griffin, 2022).

Tworek, H., and Leerssen, P., suggested a more ambitious approach for the German government, which involves encouraging and supporting the creation of research repositories, which compile data from various platforms. The repository could initially gather data on all deleted content or complaints under the NetzDG, promoting transparency from both platforms and enforcement authorities. German ministries could set an example by openly sharing submissions from their complaint bodies. This repository would serve multiple purposes, including facilitating appeal processes and providing data for researchers, regulators, and watchdogs to scrutinize platform decisions. The disclosure of such information could shed light on the impact of the law on the freedom of expression. Over time, the repository might expand its scope beyond the NetzDG (Tworek & Leerssen, 2019).

Addressing the intricate and varied structures of platform architectures and user communities presents significant challenges for regulators and scholars alike. Despite the uncertain effects of interventions in these complex sociotechnical systems, there remains an opportunity to steer their evolution toward more beneficial outcomes. Currently, platforms prioritize ad impressions and profitability in their optimization strategies. The recommended regulatory strategy emphasizes the need to ensure that public interest goals, like reducing hate speech, are properly integrated and prioritized within the platforms' design and optimization processes. However, in doing so, the regulators should ensure the protection of free speech, the abilities and control of private platforms, and the implementation strategy.

As a member of the EU, Germany is subject to regulations such as the DSA, yet the Network Enforcement Act has emerged as a prominent and controversial framework since its proposal and subsequent enactment in 2017. Despite being among the few countries grappling with extreme Internet censorship, the NetzDG has faced criticism due to its harsh penalties, tight deadlines for platforms, the delegation of significant decision-making power to private entities, and concerns over free speech and the absence of implementation safeguards. This chapter has explored how these issues affect free speech across SMPs and proposes both substantial and procedural suggestions to refine the regulatory framework. The objective is to make it more effective while safeguarding free speech rights.

References

Article 19. (2017). *Germany: The act to improve enforcement of the law in social networks*. Article 19.

Balkin, J. M. (2014). Old-school/new-school speech regulation. *Harvard Law Review, 127*(2296), 2329–2341.

Balkin, J. M. (2018). Free speech in the algorithmic society: Big data, private governance, and new school speech regulation. *UC Davis Law Review, 51*, 1149–1210.

Bayer, J. (2022). Procedural rights as safeguard for human rights in platform regulation. *Policy & Internet, 14*(4), 755–771.

Clasen, A. (2023). *Digital Services Act: Germany proposes creation of advisory board.* Retrieved January 22, 2024, from https://www.euractiv.com/section/platforms/news/digital-services-act-germany-proposes-creation-of-advisory-board/

Claussen, V. (2018). Fighting hate speech and fake news. The Network Enforcement Act (NetzDG) in Germany in the context of European legislation. *Media Laws, 3*(4), 110–136.

CMS Law Now. (2019, August 28). *Facebook fined EUR 2 m for infringement of Germany's Network Enforcement Act.* Retrieved from CMS Law Now: https://cms-lawnow.com/en/ealerts/2019/08/facebook-fined-eur-2-m-for-infringement-of-germany-s-network-enforcement-act

Danya, H. (2020). Governing hate content online: How the Rechtsstaat shaped the policy discourse on the NetzDG in Germany. *International Journal of Communication, 14*, 3746–3768.

Echikson, W., & Knodt, O. (2018). *Germany's NetzDG: A key test for combatting online hate.* Centre for European Policy Studies (CEPS).

Eifert, M., Metzger, A., Schweitzer, H., & Wagner, G. (2021). Taming the giants: The DMA/DSA package. *Common Market Law Review, 58*(4), 987–1028.

Fieselmann, J., Annac, K., Erdsiek, F., Yilmaz-Aslan, Y., & Brzoska, P. (2022). What are the reasons for refusing a COVID-19 vaccine? A qualitative analysis of social media in Germany. *BMC Public Health, 22*(1), 846–853.

Freedom House. (2022). *Freedom on the Net - Germany.* Freedom House.

Freedom House. (2023). *Freedom on the Net - Germany.* Freedom House.

Gillespie, T. (2018). *Custodians of the internet platforms, content moderation, and the hidden decisions that shape social media.* Yale University Press.

Glaun, D. (2021). *Germany's Laws on Hate Speech, Nazi Propaganda & Holocaust Denial: An Explainer.* Retrieved April 5, 2023, from https://www.pbs.org/wgbh/frontline/article/germanys-laws-antisemitic-hate-speech-nazi-propaganda-holocaust-denial/

Gorwa, R. (2021). Elections, institutions, and the regulatory politics of platform governance: The case of the German NetzDG. *Telecommunications Policy, 45*(6).

Griffin, R. (2021). *New school speech regulation and online hate speech: A case study of Germany's NETZDG.* Hertie School.

Griffin, R. (2022). New school speech regulation as a regulatory strategy against hate speech on social media: The case of Germany's NetzDG. *Telecommunications Policy, 46*(9).

Guerrinia, F. (2020). *The Problems with Germany's New Social Media Hate Speech Bill.* Retrieved October 2, 2023, from https://www.forbes.com/sites/federicoguerrini/2020/03/03/the-problems-with-germanys-new-social-media-hate-speech-bill/?sh=6d522e25592a

Haupt, C. E. (2024a). Curbing hate speech online: Lessons from the German Network Enforcement Act (NetzDG). In N. A. Eric Heinze (Ed.), *Oxford handbook of hate speech.*

Haupt, C. E. (2024b). Curbing hate speech online: Lessons from the German Network Enforcement Act (NetzDG). In N. A. Eric Heinze (Ed.), *Oxford handbook on hate speech* (p. Forthcoming).

Helberger, N. (2020). The political power of platforms: How current attempts to regulate misinformation amplify opinion power. *Digital Journalism, 8*(6), 842–854.

Helbling, M., & Tresch, A. (2011). Measuring party positions and issue salience from media coverage: Discussing and cross-validating new indicators. *Electoral Studies, 30*(11), 174–183.

Heldt, A. P. (2019). Reading between the lines and the numbers: an analysis of the first NetzDG reports. *Internet Policy Review, 8*(2).

Human Rights Watch. (2018). *Germany: Flawed Social Media Law.* Retrieved September 22, 2023, from https://www.hrw.org/news/2018/02/14/germany-flawed-social-media-law

Isabelle, C. (2022). Netzdg and the german precedent for authoritarian creep and authoritarian learning. *Columbia Journal of European Law, 28*(1), 101-[iv].

Jiménez Durán, R., Müller, K., & Schwarz, C. (2023). The effect of content moderation on online and offline hate: Evidence from Germany's NetzDG.

Kaesling, K. (2018). Privatising law enforcement in social networks: A comparative model analysis. *Erasmus Law Review, 11*(3), 151–164.

Kaufhold, M., & Reuter, C. (2016). The self-organization of digital volunteers across social media: The case of the 2013 European Floods in Germany. *Journal of Homeland Security and Emergency Management, 13*(1), 137–166.

Knight, B. (2018). *Germany implements new internet hate speech crackdown*. Retrieved April 5, 2023, from https://www.dw.com/en/germany-implements-new-internet-hate-speech-crackdown/a-41991590

Lee, D. (2017). *Germany's NetzDG and the Threat to Online Free Speech*. Retrieved March 15, 2023, from https://law.yale.edu/mfia/case-disclosed/germanys-netzdg-and-threat-online-free-speech

Library of Congress. (2022, March 30). *Germany: Administrative Court of Cologne Grants Google and Facebook Interim Relief; Holds Network Enforcement Act Partially Violates EU Law*. Retrieved from Library of Congress: https://www.loc.gov/item/global-legal-monitor/2022-03-30/germany-administrative-court-of-cologne-grants-google-and-facebook-interim-relief-holds-network-enforcement-act-partially-violates-eu-law

Maaß, S., Wortelker, J., & Rott, A. (2024). Evaluating the regulation of social media: An empirical study of the German NetzDG and Facebook. *Telecommunications Policy*.

Mchangama, J., & Fiss, J. (2019). *The digital Berlin Wall: How Germany (accidentally) created a prototype for global online censorship*. Justitia.

Moon, L. E. (2019). A new role for social network providers: NetzDG and the Communications Decency Act. *Transnational Law & Contemporary Problems, 29*(1), 611–633.

Office of the United Nations High Commissioner for Human Rights. (2017, June 1). Mandate of the Special Rapporteur on the promotion and protection of the right to freedom of opinion and expression.

Oltermann, P. (2018). *Tough new German law puts tech firms and free speech in spotlight*. Retrieved February 2, 2023, from https://www.theguardian.com/world/2018/jan/05/tough-new-german-law-puts-tech-firms-and-free-speech-in-spotlight

Otten, T. (2023, April 12). *Elon Musk's Twitter Faces Fines for Hate Speech Worth More Than the Entire Company*. Retrieved from The New Republic: https://newrepublic.com/post/171832/elon-musk-twitter-fines-hate-speech

Pfaff, K., Neumayer, E., & Plümper, T. (2021). *Querdenken: the German anti-lockdown movement that thrives on public distrust*. Retrieved February 3, 2023, from https://blogs.lse.ac.uk/covid19/2021/09/29/querdenken-the-german-anti-lockdown-movement-that-thrives-on-public-distrust/

Pillalamarri, A., & Stanley, C. (2021). *Online content regulation: An international comparison*. Retrieved September 12, 2023, from https://studentbriefs.law.gwu.edu/ilpb/2021/12/08/online-content-regulation-an-international-comparison/

Plümper, T., Neumayer, E., & Pfaff, K. G. (2021). The strategy of protest against Covid-19 containment policies in Germany. *Social Science Quarterly, 102*(5), 2236–2250.

Pohlmann, J., Barbaresi, A., & Leinen, P. (2023). Platform regulation and "overblocking" – The NetzDG discourse in Germany. *Communications, 48*(3), 395–419.

Schmitz, S., & Berndt, C. M. (2018). The German Act on Improving Law Enforcement on Social Networks (NetzDG): A Blunt Sword? *Working Paper*.

Schulz, W. (2022). Regulating intermediaries to protect personality rights online—The case of the German NetzDG. In a. I. M. Albers (Ed.), *Personality and data protection rights on the Internet: Brazilian and German approaches* (pp. 289–307). Springer International Publishers.

Schwemmer, C. (2021). The limited influence of right-wing movements on social media user engagement. *Social Media+ Society, 7*(3).

Spindler, G. (2017). *Legal expertise commissioned by BITKOM concerning the notified German Act to Improve Enforcement of the Law in Social Networks.*

Theveny, K. C., & Phillips, J. D. (2018). The case of social media censorship in Germany. In A. V. Laskin (Ed.), *Social, mobile, and emerging media around the world: Communication case studies* (pp. 175–186). Rowman & Littlefield Publishing Group.

Tworek, H., & Leerssen, P. (2019). An analysis of Germany's NetzDG law. *First session of the Transatlantic High Level Working Group on Content Moderation Online and Freedom of Expression.* Transatlantic Working Group.

Zeh, R., & Holtz-Bacha, C. (2015). Internet, social media use and political participation in the 2013 parliamentary election in Germany. In G. L. Maarek (Ed.), *Political parties in the digital age: The impact of new technologies in politics* (pp. 43–57). Deutsche Nationalbibliothek.

Zehring, M., & Domahidi, E. (2023). German corona protest mobilizers on telegram and their relations to the far right: A network and topic analysis. *Social Media + Society, 9*(1).

Zurth, P. (2021). The German NetzDG as role model or cautionary tale? Implications for the debate on social media liability. *Fordham Intellectual Property, Media & Entertainment Law Journal, 31*(4), 1084–1153.

Chapter 9
Regulation from the South: IT Rules of India

9.1 Introduction

As an emerging country from South Asia, the information technology and business process management (IT and BPM) sector has emerged as a crucial driver of growth for the Indian economy, making substantial contributions to both GDP and public well-being. In the fiscal year 2022, the IT industry constituted 7.4% of India's GDP, and there are projections that it will increase its contribution to 10% of the GDP by the year 2025 (Webber, 2023). Beyond the IT sphere, India, as the world's most populous country, has been actively engaged in various social media platforms for an extended period. Active social media penetration in India is 33.4%. According to figures, as of the beginning of 2023, there were 398.0 million users in India aged 18 years or older, constituting 40.2% of the country's entire population (Wong, 2024). This robust presence underscores India's significant and continually expanding influence in the realm of social media.

The Indian media industry has undergone significant changes due to the rise of social media, which has become an integral part of communication, marketing, and advertising. Social media has taken on various forms, including magazines, Internet forums, blogs, microblogging, and social networking sites, and has transformed the way media content is produced, consumed, and distributed. It has also had an impact on journalism, with citizen journalism and bloggers redefining the agenda of mainstream media. The digital shift and the incorporation of social media have become essential for media companies to align with the needs of tech-savvy consumers. The factors influencing an individual's online news consumption include Internet penetration, literacy in English or vernacular languages, personal interest in news types, and the reputation of news outlets (Mukerjee, 2024). The impact of digital technology on media consumption in India has disrupted traditional industries and changed consumer behavior (Ratnan, 2022).

The advent of social media has significantly expanded avenues for user expression in online spaces, promoting citizen journalism and fueling online movements

S. Balendra, *Free Speech in the Puzzle of Content Regulation*, Law, Governance and Technology Series 70, https://doi.org/10.1007/978-3-031-75813-3_9

aimed at societal improvement. However, similar to experiences in other jurisdictions, social media platforms (SMPs) have sometimes been exploited during social conflicts, leading to the proliferation of hate speech, disinformation, and harmful or unlawful content across the public domains of social media.

These incidents underscore the necessity of regulating digital spaces, leading to the development of regulatory frameworks in India. The country has a long history of such regulations, especially since the introduction of the comprehensive yet controversial provisions of the IT Act in 2000. Recognizing the need to closely monitor SMPs, the government introduced the Information Technology (Intermediary Guidelines and Digital Media Ethics Code) Rules in 2021—as an effort toward external regulation. These rules aim to regulate digital platforms, including SMPs and digital media.

The choice of the Indian jurisdiction in this book is influenced by a myriad of factors. As a country from the Global South, India represents an emerging and demanding market for social media platforms, with a vast user base, substantial advertising revenues, and active civic participation. The contemporary legislative and policy issues surrounding social media content in India, including Twitter content takedown requests during public protests and the spread of Hindutva ideologies, particularly during Modi's regime, highlight the jurisdiction's rapid move toward content regulation. Therefore, discussing issues around free speech and social media content regulation would be scrappy without exploring the Indian context.

This chapter explores the role of social media in enhancing free speech within the Indian legal framework and examines the efforts and impacts of various regulatory measures introduced by the government to govern the technology space. Specifically, this study seeks to understand the background and key features of the Information Technology (Intermediary Guidelines and Digital Media Ethics Code) Rules of 2021 and to thoroughly assess how these regulatory provisions affect free speech and other competing values, such as public trust, safety, and security across the SMPs.

9.2 The Impact of Social Media

Freedom of speech is crucial for democracies, which rely on information exchange. SMPs like Twitter and Facebook play a vital role in public discourse, enabling people to express ideas, question state actions, demand accountability, and organize movements in India. For example, social media played a significant role in organizing, communicating, and raising awareness of the India Against Corruption movement of 2011. Ranked among Time magazine's *Top 10 News Stories of 2011*, the series of ongoing demonstrations spearheaded by Anna Hazare intensified the need for robust legislation and effective enforcement to eradicate pervasive political corruption (Rodrigues, 2014).

The issue of net neutrality gained prominence after the Telecom Regulatory Authority of India (TRAI) initiated a consultation on the "Regulatory Framework for Over-the-Top (OTT) Services" in 2015. Internet service providers (ISPs) attempted to introduce a scheme allowing companies to pay for users to access their services without data charges, known as zero rating. Activists, viewing this as a violation of net neutrality, had launched protests nationwide since April 2015 to raise awareness. The trigger for the movement was TRAI's 117-page paper on OTT services, encouraging public participation. Massive online protests assisted the net neutrality movement in India, with a wide range of public participation involving stakeholders from the private sector, government, and citizens represented by civil society organizations and activists. The movement successfully led to the enactment of regulations prohibiting the differential pricing of data services, meeting the demands of the movement organizers.

These movements reaffirm that the internet and social media not only enhance the ability to organize social movements with greater logistical ease, efficiency, and impact, but also introduce deliberative processes that foster knowledge and learning among affected citizens. This approach can integrate expertise across various levels, helping movements progress toward their desired outcomes (Madhavan, 2016).

In India, the evolution of social media and the information era has been significantly shaped not only by ordinary citizens but also by public-elected representatives and diplomats. Their active participation and engagement on social media platforms have contributed to this development, facilitating direct communication and interaction with the public. Parama Sinha Palit wrote that the ability of social media to facilitate communication and create dialogue across borders is evident. While some diplomatic efforts, like Nirupama Rao's, prioritized "listening" to engage domestic and external audiences, not all diplomatic communication, such as Modi's tweets on economic initiatives, demonstrates the same commitment to hearing public concerns (Palit, 2018). It is worth pointing out that in 2023, Narendra Modi—the Prime Minister of India—was the most followed politician on the X platform (previously Twitter).[1] The fact that Modi has not held a single press conference during his eight-year tenure highlights his strategy of mobilizing social media to shape India's contemporary political and social landscape (Kutty, 2022).

However, these social media platforms are also under regulatory scrutiny due to the risks associated with the dissemination and creation of harmful and illegal content (Ashraf, 2022a, 2022b). Although the Internet is widely hailed as a tool for empowerment, it also brings with it heightened threats to security, order, and general welfare. This has led to an increasing necessity for the regulation of social media platforms (Singh, 2015). Narrain, S., examined the spread of hate speech across the country using social media platforms and technology. For example, during the Northeast exodus of 2012, the Muzaffarnagar riots of 2013, and the intergroup violence in Pune in 2014, the threatening messages and hate speech

[1] See https://medium.com/digital-diplomacy/the-most-followed-world-leaders-on-social-media-2022-193bb9d89d8d.

spread across these platforms amplified the issues in the communities (Ananth & Narrain, 2023).

A few other scholars also noted that the scenario in India involves a combination of social media illiteracy and an ineffective legislative framework for social media. This raises concerns about representation on these platforms, particularly regarding the misuse of data-based public platforms through tools like bots and web robots to manipulate content. Notably, the emergence of political bots has introduced a new dimension of computational propaganda, influencing public opinion in the political sphere (Ashwini, 2021).

These backlogs highlighted and compelled the urge to regulate these shared or circulated prohibited content via the new medium. India, as a diverse country with many ethnic, religious, and linguistic groups, started to adopt different levels of censorship laws from time to time to protect public security, morality, and peace.

9.3 Regulating Online Spaces

9.3.1 Internet Shutdowns as the Go-to Measure

Before and even after the introduction of contemporary regulations, such as the IT Rules, India has predominantly relied on Internet shutdowns as an extralegal measure to address social media content regulation. This approach has been particularly evident in situations where content is perceived to contradict public policy or threaten values like public order, security, and the economy.

Human Rights Watch documented that "Since 2018, India has shut down the internet more often than any other country in the world" (Human Rights Watch, 2023). A Study of Access Now evidently noted that in 2023, India led the world in Internet shutdowns for the sixth consecutive year, undermining democracy by suppressing free speech, information, and assembly across regions like Manipur and Punjab (Access Now, 2024). Woodhams and Migliano further note that during this time frame, the Indian government imposed 30 Internet shutdowns across various regions, lasting a total of 7821 h and resulting in a financial loss exceeding $500 million (Woodhams & Migliano, 2024).

Beyond the financial losses, Internet shutdowns are universally criticized as serious human rights violations, affecting public rights such as free speech and access to information, as well as disrupting day-to-day activities like banking services. Consider how often you use the Internet each day—for entertainment, information, job applications, education, connecting with loved ones, checking on things, ordering items, travel, ticketing, and studying. Its importance becomes starkly evident when it is taken away. In August 2019, the Indian government completely blocked all communication networks in Jammu and Kashmir, including landlines, fixed-line Internet, and mobile networks—which severely impacted the population in the territory (Human Rights Watch, 2023).

The debate is both intriguing and complex. While government authorities must address issues that contradict public policy, Internet shutdowns often infringe upon the rights mentioned above. How to address this issue remains a persistent challenge within legislative, policy, and judicial domains.

In hearing *Anuradha Bhasin v. Union of India*[2]—concerning the issue of the Internet shutdown ordered by the government in 2019—the Court ruled that the government cannot withhold Internet suspension orders from the Court but must regularly review them, and it cannot impose indefinite suspensions; while suspensions may be used to safeguard public order, they must not be arbitrary or excessive, with all orders required to be published or notified to the people via the public domain. Further, the Court affirmed that the freedom of expression guaranteed under Article 19 of India's Constitution extends to the Internet, recognizing online expression as a key means of information dissemination integral to the enjoyment of free speech under Article 19(1)(a), though it can also be restricted under Article 19(2) of the Constitution.

Juyal points out:

> Recognising access to the internet as a fundamental right is therefore crucial to enabling individuals to enjoy other guaranteed rights, like free speech, access to information, participation in the digital economy for trade, business etc. The court mandate ensures restrictions over cyberspace satisfy the proportionality test and that the state objectives are aligned with the restrictions imposed on fundamental rights, which are proportionate and reasonable (Juyal, 2023).

Following the jurisprudence, in March 2022, the State of West Bengal issued a suspension order directing the suspension of Internet services for 8 days, which was contested in the case of *Ashlesh Biradar v. State of West Bengal.*[3] The petitioner argued that the suspension order violated Articles 14, 19(1)(a), and 21 of the Indian Constitution, claiming it was arbitrary and unreasonable and infringed upon freedom of expression. Additionally, the petitioner contended that the order failed to meet the three-pronged proportionality test and did not serve a legitimate aim. The Court held that state authorities must adhere to both the Telecom Suspension Rules and the Supreme Court's directives in *Anuradha Bhasin*. The suspension orders in question were found to have violated these established directions.

In the case of *Raju Prosad Sarma v. The State of Assam*,[4] the Court extensively referenced *Anuradha Bhasin* and *Ashlesh Biradar* to examine the constitutionality of the Government of Assam's suspension order, which directed the suspension of Internet services on August 21 and August 28, 2022. The order aimed to prevent cheating during recruitment exams using mobile phones and Internet technology, ensuring a free, fair, and transparent examination process.

The case examined the constitutionality of the suspension order under Articles 14 (equality before the law), 19(1)(a) (freedom of expression), and 21 (life and

---

[2] *Anuradha Bhasin v. Union of India*, AIR 2020 SC 1308.

[3] *Ashlesh Biradar v. State of West Bengal*, PA(RB) WPA (P) 104/2022.

[4] *Raju Prosad Sarma v. The State of Assam*, WP(C)/5527/2022.

personal liberty) of the Indian Constitution, which the petitioner argued as arbitrary and unreasonable and restricted the freedom of expression. The petitioner also contended that the suspension order violated Section 5(2) of the Telegraph Act and the Telecom Suspension Rules as these provisions do not permit suspensions to prevent cheating, which fall under neither public emergency nor public safety. The Court did not address the merits of the suspension order or its constitutionality, nor did it determine whether the executive is empowered to suspend Internet services to prevent cheating in exams. Instead, the Court issued a notice on these issues and directed the Government of Assam to provide an explanation through an affidavit.

9.3.2 Evolution of Regulatory Frameworks

As technology continues to advance, it is crucial for the laws and policies governing technology to evolve in tandem. This is especially important in countries like India, where the information technology sector and related services play a significant role in the economy and facilitate widespread public engagement. Recent legislative updates in India reflect a proactive effort to align legal frameworks with the ever-changing technological landscape. However, despite numerous changes and amendments to India's regulatory environment, challenges persist in delineating boundaries that respect democratic values and online human rights, particularly freedom of speech. As technology rapidly progresses, regulatory frameworks are under pressure to refine existing structures to address the emerging challenges posed by new technologies effectively.

Below, Table 9.1 summarizes the key laws related to the technology sector discussed in this chapter.

The Information Technology (IT) Act of 2000 is India's cornerstone legislation addressing cybersecurity, data protection, and cybercrime. This Act, along with its subsequent amendments, aims to regulate various online domains, including cybercrime, electronic and digital signatures, as well as data protection and privacy. The IT Act establishes a comprehensive legal framework that encompasses a wide range of issues within cyberspace. In contrast, other South Asian countries, such as Sri Lanka, maintain separate legal and regulatory frameworks for cybercrimes, electronic commerce, and intellectual property rights. While the IT Act has been instrumental in some respects, it is somewhat outdated in others, particularly in its regulation of social media platforms and Internet intermediaries. Despite its limitations, the Act provides a few provisions that enable mechanisms to address content-related issues on social media platforms.

In a significant update, the IT Act was amended in 2008 to include Section 66A, which made posting offensive content online a criminal offense.

Section 66A of the Act provides:

> any person who by means of a computer or communication device sends any information that is: grossly offensive; false and meant for the purpose of causing annoyance, inconvenience, danger, obstruction, insult, injury, criminal intimidation, enmity, hatred or ill will;

Table 9.1 Important information technology laws and rules in India

Legislative framework	Category	Year	Scope	Status
The Information Technology Act with amendments	Legislation	2000	Electronic commerce, digital signatures, electronic documents, digital governance, computer crimes, regulating certifying authorities, intermediary liability, and procedural matters connected therein	In force (active)
Cyber Regulations Appellate Tribunal (Salaries, Allowances, and Other Condition of Service of Other Officers and Employees) Rules	Subordinate legislation	2002	Scale of pay for officers and employees of the Cyber Appellate Tribunal	In force (active)
Information Technology (Certifying Authorities) Amendment Rules	Subordinate legislation	2009	Amendment to the certifying authorities' rules	In force (active)
Information Technology (Intermediaries Guidelines) Rules	Subordinate legislation	2011	Regulating Internet intermediaries	Repealed (not active)
The Information Technology (the Indian Computer Emergency Response Team and Manner of Performing Functions and Duties) Rules	Subordinate legislation	2013	Establishment, function, powers, procedures, and responsibilities of the Indian Computer Emergency Response Team (Cert-In)	In force (active)
The Information Technology (Intermediary Guidelines and Digital Media Ethics Code) Rules with amendments	Subordinate legislation	2021	Regulating Internet intermediaries and online gaming and superseding the Information Technology (Intermediaries Guidelines) Rules, 2011	In force (active)
Digital Personal Data Protection Act	Legislation	2023	Privacy and data protection	In force (active)

meant to deceive or mislead the recipient about the origin of such messages, etc, shall be punishable with imprisonment up to three years and with fine.

Although initially aimed at combating spam, the amendment was often applied to content deemed to potentially disturb public order. This *vague*, *broad*, and *undefined* provision seemingly ignored the parameters set down by the Supreme Court in the 1978 judgment of *Maneka Gandhi v. Union of India*,[5] which emphasized that a statute would violate Article 14 of the Constitution if its language is vague and undefined (Yadav, 2022). The excessive power conferred by the provision upon the executive to arbitrarily and unapologetically act on content across online platforms is clearly a sharp-edged sword against free speech. The provision is metaphorically

[5] *Maneka Gandhi v. Union of India* (1978) 1 SCC 248.

termed a "legal zombie" because, akin to the concept in popular culture, particularly Romero's *Night of the Living Dead* movies, it symbolizes a legal entity that persists despite being declared obsolete or problematic (Sekhri & Gupta, 2018).

The use of Section 66A to clamp down on public expression via online platforms, including social media, has led to several controversial incidents. For instance, in 2012, Ravi Srinivasan was arrested for tweeting about the alleged corruption of Karti Chidambaram, son of the then Finance Minister, P. Chidambaram.[6] In a separate event, a 20-year-old woman was arrested simply for "liking" a Facebook post that criticized the shutdown of Mumbai for Bal Thackeray's funeral.[7] Furthermore, Ambikesh Mahapatra, a professor at Jadavpur University, was detained by West Bengal police for emailing cartoons that mocked Chief Minister Mamata Banerjee.[8] These are a few examples underscoring the contentious enforcement of Section 66A to stifle free speech online.

While it is essential to eliminate hate speech, defamation, and misinformation from online spaces and hold perpetrators accountable, the broad powers granted by this provision have drawn significant criticism from human rights defenders, judges, academics, legal practitioners, and civil society. In response to the widespread concern over the potentially harmful impacts of this provision, efforts were made to amend Section 66A of the IT Act. In December 2012, P Rajeev, a Rajya Sabha member from Kerala, proposed a resolution to revise Section 66A.[9] He highlighted that the law, introduced in December 2008, was enacted without adequate debate and resulted in the censorship of cartoons and editorial content on new media platforms, a restriction not imposed on traditional media.

In this prolonged debate, the *Shreya Singhal* case[10] has made a prominent change in the Indian Internet regulatory landscape. Shreya Singhal, a student, challenged three key provisions of the IT Act: Section 66A, which prohibited "grossly offensive" and "menacing" content; Section 69A, granting the government authority to block content; and Section 79, outlining legal standards for Internet intermediaries. The case gained attention due to arrests of artists, students, and critics under Section 66A, leading to widespread criticism from civil society and human rights organizations, particularly those focused on technology and human rights. Hearing this, in 2015, the Indian Supreme Court declared Section 66A *unconstitutional*, citing violations of the right to freedom of speech and expression (Narrain, 2019). The Court ruled that the provision is deficient because it does not provide clear definitions for terms like inconvenience or annoyance—"a very large amount of

[6] See https://www.bbc.com/news/world-asia-india-20202275.

[7] See https://www.washingtonpost.com/news/worldviews/wp/2012/12/01/when-and-where-posting-the-wrong-thing-to-facebook-can-get-you-arrested/.

[8] See https://timesofindia.indiatimes.com/india/jadavpur-university-professor-arrested-over-anti-mamata-cartoons/articleshow/12647712.cms.

[9] See https://timesofindia.indiatimes.com/india/section-66a-of-it-act-undemocratic-rs-mps/articleshow/17623782.cms.

[10] *Shreya Singhal v. Union of India*, AIR 2015 SC 1523; Writ Petition (Criminal) No. 167 OF 2012.

protected and innocent speech" could be curtailed. The Court stated that Section 66A of the IT Act unreasonably, excessively, and disproportionately infringes upon the freedom of speech guaranteed by Article 19(1) of the Constitution of India. This Supreme Court decision had a substantial impact on shaping the regulatory framework for the Internet in India.

Currently, India has initiated a substantial overhaul of its technology law framework, realizing the need for replacing the two-decades-old IT Act. The Digital India Act is drafted with the objectives of addressing various competing rights over the Internet, including consumer rights; making the Internet an open, safe, trusted, and accountable environment; promoting the advancement of the innovation and technology ecosystem at an accelerated pace; establishing a structure to expedite the digitization of government processes; enhancing democracy and governance in the government-to-citizen (G2C) context; and addressing emerging technologies and risks (MEITy, 2023). The Act is expected to be passed before the 2025 general elections in India. Further, after a prolonged discussion, in August 2023, the Indian Parliament approved the Digital Personal Data Protection (DPDP) Act, marking the country's inaugural cross-sectoral legislation on the protection of personal data. In 2021, pursuant to the powers conferred by Section 87 of the Information Technology Act,[11] India passed the Information Technology (Intermediary Guidelines and Digital Media Ethics Code) Rules of 2021 (hereinafter "IT Rules"), with the objective of the government to enhance the accountability of intermediaries. The rationale behind this regulatory framework was rooted in the understanding that intermediaries lack direct control over the content posted on their platforms.

This chapter delves deeper into the debate surrounding the IT Rules in India, focusing on how intermediary liability arrangements affect free speech across SMPs.

9.4 The IT Rules of India

9.4.1 Background of the Framework

Regulating social media in countries of the Global South is a complex challenge, often entangled in debates over power asymmetries between private technology platforms and government regulatory bodies. Additionally, given that India represents one of the largest markets for many social media companies, these tech giants are sometimes compelled to make compromises or be persuaded by the government to adapt their practices in order to maintain and expand their market presence within the jurisdiction.

In 2021, events in India highlighted concerns regarding the real dedication of both the government and SMPs to speech regulation. A significant issue occurred in

[11] Section 87 grants authority to the Central Government of India to create rules for implementing the provisions of the Information Technology Act, 2000.

February between the Indian government and Twitter, which stemmed from the platform's refusal to block accounts critical of the government's management of farmer protests. Despite initially resisting, Twitter ultimately yielded to the removal demands under the prospect of legal repercussions. This episode stood out as a rare instance of pushback by SMPs against governmental directives (Soni, 2021).

In April 2021, platforms such as Facebook and Twitter complied with directives to delete posts criticizing the government's management of the COVID-19 pandemic. These actions indicate that SMPs frequently adhere to government requests for content removal, triggering discussions about the appropriateness and validity of these censorship measures (Daniyal, 2021). Twitter's initial reluctance to delete specific tweets, combined with Facebook's uneven approach to removing hate speech, misinformation, and fake news—particularly content targeting Muslims and the promotion of such material in 2021—underscored the need for regulatory oversight of these large tech platforms through legislative action (Frenkel & Alba, 2021).

Against the backdrop of the rampant misuse of the Internet for spreading fake news, Ashvini Vaishnaw, the Minister of Electronics and Information Technology, highlighted the need for a legal framework for social media platforms in 2018.[12] Building on this context, in 2021, the Indian government introduced new regulations, superseding the IT Rules of 2011, to govern digital content platforms, including social media intermediaries, OTT services, and digital news outlets. Although the constitutionality of these rules was challenged in the High Court of Madras,[13] the government submitted a counteraffidavit asserting that such regulations are crucial to combatting severe online threats, such as child pornography, rape-related content, and messages that might incite violence or crime, thereby safeguarding India's sovereignty and integrity.

The Rules were drafted with the following primary objectives: combating the propagation of fake news, controlling the spread of obscene materials across the Internet, preventing the abuse of social media, and enhancing the security of Internet users. While the initial rationale did not explicitly mention "fake news," one of the primary motivations behind the new rules was to combat the spread of misinformation across cyberspace (Abhishek, 2023). Furthermore, the regulations were not limited to social media platforms alone; they were also extended to include digital news providers, broadening the scope of their application.

Parthasarathi and Agarwal pointed out that the Indian government exerts control over the news media sector through three legal avenues: colonial laws from the preindependence period, regulations enacted by the Indian parliament, and executive directives, like the IT Rules 2021, which may lack democratic legitimacy as they are frequently implemented to circumvent the scrutiny of time-consuming legislative

[12] See https://www.meity.gov.in/content/comments-suggestions-invited-draft-%E2%80%9C-information-technology-intermediary-guidelines.

[13] See https://economictimes.indiatimes.com/tech/technology/madras-high-court-stays-certain-sub-clauses-of-new-it-rules/articleshow/86265232.cms?from=mdr.

processes (Parthasarathi & Agarwal, 2020). Therefore, legal scrutiny related to standards and processes in the digital news sphere under the application of the IT Rules plays a vital role in a democratic penumbra.

Facing legal challenges from digital news organizations in the Delhi High Court against the IT Rules, the Ministry of Information and Broadcasting (MIB) and the Ministry of Electronics and Information Technology (MEITY) argued that the proliferation of misleading and false audiovisual content has resulted in the loss of lives and public disturbances. They emphasized that a competitive economic environment vying for audience attention, coupled with the lack of regulation for digital media content, has enabled the widespread dissemination of fake news and other detrimental content. This has allowed digital news publishers to operate without sufficient accountability (Abhishek, 2023). Scholarly discussions, research findings, and critiques highlighted a gap in India's digital regulatory landscape, especially concerning online news publishers and social media platforms. Conversely, some scholars argued that these regulatory efforts represent an attempt by the government to control the political discourse circulating within cyberspace (Karanicolas, 2021).

9.4.2 Salient Features of the IT Rules

Though the IT Rules 2021 represents India's first substantial regulatory effort to govern Internet intermediaries, the framework has introduced many strong features to regulate digital platforms. The IT Rules introduce several key features, including assigning additional responsibilities to Internet intermediaries, amending *safe harbor* provisions, distinguishing between social media intermediaries and significant social media intermediaries, and establishing a three-tier governance structure for digital media, among others.

Intermediaries are entities that offer services facilitating the distribution of online content to end users. This encompasses Internet service providers, search engines, Domain Name System (DNS) providers, and social media platforms.

Previously, the IT Act of India defined intermediaries as:

> Intermediary with respect to any particular electronic records, means any person who on behalf of another person receives, stores or transmits that record or provides any service with respect to that record and includes Telecom service providers, network service providers, internet service providers, web-hosting providers, search engines, online payment sites, online-auction sites, online-market places and cyber cafe.[14]

Entities like ISPs, social media platforms, and search engines are crucial for information dissemination, but they lack editorial control over the content circulated on their platforms. They function solely as conduits for information transmission and, consequently, benefit from a *safe harbor* provision that shields them from legal liability arising from third-party content.

---

[14] Information Technology Act 2000, Section 2(w).

Prior to the introduction of the new IT Rules, Section 79 of the IT Act of India,[15] which is the *safe harbor* provision similar to Section 230 of the Communication Decency Act (CDA) of the United States (*though the CDA provides a broader immunity model*). The provision exempts Internet intermediaries from liabilities for content created or shared across platforms to the extent that they comply with the provisions laid down by the IT Act.

Yet, recognizing the squealing growth of the social media regime, the newly introduced rules have imposed additional obligations on social media intermediaries. The IT Rules impose substantial due diligence obligations on intermediaries, including significant social media intermediaries (SSMI) and news content intermediaries, potentially compromising their *safe harbor* protection previously outlined in Section 79 of the IT Act. Failure to comply with the rules would result in the removal of the *safe harbor* shield underlined in Section 79(1) and would render the intermediary liable to punishment under existing laws, including the IT Act and the Indian Penal Code.[16]

The IT Rules mandate certain obligations[17] for the intermediaries to qualify for the requirement of *due diligence* in order to secure the *safe harbor* immunity. This includes:

(i) specifying, in service agreements, the categories of content that users are not allowed to upload or share, (ii) taking down content within 36 h of receiving a court or government order, (iii) taking down a content within 24 h where the complaint is from an individual about sexual imagery, (iv) assisting law enforcement agencies, (v) retaining blocked content and associated records for 90 days, and (vi) providing a grievance redressal mechanism for users and affected persons and designating a grievance officer.[18]

---

[15] Section 79 provides:

(1) Notwithstanding anything contained in any law for the time being in force but subject to the provisions of sub-sections (2) and (3), an intermediary shall not be liable for any third-party information, data, or communication link made available or hosted by him. (2) The provisions of sub-section (1) shall apply if—(a) the function of the intermediary is limited to providing access to a communication system over which information made available by third parties is transmitted or temporarily stored or hosted; or (b) the intermediary does not—(i) initiate the transmission, (ii) select the receiver of the transmission, and (iii) select or modify the information contained in the transmission; (c) the intermediary observes due diligence while discharging his duties under this Act and also observes such other guidelines as the Central Government may prescribe in this behalf. (3) The provisions of sub-section (1) shall not apply if—(a) the intermediary has conspired or abetted or aided or induced, whether by threats or promise or otherwise in the commission of the unlawful act; (b) upon receiving actual knowledge, or on being notified by the appropriate Government or its agency that any information, data or communication link residing in or connected to a computer resource controlled by the intermediary is being used to commit the unlawful act, the intermediary fails to expeditiously remove or disable access to that material on that resource without vitiating the evidence in any manner.

[16] IT Rules 2021, Rule 7.

[17] IT Rules 2021, Rule 3.

[18] IT Rules 2021, Rule 3(1).

Further, the rules also insist that the intermediaries adhere to the provisions of the Constitution of India as follows:

> The intermediary shall respect all the rights accorded to the citizens under the Constitution, including in the articles 14, 19 and 21.[19]

Under the new IT Rules, intermediaries are obliged to preserve, maintain, and/or store the following information for 180 days: (a) any information that has been removed or access to which has been disabled under certain provisions of the Rules and (b) user's information regarding registration, after cancellation or withdrawal of such registration.[20]

Another key feature of the IT Rules is the distinction made between a social media intermediary (SMI) and a significant social media intermediary (SSMI). The IT Rules define a social media intermediary as "an intermediary which primarily or solely enables online interaction between two or more users and allows"[21] and a significant social media intermediary as "a social media intermediary having some registered users in India above such threshold as notified by the Central Government."[22] The current threshold of registered users in India is 5 million or more.

As additional due diligence measures, these rules mandate that significant SMIs appoint a chief compliance officer[23] to ensure compliance, a nodal contact person to ascertain 24 × 7 coordination with law enforcement agencies,[24] and a grievance officer[25] to perform the functions required by the rules. It also mandates that all of them reside in India. Furthermore, the regulations provide additional obligations related to the user agreement, technical measures, and user information. If an intermediary fails to follow due diligence, the chief compliance officer will be held accountable.

SSMIs are also required to employ technology, such as automated tools, to detect content depicting rape or child sexual abuse or removed material. Drawing significantly on this, unlike the 2011 Rules, the 2021 Rules recognize SMPs' ability to self-moderate content without forfeiting their immunity.[26] The 2021 Rules emphasize the necessity for consistent human oversight and a periodic review of automated tools. Further, significant social media intermediaries are mandated to release a monthly report, including information on (a) received complaints, (b) actions taken, and (c) the number of links/information removed or disabled. The report should also include any other pertinent details resulting from proactive monitoring

---

[19] IT Rules 2021, Rule 3(1) (n).

[20] IT Rules 2021, Rule (3)(1)(h).

[21] IT Rules 2021, Rule 2(1) w.

[22] IT Rules 2021, Rule 2(1) v.

[23] IT Rules 2021, Rule 4(a).

[24] IT Rules 2021, Rule 4(b).

[25] IT Rules 2021, Rule 4(c).

[26] IT Rules 2021, Rule 3(1) b.

by automated tools.[27] The Rules do not prescribe a specific format for monthly compliance reports, but they should include the essential elements outlined in the Rules. Additional details in the report are at the discretion of the SSMI. Regarding user complaints, the report should offer concise information, such as the subject of the complaint (e.g., copyright) and actions taken, possibly in an aggregated form without disclosing specific case details (Sahni & Manisha, 2021). Major SSMIs in India, such as Google (including YouTube), Koo, Meta (Facebook and Instagram), ShareChat, Snap Chat, and Twitter, have already commenced the release of monthly compliance reports.

Rule 4(6) mandates intermediaries to provide complainants with reasonable explanations for actions taken or not taken, depending on the nature of the complaint. The guidelines afford intermediaries the flexibility to choose an appropriate manner to deliver explanations while ensuring the safety of the reporting party. Rule 4(8) requires significant social media intermediaries to notify users whose information is removed or inaccessible, providing them with a fair chance to contest the action.

The 2021 Rules, in approaching the regulatory regime of online news websites and handles as part of digital media, impose some requirements online. A *three-tier structure* has been introduced to ensure compliance with the Code of Ethics by digital media publishers and the grievance-addressing mechanisms of these digital media: (i) self-regulation by publishers, (ii) self-regulation by associations of publishers, and (iii) oversight by the central government.[28] The Code of Ethics is governed by (i) norms of journalistic conduct formulated by the Press Council of India and (ii) a program code under the Cable Television Networks Regulation Act, 1995, and (iii) content that is prohibited under any law for the time it is in force shall not be published or transmitted.[29] This Code further requires publishers to enforce certain responsibilities, such as content classification,[30] abiding by laws or court orders for transmitting content,[31] and adhering to general principles, such as integrity, security, and public order.[32]

The rules provide that where a person is affected by any content shared, they may file a complaint with the publisher, which must address it within 15 days. In cases where the person is not satisfied with the decision or the complaint is not responded to within the stipulated time, it may be escalated to the association of publishers, which must also address the complaint within 15 days. Finally, the complaint will be considered by an interdepartmental committee constituted by the Ministry of Information and Broadcasting if it is (i) escalated by the complainant or the association under certain conditions or (ii) referred by the Ministry itself.[33]

[27] IT Rules 2021, Rule 4(1) d.

[28] IT Rules 2021, Rule 9(3).

[29] IT Rules 2021, Appendix (I).

[30] IT Rules 2021, Appendix (II) (b).

[31] IT Rules 2021, Appendix (II) (A) (a).

[32] IT Rules 2021, Appendix (II) (A) (b).

[33] IT Rules 2021, Rules 2 and 3.

Chapter IV of the Rules provides for an oversight mechanism, which empowers the Ministry of Information and Broadcasting to perform the following functions: (a) publishing a charter for self-regulating bodies, including Codes of Practices for such bodies; (b) issuing appropriate guidance and advisories to publishers; (c) establishing an Inter-Departmental Committee for hearing grievances; and (d) issuing orders and directions to the publishers for the maintenance and adherence to the Code of Ethics.[34]

9.4.3 Applications of the IT Rules

Soon after the rules were passed, in May 2021, WhatsApp instituted an action[35] against the government of India alleging that under the new law, WhatsApp would have to compromise its *end-to-end encryption*, potentially requiring the collection of data on all messages exchanged among users. This would undermine the privacy of billions of users and infringe upon their fundamental rights recognized under Articles 14, 19(1)(a), 19(1)(g), and 21 of the Indian Constitution, including the right to privacy (Pratap, 2021).

Particularly, WhatsApp underscored IT Rule 4(2) (well known as the *traceability clause)*—which provides:

> A significant social media intermediary providing services primarily in the nature of messaging shall enable the identification of the first originator of the information on its computer resource as may be required by a judicial order passed by a court of competent jurisdiction.

The rule requires companies, such as WhatsApp, to implement a mechanism enabling either the companies themselves or the government to trace a message back to its original sender. WhatsApp alleged that the IT Rules would compel WhatsApp to compromise its end-to-end encryption, violating the fundamental right to privacy and free speech for hundreds of millions of users.

However, in response to WhatsApp's concerns, the Union of India emphasized its respect for the right to privacy, stating that the intention is not to violate it when seeking the origin of a specific message. The disclosure requirements apply "only" in cases related to the prevention, investigation, or punishment of serious offenses concerning the sovereignty and integrity of India, state security, foreign relations, or public order or offenses like incitement, rape, sexually explicit material, or child sexual abuse material. The government highlighted that no fundamental right is absolute, and the test of proportionality, as outlined in *KS Puttaswamy v. Union of India*,[36] is applicable in this context.

[34] IT Rules 2021, Rule 13.

[35] *Whatsapp v. Union of India*, W.P.(C) No. 7284/2021.

[36] *KS Puttaswamy v. Union of India*, AIR 2017 SC 4161.

Similarly, Facebook also filed a suit[37] under the same *traceability* clause based on similar issues. Both of these petitions are pending in the High Court of Delhi. India's traceability requirement, aimed at regulating social media companies to address concerns like mob lynchings and child pornography, is considered a bold move. However, the mandate for messaging platforms to implement widespread traceability indefinitely may face challenges due to concerns about its constitutionality (Kumar, 2022).

The legal and technological challenges outlined present a significant test to the clarity, implementation, and inclusiveness of the IT Rules. These challenges also raise questions about various technical elements within the regulatory framework. Moreover, when viewed from a different angle, the *traceability* requirement under these rules sparks concerns over possible abuses that could infringe upon personal rights safeguarded by the Indian Constitution. Although the new rules mandate intermediaries to adhere to constitutional provisions,[38] the sweeping nature of these regulatory measures prompts a critical inquiry into the extent to which the regulatory authority is committed to upholding and respecting fundamental rights and democratic values enshrined in the Indian Constitution.

In July 2022, X (formerly known as Twitter) filed a lawsuit against the Indian government in the Karnataka High Court in Bengaluru. The platform accused the government of overstepping its authority by issuing orders to remove numerous tweets in an arbitrary and excessive manner, as per Section 69A of the IT Act.[39] X argued that some of these orders targeted political content from official party accounts. The company also highlighted threats of criminal proceedings against its chief compliance officer in India should X fail to adhere to these government directives. Notably, under India's updated IT Rules, X is significantly restricted in challenging individual takedown orders, risking legal consequences for its compliance officer for noncompliance.

In response, in July 2023, the Court ruled against X, imposing a penalty of Rs 50 lakh (INR) on Twitter Inc. The verdict reinforced the government's power to block entire X accounts under Section 69A of the IT Act, viewing it as a stronger deterrent than removing specific tweets. This approach, according to the Court, is essential for dealing with users who persistently post highly objectionable content. The Court noted that while Section 69A requires the reasons for such actions to be recorded in writing, it does not obligate the authorities to communicate these reasons, leaving it to their discretion. This judgment highlights the limited scope for social media intermediaries to resist compliance with the blocking orders of the government.

This recent judicial decision calls for a thorough analysis as it signifies an expansion of governmental control over online platforms in India. The ruling contrasts with the principles established in the *Shreya Singhal* case, where it was

[37] *Facebook LLC v. Union of India*, W.P.(C) No. 7281/2021.

[38] IT Rules 2021, Rule 3(1).

[39] *X Corp. v. Union of India*, W.P. No. 13710 of 2022.

argued that platforms, being private entities, do not have the jurisdiction to adjudicate on human rights matters. However, this latest judgment limits the autonomy of these platforms by compelling them to comply strictly with government directives, thus raising concerns about the impact on the social media landscape and the resilience of democracy in India.

The judgment serves as a cautionary signal, with profound implications for the future of social media, especially as it sets a precedent that could undermine the democratic structure of the nation. In a time when social media is crucial for enhancing public discourse and scrutinizing government policies, this decision threatens to erode democratic values. The potential to suppress dissenting voices online, under the guise of following government orders, especially when social media is used as a platform for protest and organizing movements against governmental policies, poses a significant risk. This scenario underscores the need for a delicate balance between enforcing governmental authority and preserving democratic freedoms in the sphere of online communication.

In January 2023, leveraging the newly implemented regulations, India imposed a ban on a BBC documentary that scrutinized the involvement of Indian Prime Minister Narendra Modi in the 2002 Gujarat riots. This action was taken under Rule 16 of the 2021 IT Rules (Ellis-Petersen, 2023), which authorizes officials to urgently block content under Section 69A of the IT Act. This episode starkly illustrates the diminishing civic freedoms in India, particularly evident in instances where dissenting voices emerge. Subsequently, in February, the Income Tax Department conducted operations at the BBC's offices in what seemed to be a governmental reprisal, further underscoring the constrained environment for journalism within the country.

The IT Rules primarily facilitate a link between *state-enforced* censorship and actions motivated by online vigilantism. Criticism surrounding these rules focuses on the belief that they serve as a tool for the Indian government to censor the press, in line with the biases of vigilante groups, under the misleading guise of promoting news media accountability to the public (Abhishek, 2023).

Against this backdrop, in early 2023, the Ministry of Information and Broadcasting of India announced that 3101 digital news media publishers[40] and 57 OTT platforms[41] had registered their details in accordance with the IT Rules 2021. Prominent digital media outlets such as India Mix, IBC 24, and Kalaignar TV, among other leading channels, have complied with the regulations. Likewise, OTT platforms like Amazon, Disney+ Hotstar, and Jio have also followed suit in adhering to these rules.

[40] Available at https://drive.google.com/file/d/1_RvZQyinLgWGC8X9xuidjHm2K8WuqJ_a/view?ref=static.internetfreedom.in.

[41] Available at https://drive.google.com/file/d/1Dz9aPB2yMd1xalK4BodPdIev-ICL5QZi/view?ref=static.internetfreedom.in.

On April 6, 2023, India introduced amendments to the existing IT Rules,[42] establishing a "fact check unit" under the central government's authority to identify and mark online content concerning any central government business as "fake, false, or misleading." These amendments require online intermediaries, such as social media platforms and Internet service providers, to quickly remove content flagged by this unit. Failure to do so jeopardizes their safe harbor protections, exposing them to potential legal liability for hosting third-party information. Critics have denounced the amendment for granting the government broad and unchecked censorship powers, threatening the constitutionally and internationally recognized freedoms of expression and opinion. Ostensibly designed to combat misinformation online, these rules endow the government with the subjective power to decide which content is considered misleading or false. This grants the government unprecedented control over online discourse, significantly hindering the freedom of various entities, including journalists, activists, and human rights defenders, to express their views on the Internet, according to Amnesty International (Amnesty International, 2023).

9.5 Scholarly and Policy Debates Around the IT Rules

The adoption of a conditional immunity model for intermediary liability on digital platforms marks a pivotal shift in legal approaches to user-generated content. Under the IT Rules of India, this model provides intermediaries, such as social media platforms and Internet service providers, with legal protections against liability for user-posted content, contingent upon meeting specific conditions. On one hand, this model aims to foster a more responsible and accountable digital environment by mandating that intermediaries take on greater oversight duties. This is intended to curb the spread of harmful or illegal online content, including hate speech, misinformation, and copyright-infringing material.

On the other hand, the model presents a challenge to free speech and expression due to the tight deadlines for content moderation imposed on these intermediaries. The pressure to act swiftly may lead platforms to overzealously censor content, erring on the side of caution to avert legal penalties. This approach risks silencing legitimate discourse as platforms might choose to remove content hastily instead of facing the potential legal ramifications of hosting contentious material (Rodriguez et al., 2021). Moreover, achieving a balance between safeguarding a safe online ecosystem and maintaining the Internet's openness remains a universal dilemma. The rigorous demands for content removal risk impeding the free exchange of ideas and information, potentially stifling the Internet's unfettered access and openness (Biyani & Choudhury, 2021).

Criticism of the oversight mechanisms introduced by the IT Rules focuses on their perceived lack of neutrality and independence, pointing to a significant flaw in

[42] Information Technology (Intermediary Guidelines and Digital Media Ethics Code) Amendment Rules, 2023 (IT Rules, 2023).

the regulatory framework that threatens to undermine democratic principles. Concerns arise over the potential for these mechanisms to be influenced by government entities or other powerful groups. Without genuine neutrality and independence, these oversight bodies risk failing to oversee the implementation of the rules objectively and impartially.

Moreover, the IT Rules of 2021 failed to invoke a crucial feature present in the IT Act: they do not allow intermediaries or content creators to respond to content removal notifications (Biyani & Choudhury, 2021). The guidelines vaguely define "objectionable content," encompassing a wide range of categories such as sovereignty and integrity, national security, public order, and morality. This broad categorization can lead to unwarranted content restrictions, shutdowns, and removals, even when the content is lawful, adversely affecting freedom of speech, expression, and the public's access to information and resources online.

On February 11, 2024, in anticipation of protests called for by the Samyukta Kisan Morcha and Kisan Mazdoor Morcha, the Haryana government implemented a suspension of mobile data services from February 11 to 13. This decision was made in light of over 200 farmers' unions announcing the *Delhi Chalo* march.[43] Citing the Indian Telegraph Act, 1885, and the Temporary Suspension of Telecom Services (Public Emergency or Public Safety) Rules, 2017,[44] the government described the Internet shutdown as a precautionary measure to curb the "spread of misinformation and rumors through various social media platforms" and to prevent the "facilitation and mobilization of mobs, agitators, and demonstrators." Beyond significantly infringing on the constitutional rights to free speech, information, and assembly, the Internet shutdown provided the state with a pretext to commit human rights violations amidst the protests by stifling the flow of information and impeding fact-checking processes.

While existing legislation permits state governments in India to interrupt Internet services under the guise of public interest, the proposed IT Rules introduce the possibility of nationwide Internet shutdowns and the blocking of access during pivotal moments, such as protests and elections. These measures, justified as necessary for maintaining public order, threaten the fundamental circulation of information vital to public awareness and the democratic process. Notably, studies have consistently ranked India as the leading country in terms of Internet shutdowns, indicating a pattern of frequent and extensive use of this measure, surpassing that seen in other nations (Andrabi, 2024).

As the Rules extend their application to online media, they may lead to mob censorship of digital media (Abhishek, 2023) and may reflect a selective application of these laws to certain media publications or to stifle the voice of marginalized people, causing them to dissent against the government. Scholar Mahapatra, drawing from the foundation laid by the IT Act, raised alarms over the possibility of digital

---

[43] See https://www.moneycontrol.com/news/business/farmers-delhi-chalo-call-haryana-govt-orders-suspension-of-mobile-internet-bulk-sms-in-7-districts-12240031.html.

[44] See https://homeharyana.gov.in/pdfs/Orders/Telecom%20Suspension%2017.02.pdf.

surveillance by government agencies under the proposed framework. She cautioned that this framework could be leveraged to monitor individuals who critique the government, permitting the lawful surveillance of digital content across various platforms and devices (Mahapatra, 2021).

Mahapatra further pointed out the potential for prosecuting individuals based on vaguely defined offenses, such as threats to national sovereignty or damaging international relations. She emphasizes that the current framework could replicate past abuses seen with the IT Act, where satire or criticism of the government led to arrests, marking a new wave of repression in India (Mahapatra, 2021). She referred to instances of the IT Act's misuse, including arrests over social media posts and the blocking or removal of web pages and accounts, to illustrate the threat to free speech and media freedom in the digital sphere. Moreover, Mahapatra warns of the larger ramifications, indicating that these rules could lead to an escalation in monitoring and digital surveillance, reminiscent of previous situations under the IT Act.

Another concern she raised involves the requirement for messaging platforms to identify the first originator of information. This mandates that service providers store extensive data, including message details and identifiers, indefinitely, without a clear limit for how long to check for the first originator. Such a requirement forces the retention of vast amounts of personal data, challenging the principle of data minimization and exceeding what is technologically necessary for providing messaging services.

The Rules introduced a commendable requirement for significant social media intermediaries to establish transparent and fair processes for content removals. Nonetheless, there is a looming concern over the potential for abuse of power, given that the capability to modify or delete online content, including digital media, is conferred upon a government committee. While the Rules recognize the self-regulatory obligations of platforms, centralizing content oversight within a government committee sparks doubts regarding the underlying objectives and efficacy of these regulations. The recent judgment in the *Platform X* case in Bangalore serves as a pertinent illustration of these issues.

The introduction of these Rules undermines the principle of self-regulation by granting an Inter-Departmental Committee, organized by the Ministry of Information and Broadcasting, the authority to supervise and potentially overturn the self-regulatory bodies' decisions concerning platforms. This shift in power compromises the effectiveness of platforms' own content moderation and dispute resolution mechanisms as the ultimate decision-making power is vested in a government entity. This committee's ability to intervene in content disputes and possibly alter or remove content, essentially transferring control from private platforms to a governmental body, exemplifies a significant change in the regulatory landscape for digital content (Karanicolas, 2021; Abhishek, 2023).

Ashraf's argument also highlighted a significant oversight in addressing the concerns of scholars like Lessig and Reidenberg about the potential for technology to be used as an instrument of tyranny and control. Moreover, it fails to consider the apprehensions of critical cyberspace theorists who worry that the state could exploit technologies to bypass constitutional limits on its legal powers. This neglect leads to a decrease in the online freedom of speech, potentially diminishing opportunities for democratic self-governance and the creation and sharing of culture (Ashraf, 2022a, 2022b).

From my argument, the introduction of stringent regulations by India's IT Rules, which place extra obligations on intermediaries, represents a step in the right direction. Platforms like social media, which generate profit from their user base, should indeed shoulder a certain degree of responsibility. For instance, performing "due diligence" is a reasonable expectation to earn "safe harbor" protections. This view contrasts with the more lenient immunity model in the United States, specifically Section 230 of the CDA, and it brings into focus the ongoing debate about how intermediaries should navigate the fine line between free speech and the trust and safety of digital environments while also considering other rights and values. In the contemporary era, where debates are going around amending the broader immunity model laid down by Section 230 of CDA, I trust that the IT Rule of India have been in the right direction in terms of adding responsibilities to intermediates.

Similarly, when comparing Germany's Network Enforcement Act (NetzDG) framework with India's IT Rules, significant differences and flexibility in certain aspects become apparent. For instance, while NetzDG requires platforms to remove illegal content within 24 h—a deadline criticized for being excessively tight, discussed in Chap. 8 of this book—India provides a slightly longer time frame of 36 h for content takedown. Additionally, the threshold for what constitutes a significant social media intermediary differs between the two countries: in India, it is set at platforms with over 5 million users, whereas in Germany, the threshold is lower at 2 million users.

Yet a few responsibilities, such as the introduction of specific obligations by the Rules—such as the requirement for social media companies to appoint compliance officers based in India, adhere to the traceability of the first originator requirement, use automated filtering technologies, and disclose users' physical addresses—have met with resistance from the tech giants in India. These platforms view the added requirements as overly burdensome. An illustrative case of the difficulty of the challenges posed by these new rules is the resignation of Twitter's interim resident grievance officer in June 2021, merely 4 weeks after taking up the position.

Balkin's perspective on leveraging intermediary immunity to encourage more socially responsible behavior (Balkin, 2021) among social media companies is reflected in the IT Rules. However, the framework does not adequately address the role of the government in motivating platforms to enhance their moderation practices, such as by increasing moderator numbers and ensuring fair due process for users.

Implementing these strategies would significantly bolster social media governance in India, a country where platforms are navigating the complexities of localizing their operations in today's dynamic environment. Furthermore, the application of these rules to digital media is criticized as an excessive expansion of central government authority, perceived as a veiled effort to control online news outlets through delegated legislation. In my opinion, the intervention by government authorities aims to override the outcomes of private governance by platforms due to their extensive authority over the platforms and their content. I recommend that while adhering to the standards set by the IT Rules, India should consider the practicality of the structural frameworks surrounding significant social media platforms. This approach would help in developing a regulatory model that not only is feasible and effective but could also serve as a benchmark for other jurisdictions in the Global South.

In my view, introducing a Code of Ethics for digital news platforms through the IT Rules is a clear indication of India's intent to incorporate a coregulation model into social media regulation—a promising development from the Majority World. While coregulation systems have been predominantly introduced in Western jurisprudence, this initiative could serve as a guide for other countries to explore similar approaches. In the future, this may lead to the development of coregulatory models, potentially combined with external regulation, that address the shortcomings of the other two models.

I suggest a detailed reform involving a shift in regulatory authority from the government to both private platforms and independent entities. This redistribution aims to mitigate fears of governmental overreach. Additionally, by offering incentives to social media platforms to improve their content moderation efforts, the government can promote a more equitable and efficient social media governance framework within Indian legislation. Such incentives would encourage platforms to proactively participate in content moderation, thereby finding a middle ground between safeguarding free speech and reinforcing democratic principles.

References

Abhishek, A. (2023). The state deputizing citizens to discipline digital news media: The case of the IT rules 2021 in India. *Digital Journalism, 11*(10), 1769–1787.

Access Now. (2024, May 15). *Unabashed and unabated: India leads the world shutdown count for sixth year.* Retrieved from https://www.accessnow.org/press-release/india-keepiton-internet-shutdowns-2023-en/

Amnesty International. (2023, May 2). *India: New amendment to the information technology rules that threatens press freedoms must be withdrawn.* Retrieved from Amnesty International: https://www.amnesty.org/fr/wp-content/uploads/2023/05/ASA2067342023ENGLISH-1.pdf

Ananth, A., & Narrain, S. (2023). Facebook's crowds and publics: Law, virality and the regulation of hate speech online in contemporary India. Sydney.

Andrabi, K. (2024, February 23). *Rising internet shutdowns in India spark fears of authoritarianism before election.* Retrieved from South China Morning Post: https://www.scmp.com/week-asia/politics/article/3252997/rising-internet-shutdowns-india-spark-fears-authoritarianism-election

Ashraf, M. M. (2022a). Reimagining regulation of speech on social media platforms in India. *NUJS Journal of Regulatory Studies, 7*(4), 21–53.

Ashraf, M. M. (2022b). Reimagining regulation of speech on social media platforms in India. *NUJS Journal of Regulatory Studies, 2*(4), 21–54.

Ashwini, S. (2021). Social media platform regulation in India–A special reference to the information technology (Intermediary Guidelines and Digital Media Ethics Code) rules. *Perspectives on Platform Regulation, 12*(2), 215–232.

Balkin, J. M. (2021). How to regulate (and not regulate) social media. *Journal of Free Speech Law, 1*(1), 71–96.

Biyani, N., & Choudhury, A. (2021). *Indian intermediary guidelines and the internet experience in India*. Internet Society.

Daniyal, S. (2021, July 8). *Why is the Indian government at war with Twitter?*. Retrieved from Scroll.in: https://scroll.in/article/999171/why-is-the-government-of-india-at-war-with-twitter

Ellis-Petersen, H. (2023, January 23). *India invokes emergency laws to ban BBC Modi documentary*. Retrieved from The Guardian: https://www.theguardian.com/world/2023/jan/23/india-emergency-laws-to-ban-bbc-narendra-modi-documentary

Frenkel, S., & Alba, D. (2021, October 23). *In India, Facebook grapples with an amplified version of its problems*. Retrieved from New York Times: https://www.nytimes.com/2021/10/23/technology/facebook-india-misinformation.html

Human Rights Watch. (2023, June 14). *"No Internet Means No Work, No Pay, No Food": Internet shutdowns deny access to basic rights in "Digital India"*. Retrieved from https://www.hrw.org/report/2023/06/14/no-internet-means-no-work-no-pay-no-food/internet-shutdowns-deny-access-basic

Juyal, R. (2023). Constitutional liberties and cyberspace: Analysing the Anuradha Bhasin v Union of India Case and its impact on fundamental rights. *Legal Information Management, 23*(4), 276–281.

Karanicolas, M. (2021). Authoritarianism as a service: India's moves to weaponize private sector content moderation with the 2021 Information Technology Rules. *Indian Journal of Law and Technology, 17*(2), 25–43.

Kumar, S. (2022). Traceability and end-to-end encryption: An analysis of India's intermediary rules mandating traceability.

Kutty, S. (2022, May 30). *Why hasn't PM Modi taken a single press conference in 8 years, and why isn't press driving this message home?* Retrieved from National Herald: https://www.nationalheraldindia.com/opinion/why-hasnt-pm-modi-taken-a-single-press-conference-in-8-years-and-why-isnt-press-driving-this-message-home

Madhavan, E. (2016). Internet and social media's social movements leading to new forms of governance and policymaking cases from India. *Glocalism*, 1–32.

Mahapatra, S. (2021). *Digital surveillance and the threat to civil liberties in India.* Social science open access repository.

MEITy. (2023). *Proposed Digital India Act, 2023.* Retrieved from Ministry of Electronics and Information Technology: https://www.meity.gov.in/writereaddata/files/DIA_Presentation%2009.03.2023%20Final.pdf

Mukerjee, S. (2024). Online news in India: A quantitative appraisal of the digital news consumption landscape in the world's largest democracy (2014–2018). *Information, Communication & Society*, 1–21.

Narrain, S. (2019). Social media, violence and the law: 'Objectionable Material' and the changing countours of hate speech regulation in India. *Culture Unbound, 10*(3), 388–404.

Palit, P. (2018). India's use of social media in public diplomacy. *Public Diplomacy of Rising and Regional Powers, 3*(3), 151–171.

Parthasarathi, V., & Agarwal, S. (2020). Rein and Laissez Faire: The dual personality of media regulation in India. *Digital Journalism, 8*(6), 797–819.

Pratap, A. (2021, June 15). *WhatsApp's fight with the Indian Government over its data privacy rules may have global reverberations.* Retrieved from Forbes: https://www.forbes.com/sites/aayushipratap/2021/06/15/whatsapps-fight-with-the-indian-government-over-its-data-privacy-rules-may-have-global-reverberations/?sh=3205c6965a7a

Ratnan, G. G. (2022). Significance of social media and its revolution in India. *International Journal of English and Studies (IJOES), 4*(3), 96–101.

Rodrigues, U. (2014). Social media's impact on journalism: A study of media's coverage of anti-corruption protests in India. *Global Media Journal - Australian Edition, 8*(1), 1–10.

Rodriguez, K., Mathew, S., & Schmon, C. (2021, April 7). *India's strict rules for online intermediaries undermine freedom of expression*. Retrieved from Electronic Frontier Foundation: https://www.eff.org/deeplinks/2021/04/indias-strict-rules-online-intermediaries-undermine-freedom-expression

Sahni, S., & Manisha, A. T. (2021). Intermediary liability & the media rules. *Webology, 18*(2), 1554–1559.

Sekhri, A., & Gupta, A. (2018). *Section 66A and Other Legal Zombies*. FF Working Paper No. 2/2018. Available at SSRN: https://ssrn.com/abstract=3275893 or https://doi.org/10.2139/ssrn.3275893

Singh, A. P. (2015). Regulation of social media in cyber space a critical study of regulatory mechanism with special reference to India.

Soni, P. (2021, December 14). *Online censorship is growing in Modi's India*. Retrieved from Columbia Journalism Review: https://www.cjr.org/investigation/modi-censorship-india-twitter.php

Webber, E. (2023, March 15). *Information technology sector of India*. Retrieved from Ensure IAS: https://ensureias.com/blog/information-technology-sector-of-india#:~:text=Facts%20about%20IT%20sector%20of,to%20India's%20GDP%20by%202025. https://oosga.com/social-media/ind/#:~:text=Social%20Media's%20User%20Demographics%20in,of%20users%20has%20grown%204

Wong, B. (2024, February 6). *Top social media statistics and trends*. Retrieved from Forbes: https://www.forbes.com/advisor/in/business/social-media-statistics/#:~:text=Active%20Social%20Media%20Penetration%20in,of%20the%20country's%20entire%20population

Woodhams, S., & Migliano, S. (2024, May 8). *The global cost of internet shutdowns*. Retrieved from Top10VPN: https://www.top10vpn.com/research/cost-of-internet-shutdowns/

Yadav, N. (2022). Freedom of Speech and Section 66A of IT Act, 2000: Disputed Path of Indian Law. *Indian Journal of Law and Legal Research, 4*(4), 1–10.

Chapter 10
Continuing Repression: The Online Safety Act of Sri Lanka

10.1 Introduction

Sri Lanka, despite its geographical proximity to India within the South Asian region, boasts a distinct social, political, and cultural context. With a relatively small population, the country is characterized by a multiethnic society and a rich tapestry of diverse religions. Its history is marked by a challenging period, enduring a devastating 3-year local war until 2009. Presently, Sri Lanka finds itself in the complex landscape of postbellum governance, grappling with the aftermath of conflict and engaging in a *transitional justice* process. The scars of the conflict have left an indelible impact on the nation, necessitating a thoughtful and comprehensive approach to rebuilding and reconciliation. As Sri Lanka navigates through this postconflict period, it faces the intricate task of addressing the grievances of various communities, fostering unity, and establishing a foundation for sustainable peace. The challenges and opportunities inherent in the postwar era underscore the importance of inclusive policies that respect the diversity of the population. Efforts toward *transitional justice*, which involves acknowledging past wrongs, ensuring accountability, and promoting healing, become pivotal in shaping a harmonious and equitable society. Sri Lanka's journey toward reconciliation reflects the resilience of its people and the commitment to forging a shared future despite the complexities arising from its unique historical and cultural context (Grewal, 2023).

In addition to the existing challenges, within the last few years, Sri Lanka has undergone a severe constitutional, political, and economic crisis. These crises contribute to the fragile nature of the state, particularly within the global context of the South. Despite facing economic challenges due to pandemic-related policy mistakes, resulting in consecutive years of a shrinking economy and slow growth projections for 2023–2025, Sri Lanka is witnessing a notable surge in Internet usage. Over the past 6 years, the number of Internet users has more than tripled, reaching nearly 40% of the population (OOSGA, 2023). This growth is attributed to a robust mobile-first Internet economy, fostering innovative applications and attracting

S. Balendra, *Free Speech in the Puzzle of Content Regulation*, Law, Governance and Technology Series 70, https://doi.org/10.1007/978-3-031-75813-3_10

significant investment. According to a United Nations Conference on Trade and Development (UNCTAD) report, digital investment in Sri Lanka surpasses that of larger economies such as China and India, marking a distinctive trend in both emerging and developed markets in the broader Asia region (Wattegama, 2021).

During and after the local war, Sri Lanka has been marked by *severe restrictions on freedom of opinion and expression*, particularly targeting the ethnic minority of the country. This includes the excessive use of force by police to disperse peaceful assemblies and the application of counterterrorism laws against protesters (Human Rights Watch, 2024).

To address these challenges, social media has seen substantial growth in Sri Lanka, providing a platform for citizens to express their opinions online, especially in a jurisdiction where human rights are sometimes suppressed or infringed upon by legislation such as the Prevention of Terrorism Act (PTA). Social media platforms (SMPs) are used by civil society activists, and citizens to engage in the democratic process, with the larger community within and beyond Sri Lanka.

However, since 2018, amid events such as the *anti-Muslim* riots,[1] the Easter Sunday attacks (Amarasingam & Rizwie, 2020), the *Aragalaya* protest (Center for Policy Alternatives, 2023), etc., the Sri Lankan government has intermittently shut down public access to social media, citing it as a preventive measure against hate speech and misinformation to protect the public good. Meanwhile, law enforcement authorities also persist in arresting, detaining, and intimidating individuals, including journalists, for online posts on SMPs. This is done by applying existing regulatory frameworks such as the Prevention of Terrorism Act (PTA)[2] and the International Covenant on Civil and Political Rights (ICCPR) Act[3] (Freedom House, 2024), owing to the *broad* nature of the provisions of these statutes.

This chapter of the book explores the Sri Lankan context from the perspective of the Majority World, alongside India, for several reasons. While the political, legal, and social landscapes of Sri Lanka differ significantly from those of India, there are also notable similarities. For instance, both countries are characterized by multiethnic, linguistic, and culturally diverse populations, yet the challenges they face are markedly distinct. In the preceding chapter, I discussed India; in this chapter, I will conduct an in-depth examination of the Sri Lankan context. Sri Lanka has endured a civil war lasting over 3 decades, which deeply impacted its various ethnic communities. Currently, the country is navigating a transitional justice process, criticized for the state's heavy-handed regulations that often infringe upon human rights. This case study will explore how social media content regulation is influenced in a majoritarian country undergoing transitional justice, marked by significant state interference in individual freedoms.

---

[1] See https://www.theguardian.com/world/2019/apr/21/social-media-shut-down-in-sri-lanka-in-bid-to-stem-misinformation.

[2] Prevention of Terrorism (Temporary Provisions) Act, No. 48 of 1979 (PTA).

[3] International Covenant on Civil and Political Rights Act, No.56 of 2007 (ICCPR Act).

Against this backdrop, after the prolonged discussions to regulate the online spaces of Sri Lanka over 4 years, in 2024, Sri Lanka enacted its Online Safety Act (OSA) to regulate content across the Internet space, primarily through SMPs. This chapter will delve into the details of the OSA and its implications for online speech, expression, and safety in a jurisdiction that is in the postconflict era, marching through the *transitional justice* process.

10.2 Rise of Social Media and Recurring Challenges

As of January 2024, Sri Lanka reported having 7.50 million users on various social media platforms, which represents 34.2 percent of the country's total population (Data Reportal, 2024). SMPs have significantly contributed to the business and enterprise landscape of Sri Lanka. From the perspective of a developing country, these platforms have enabled Sri Lankan businesses to reach out to potential investors, clients, and outsourcing opportunities, both domestically and internationally. Social media outlets such as Facebook and Instagram are increasingly being used by micro, small, and medium enterprises (MSMEs) in the country (Jayasuriya et al., 2017; Hewage & Weerasekera, 2021). Evidencing the continuous growth of social media, the social media advertising market in Sri Lanka is projected to grow by 5.09% (2024–2028), resulting in a market volume of US$93.6M in 2028 (Statista, 2023).

Beyond serving as a marketing strategy, social media's role in public interaction has been significant. Furthermore, it plays a vital role in the mobilization and expression of views concerning the democratic process on digital platforms. This fundamentally enhances free speech and expression through these platform handles, highlighting their importance beyond mere communication tools (Soorya, 2021). As a country grappling with severe human rights violations and limitations during the *postconflict* era, Sri Lanka witnessed numerous human rights violations, especially regarding free speech, association, and expression. These violations were perpetrated through repressive administrative and governmental actions, as well as through legislation, such as the Prevention of Terrorism Act (PTA) of Sri Lanka (DeVotta & Ganguly, 2019). In the contemporary Internet era, particularly through SMPs, the amplification of minority voices in Sri Lanka has become more noticeable. This phenomenon continues despite physical restrictions resulting from authoritarian approaches employed by the government. The Internet, especially via SMPs, emerges as a resilient platform, acting as a vital channel for protecting human rights within the country.

As a tool for citizen journalism, SMPs have *prima facie* played a significant role in facilitating numerous social media movements within the Sri Lankan landscape. The features, easy access, and global reach of SMPs have tremendously contributed to the amplification of human rights, political discourse, and democratic values in Sri Lanka. These platforms often become integral to the broader domain of digital activism, significantly contributing beyond mainstream media in promoting such activism. This is particularly true for issues related to the government, where mainstream media faces the risk of *a state-controlled* trajectory (Gunatilleke, 2017).

The mobilization enabled by the features of these platforms has led to an amplification of free speech and the right to information, contributing to the organization of movements in the country. In Sri Lanka, social media has emerged as a significant tool for organizing protests against the military regime. Activists have effectively utilized platforms like Facebook in recent years to mobilize people for various protests throughout the country (Nifra, 2022).

Similar to the United States (US), the alliance between social media and citizen participation significantly impacted Sri Lankan politics during the 2015 presidential election. In that pivotal election, the extensive use of social media by citizens and civil society organizations played a strategic role in the surprising defeat of the two-time incumbent president (Anuradha Rao, 2018). These movements gained further momentum after the COVID-19 pandemic, during which the government imposed various physical restrictions. Notable social media movements include the dissemination of information across SMPs following the 2019 Easter Sunday bombings, the 2019 presidential election, and the *Aragalaya* movement.

Sri Lanka witnessed a potential shift in political dynamics spurred by the 2022 *Aragalaya* movement, named after the Sinhala word for "struggle." Originating in March 2022, the movement brought together thousands of people protesting against power cuts; shortages in fuel, food, medicine; and rising prices. Social media played a significant role in mobilization, enabling activists to live-stream events and attract thousands to join online protests. This digital activism not only heightened public awareness but also popularized slogans like "Gota Go Home" and "Kaputu Kaak" (Center for Policy Alternatives, 2023). Unprecedentedly, Sri Lankans from diverse backgrounds collectively rallied against the government led by Gotabaya Rajapaksa, marking a historic moment in the country's history. The predominantly nonviolent protests achieved a notable outcome: the removal of the entrenched Rajapaksa family from power, with Prime Minister Mahinda Rajapaksa resigning in May 2022, followed by President Gotabaya Rajapaksa's resignation in July 2022.

In Sri Lanka, SMPs have become inevitably necessary to uphold the democratic pillars of jurisprudence, particularly in response to the heavy-handed treatment of human rights. The increase in citizen participation is seen as a strong defense of democracy, responding to perceived threats to the foundational principles of Sri Lanka's democratic system (Gunatilleke, 2017). On the flip side, these platforms have also frequently impacted Sri Lanka's online sphere with issues such as fake news, information manipulation, cyber defamation, and hate speech. This has significantly undermined the resilience of the Internet, electoral integrity, public security, and various other essential public values.

For the first time, social media *infodemic* cohesion was experienced in Sri Lanka following a confrontation on February 23, 2018, in *Digana*, which resulted in the death of a Sinhalese individual, Kumarasinghe, on March 3. Meetings aimed at de-escalation and compensation by a local mosque ensued but faced difficulties. Sinhala Buddhist nationalist leaders, including Gnanasara Thero and Amith Weerasinghe, visited Kumarasinghe's house. Ampitiye Sumanarathna Thero, part of the group, was filmed verbally abusing and assaulting Christians. Following Kumarasinghe's death, leaders, notably Amith Weerasinghe, utilized SMPs to share content containing anti-Muslim statements. The incident also involved the demolition of a Muslim-owned grocery and subsequent protests against the arrests (Law & Society Trust, 2018). The *Digana* incident was amplified through SMPs, which provided a channel to incite hate and mob violence against the minority community in the country, severely used as propaganda by Sinhalese extremist groups across the country. Although the incident occurred in the Kandy district, after the content spread across various SMPs, minor incidents targeting Muslims were reported in various districts. This seriously harmed the existence of public safety, peace, and religious harmony, particularly in a country navigating through a *transitional justice* and *peace-building* process.

Months after, in the aftermath of the *Easter Sunday attacks* on April 21, 2019, in Sri Lanka, a series of bombings targeted churches and hotels, resulting in at least 290 deaths and numerous injuries. Social media content distributed across the island discussed potentially polarizing topics such as national security narratives, political criticism of a party or politician, and government negligence in implementing security measures (Democracy Reporting International, 2021). In the aftermath of the attacks, a significant portion of Sri Lanka's 15 million Buddhists became apprehensive about potential targeting by *jihadists*, fueled by rumors within the community and online discussions through SMPs. Simultaneously, Muslims began to be targeted as *potential terrorists* by other religious groups, fostering an atmosphere of *Islamophobia* after the incident. While Muslims condemned the senseless killings, some Sinhalese extremists remained unsatisfied with this rejection of violence. Following the Easter Sunday attacks, Muslim women wearing traditional Islamic dress were targeted as the government banned face coverings in public for security reasons.[4] The ban, while not specifying the *niqab* and *burka*, led to harassment even for those wearing headscarves, according to rights groups. The community attributes actions like boycotts of Muslim businesses to messages from local Buddhist clergy, influenced by senior monks. The spread of *Islamophobia* across SMPs not only affected the common good of the country but also seriously harmed the dignity and freedom related to cultural practices and engagement in business, as recognized under Articles 14(1)(f) and 14(1)(g) of the Constitution of Sri Lanka.

Article 14(1)(f) of the Constitution provides:

> Every citizen is entitled to the freedom by himself or in association with others to enjoy and promote his own culture and to use his own language.

Article 14(1)(g) reads as follows:

[4]President of Sri Lanka Maithripala Sirisena has invoked emergency law to enforce a restriction, banning any face garment that "hinders identification" for security reasons in the aftermath of the Easter Sunday attack.

> Every citizen is entitled to the freedom to engage by himself or in association with others in any lawful occupation, profession, trade, business or enterprise.

This trend of *Islamophobia* continued even during the COVID-19 pandemic when significant restrictions on physical movement were enforced in adherence to the health measures of the authorities, and the Internet became even more prevalent in spreading information within and beyond the country. The pandemic has exacerbated the prevalence of conspiracy theories. In Sri Lanka, misinformation has been widespread, and the virus has been weaponized to target Muslim communities, with the minority population falsely accused of spreading the virus (Tazamal, 2021). Furthermore, the government's imposition of a forced cremation policy, justified for public health reasons without evidence, contradicts international advice, including that of the WHO, which supports permitting burials. This policy is considered a violation of several articles of the International Covenant on Civil and Political Rights (ICCPR). Instances of Muslims being forcibly cremated without COVID-19 testing raise concerns, and the disproportionately higher number of Muslim deaths from the virus lacks a reasonable explanation. This could potentially stem from factors such as access to healthcare, discriminatory treatment, or disparities in testing, as authorities fail to provide clarification (Mihlar, 2019). During and after the pandemic, SMPs were inundated with anti-Muslim and antiminority content circulating widely. However, it is worth pointing out that, in the Sri Lankan context, case studies reveal that restrictions on the fundamental freedoms of minorities and satirists, both *online* and *offline*, are often imposed in alignment with the preferences of the *Sinhala-Buddhist* majority. This contrasts with petitioners from the majority community, whose actions align with majoritarian interests and who are more successful in vindicating their fundamental freedoms before the courts (Gunatilleke, 2023).

During the pandemic, Sri Lanka encountered another challenge of an *infodemic*, which hindered both medical efforts and information management. The infodemic was fueled by two primary sources: (i) mainstream media, which willfully spread disinformation, and (ii) websites and social media users who created and widely shared disinformation without critical assessment (Nayakarathna, 2021). Vaccine misinformation and language barriers contributed to widespread vaccine hesitancy and the emergence of an antivax movement. Limited access to accurate COVID-19 information, primarily available in English, further exacerbated the issue. The spread of mis-/disinformation fostered distrust in the health sector and unfairly stigmatized minority groups as potential virus spreaders.

Initially, online discourse in Sri Lanka was opposed to holding elections during the health crisis, especially between March and May 2020, reflecting a prioritization of public safety and health. However, support for holding elections increased from June 2020 onward as the public adapted to living with the ongoing COVID-19 pandemic (Democracy Reporting International, 2020). SMPs, specifically Facebook, began to play a significant role in election campaigns in Sri Lanka, capitalizing on their respective candidates through pages and profiles. However, beyond the motive of campaigning, numerous cases alleged that SMPs were weaponized to *discredit* opponent parties/candidates through malpractices. During the 2019 presidential election in Sri Lanka, Democracy Reporting International identified the significant role of SMPs and gossip domains in disseminating *politically manipulated narratives* that often disregarded factual accuracy (Democracy Reporting International, 2020). These narratives spanned various topics, including national security and religious and ethnic issues. Additionally, there was a notable increase in targeted hate speech against minority groups—studies point out that this surge in hate speech may have contributed to a divisive atmosphere during the election period (Commonwealth Observer Group, 2019).

Similar to the elections in the United States and *Brexit*, the prevalence of fake accounts, particularly bots, on Twitter in Sri Lanka remains a significant challenge despite measures taken to address it. A preliminary analysis of 1262 accounts showed that a majority of the suspicious accounts following Twitter users were indeed *bots* (Hattotuwa et al., 2018). Prominent figures such as diplomats, ambassadors, politicians, media institutions, civil society organizations, journalists, cricketers, and others were found to have a substantial number of bot followers. This situation suggests that bots have become a permanent and growing presence in Sri Lanka's Twitter landscape, raising concerns about their impact during elections or referendums. The challenge now is to find effective ways to address this issue on a larger scale, considering the substantial number of citizens directly connected to or influenced by these fake accounts.

While the enduring opportunities afforded to Sri Lankan citizens allow for significant participation in democratic discourses through SMPs, the discussions above underscore the urgent need and rationale for regulating content across online spaces. In the coming section, I argue how regulations over SMPs have evolved in Sri Lanka through administrative and legislative efforts. This evolution demonstrates a jurisdiction's approach that often leans toward a heavy-handed restriction of fundamental freedoms, accompanied by a majoritarian perspective.

10.3 Disruption of Social Media as a Measure

Over the past 5 years, amid social media movements against the backdrop of tensions in Sri Lanka, the government has resorted to employing *extralegal* measures to regulate and govern online spaces. Instead of relying on existing legal and regulatory frameworks, these unconventional approaches have been implemented to exert control over digital platforms.

Commencing with the "Digana" *anti-Muslim* riots in 2018, which were exacerbated by the amplification of inflammatory social media posts leading to violence across the island, the government opted to *restrict* or *block* access to Facebook and other social media services. This action was taken to mitigate the dissemination of *anti-Muslim* content, believed to be a contributing factor to the escalating violence.[5] These measures persisted during the Easter Sunday attacks of 2019, affecting almost all social media platforms except Twitter. The government justified these restrictions as a means to prevent the spread of unverified reports and speculations.[6]

Later, during the *Aragalaya* protest in 2022, several social media platforms, including Facebook, Twitter, WhatsApp, Viber, and YouTube, were restricted after midnight on April 3, 2022, Sunday. This decision coincided with a *state of emergency* declared by the government in response to widespread protests over the economic crisis. The restrictions endured for approximately 16 h, with services being largely restored thereafter. Despite the ban, users found ways to access the platforms indirectly using VPN services that circumvented government-imposed Internet restrictions. Some mobile app versions of the services remained accessible on certain devices due to the partial implementation of the ban.[7]

10.3.1 Is Restricting Access to SMPs or Blocking Them a Good Idea?

In scenarios of widespread violence, when platforms are reluctant or negligent in moderating content, allowing the unchecked spread of extremely violent, hateful, or false material with serious consequences for public welfare and governance, there is a pressing need for jurisprudence to implement immediate measures. These measures often result in social media bans. Paul Bischoff warns about the peril of online censorship becoming a *norm*, citing statistics that show an increase in Internet censorship in over 50 countries in 2023, a notable rise from the 27 countries reported in the previous year (Bischoff, 2023).

While social media bans can effectively control content contributing to violence and conflicts, as witnessed in the 2018 riots, they pose significant drawbacks when SMPs play a crucial role in aiding organizations, foreign governments, and public service agencies in *crisis response*. These platforms have facilitated coordination, aid distribution, and information sharing during periods of unrest. In situations where traditional media lacks public trust, these platforms have allowed independent reporting free from government censorship and served as vital communication tools during Internet bans (Byman & Joshi, 2021). All these accesses are severely affected by the banning of social media in Sri Lanka.

Furthermore, such actions are perceived as authoritarian, reflecting the government's dictatorial measures over the digital platforms of Sri Lanka. The shutdown of

---

[5] See https://www.aljazeera.com/news/2018/3/14/did-sri-lankas-facebook-ban-help-quell-anti-muslim-violence.

[6] See https://www.bbc.com/news/technology-48022530.

[7] See https://netblocks.org/reports/social-media-restricted-in-sri-lanka-as-emergency-declared-amid-protests-JA6ROrAQ.

social media access in Sri Lanka has been criticized by many human rights organizations, particularly by the Office of the United Nations High Commissioner for Human Rights (OHCHR).

During the 51st session of the Human Rights Council in September 2022, it pointed out the action as a serious violation, stating:

> Periodic internet and social media shutdowns have been used to curb the protests and the Government is proposing new laws to regulate the digital civic space. The High Commissioner stresses the importance of maintaining an environment for freedom of expression, peaceful assembly, and democratic debate, both on and off-line (OCHCR, 2022).

I argue that while moderating and regulating content across SMPs has been acknowledged as necessary amid the information chaos in Sri Lanka over the past few years, the governmental approach of shutting down the Internet or SMPs cannot be justified on *any grounds* for two primary reasons.

First, such shutdowns constitute a clear violation of basic human rights, including free speech and expression, recognized by international instruments[8] and the Sri Lankan Constitution.[9] Additionally, the right to information is a fundamental right enshrined in the Sri Lankan Constitution[10] through the Nineteenth Amendment. Shutdowns infringe upon this right as many people rely on SMPs to access information, including media handles. Furthermore, shutting down or banning social media impedes individuals' ability to engage and associate with others, which is another basic human right recognized in the Sri Lankan Constitution.[11]

Internationally, for a restriction on human rights, such as free speech and expression, to be considered legitimate, it must pass a *three-part* test: the interference must be provided for by law, pursue a legitimate aim, and be necessary to achieve that aim. However, the reality behind SMP shutdowns in Sri Lanka often reveals political motives, suppressing protests and free association and stifling voices across platforms. Therefore, such shutdowns are considered *illegitimate* as they do not fulfill the criteria outlined.

Moreover, invoking Article 15 of the Sri Lankan Constitution, restrictions on free speech and expression can only be justified in specific instances, such as racial and religious harmony, parliamentary privilege, or contempt of court.[12] Similarly, restrictions on the freedom of assembly and association are permissible only in the interests of racial and religious harmony or the national economy.[13] However, SMP

---

[8]Universal Declaration of Human Rights, Article 19; International Covenant on Civil and Political Rights (ICCPR), Article 19; African Charter on Human and Peoples' Rights, Article 9; European Convention for the Protection of Human Rights and Fundamental Freedoms, Article 10; American Convention on Human Rights, Article 13; ASEAN Human Rights Declaration.

[9]Constitution of Sri Lanka 1978, Article 14(1)(a).

[10]Constitution of Sri Lanka 1978, Article 14A.

[11]Constitution of Sri Lanka 1978, Article 14(1)(b) and (c).

[12]Constitution of Sri Lanka 1978, Article 15(2).

[13]Constitution of Sri Lanka 1978, Article 15(2) and 15(3).

shutdowns extend beyond these limited instances and severely impact the enjoyment of fundamental rights.

Second, government intervention through administrative measures represents a clear *authoritarian* ideology within the digital realm. Decisions made solely by administrative bodies without judicial intervention infringe upon the fundamental human rights of millions of people. The normalization of Internet shutdowns opens the floodgates for continued abuse during critical times such as elections, as observed in Bangladesh in 2019 and in various African countries.

Internet shutdowns, whether occurring before, during, or after an election, would have serious detriments on democratic values. They undermine the ability of political parties and candidates to campaign and mobilize voters, hinder voter access to information, inhibit political debate, and restrict the free expression of political affiliations (Afef Abrougui & Access Now, 2021).

While advocating for SMP regulations and content moderation, I completely oppose Internet shutdowns as a measure, particularly in a country like Sri Lanka, which is known for its heavy-handed approach toward fundamental human rights and the lack of rule of law.

10.4 Laws Regulating the Social Media Domain

Sri Lanka, seeking to regulate SMPs and moderate content across various platforms, enacted its first regulatory framework, the Online Safety Act (OSA), on 24 January 2024, following prolonged discussions in 2018. However, before the introduction of the OSA, Sri Lanka had a few other legal frameworks that could potentially regulate SMPs in certain aspects.

Before the introduction of the Online Safety Act, Sri Lanka attempted to address the issues related to online content, which was regulated through a few *traditional* legal frameworks. These included the Press Council Law No. 5 of 1973, the International Covenant on Civil and Political Rights (ICCPR) Act No. 56 of 2007, and the Computer Crimes Act No. 24 of 2007.

10.4.1 Press Council Law No. 5 of 1973

The Press Council Law No. 5 of 1973 was enacted with the objective of regulating and advising on matters related to the press while also conducting investigations into printed materials and newspapers—primarily the *printed* media.[14] The Council,

[14] Press Council Law 1973 Long Title.

acting upon the powers conferred by the Act,[15] addresses instances of publication that involve untrue, distorted, and improper content or breaches of ethics. Specifically, the Act empowers the Council to either (a) order the publication of a correction, subject to its approval, in such a media; (b) censure the proprietor, printer, publisher, editor, journalist, or other officer or authority of such media; or (c) order that an apology be tendered by these individuals to the appropriate party.[16]

Another significant document in this context is the *Code of Ethics for Journalists*, introduced through the rules set out by the *Extraordinary Gazette*[17] in 1981 pursuant to Section 30 of the Sri Lanka Press Council Law No. 5 of 1973. This Code provides regulations and guidelines to appropriately balance the interests of different parties. It includes guidelines on various matters, such as preventing false or inaccurate reporting by journalists,[18] correcting any false or inaccurate reports within a possible short span of time,[19] and refraining from publishing content that offends public taste or morality.[20] Additionally, the ethics guide certain matters related to the publication of criminal cases,[21] matrimonial proceedings,[22] plagiarism,[23] etc. The Code clearly illustrates that individual life matters *shall not be published* in a manner that affects the respect toward or reputation of the individual unless it is for the public benefit.[24] Furthermore, it mandates journalists to safeguard the dignity of the profession[25] and prohibits publications that promote violence.[26] It represents one of the most comprehensive acts in terms of media regulations; however, its efficacy in regulating online content disseminated across social media platforms and websites remains limited due to the complex nature of the Internet and technology.

Furthermore, in February 2021, the government proposed amending the outdated Press Council Act No. 05 of 1973 to encompass electronic news and social media. However, this move faced significant opposition from media and civil society organizations. The resistance to the proposed amendment led to a slowdown in the calls for its implementation (Herath, 2022).

---

[15] Section (11) provides: "For the purpose of any inquiry held by the Council under this Law, the Council shall have all the powers of a District Court—(a) to summon and compel the attendance of any person; (b) to compel the production of documents; and (c) to administer any oath or affirmation to any person."

[16] Press Council Law 1973, s 9(1).

[17] No 162/5 A of 1981.

[18] Press Council Rules 1981, Rule 2(b).

[19] Press Council Rules 1981, Rule 2(d).

[20] Press Council Rules 1981, Rule 2(e).

[21] Press Council Rules 1981, Rule 6(1).

[22] Press Council Rules 1981, Rule 6(2).

[23] Press Council Rules 1981, Rule 7.

[24] Press Council Rulcs 1981, Rule 5.

[25] Press Council Rules 1981, Rule 11.

[26] Press Council Rules 1981, Rule 8.

Critics argued that applying the antiquated Press Council Act, originally designed for print media, to the diverse landscape of broadcasting and online platforms would introduce an impractical regulatory landscape and lead to new challenges.

10.4.2 ICCPR Act No. 56 of 2007

The International Covenant on Civil and Political Rights (ICCPR) Act of 2007 aligns domestic law with Sri Lanka's international human rights obligations concerning civil and political rights. Under the ICCPR Act, there is a categorical prohibition against the advocacy of "national, racial, or religious hatred that constitutes incitement to discrimination, hostility, or violence."[27] This prohibition is particularly relevant to addressing the dissemination of fake news and inaccurate information through media that offends the basis of race, religion, and nationality. For instance, publications related to the *Easter Sunday attack of 2019* were scrutinized under this provision as they predominantly targeted the Muslim minority community, leading to *anti-Muslim* sentiment. Similarly, certain allegations regarding political concerns have been challenged under the scope of this Act when they align with these prescribed grounds. However, the Act's scope does not extend to standards protecting an individual's reputation and dignity unless they intersect with these *three* specific grounds.

Notwithstanding, the ICCPR Act has faced criticism for its selective application, particularly in instances that challenge the majoritarian perspective, thereby undermining the Act's original intent (Satkunanathan, 2020). For example, the Act was not invoked in response to the 2014 incident in Kalutara, where a group of racist monks affiliated with *Bodu Bala Sena* incited violence, leading to the death of two Muslims attacked by a mob. Despite the clear incitement and subsequent violence, no arrests were made under the ICCPR Act or any other law, and to date, none of the perpetrators or those who incited the violence have been held accountable.

Moreover, Section 3 of the Act, plagued by both substantive and procedural shortcomings, faces a more significant issue with its misuse for an unintended purpose: the prohibition of *blasphemy* (Gunatilleke, 2021). This was evidenced in June 2023 when comedian Nathasha Edirisooriya and SLVlog YouTube Channel owner Bruno Diwakara were arrested under the ICCPR Act without bail, having been accused of insulting religions, including Buddhism and Christianity, during a stand-up comedy show.[28]

Critics argued that the state machinery weaponizes the ICCPR Act's provisions related to the incitement of national, racial, or religious hatred to suppress freedom of expression. Studies point out that the arrests, detentions, and threats by police and

[27] ICCPR Act 2007, s 3.

[28] See https://archives1.dailynews.lk/2023/06/02/law-order/304760/sl-vlog-owner-bruno-divakara-remanded-till-june-7?page=18.

religious authorities have sparked a debate in society regarding whether the enactment of certain acts is intended to protect civil and political rights, including the freedom of speech and expression, or to suppress them (Dasanayaka, 2023).

10.4.3 The Computer Crimes Act No. 24 of 2007

The Computer Crimes Act (CCA) No. 24 of 2007 is pertinent in this context as online websites and social media platforms fall under its jurisdiction. However, the CCA of Sri Lanka does not address the role of Internet intermediaries, which is a major oversight compared to the Indian IT Act, which does include provisions for such intermediaries. This absence is a notable shortcoming in extending the Act's application to SMPs. Furthermore, the CCA does not recognize "fake news," "misleading content," or "defamatory" publications as offenses. Criminal prosecutions under the CCA are typically filed against the alleged individual within the scope of Section 6 of the Act,[29] which applies when the publications are deemed to threaten the public at large under one of three criteria: (a) national security, (b) the national economy, or (c) public order. Recently, numerous cases have been filed under this Act for publications made regarding COVID-19 that were deemed "false" and "misleading." The application of the CCA proves futile unless the content relates to one of these specified grounds.

Prior to the enactment of the Online Safety Act, the regulatory frameworks discussed above were not effective in addressing issues arising from social media content, within the purview of these three regulatory frameworks. However, in addition to these three frameworks, the government and authorities have utilized various other regulations, such as the Penal Code, No. 2 of 1883; the Sri Lanka Telecommunications Act, No. 25 of 1991; and the Prevention of Terrorism (Temporary Provisions) Act, No. 48 of 1979, to arrest and charge numerous individuals and organizations in Sri Lanka, alleging that they have committed civil or criminal wrongs through their social media activity. Some key incidents include the arrest of consumer rights activist Asela Sampath in June 2021 for allegedly spreading misleading information about vaccines on social media,[30] the arrest of a 28-year-old individual in July 2022 for hate speech against the military on Facebook,[31] the arrest of social media activist and YouTuber Darshana Handunugoda in February 2023 for

[29] Section 6(1) provides: "Any person who intentionally causes a computer to perform any function, knowing or having reason to believe that such function will result in danger or imminent danger to—(a) national security; (b) the national economy; or (c) public order, shall be guilty of an offence and shall on conviction be punishable with imprisonment of either description for a term not exceeding five years."

[30] See https://www.adaderana.lk/news.php?nid=74940.

[31] See https://www.tamilguardian.com/content/another-arrest-over-facebook-post-sri-lankan-police-detain-man-hate-speech-against-army.

Table 10.1 Number of incidents in the year 2021 (Sri Lanka CERT, 2023)

Incident type	No. of incidents 2021
DDOS	13
Ransomware	45
Abuse/hate/privacy violations	182
Malicious software issues	10
Phone hacking	7
Scams	322
Phishing	98
Website compromise	282
Financial/email frauds	115
Intellectual property violations	8
Server compromised	13
Social media	**16975**
Others	144

posting a live video near the Prime Minister's official residence,[32] the arrest of social media activist Piyath Nikeshala in June 2023 for live streaming protesters setting fire to the President's private residence,[33] and the arrest of activists from Aragalaya in 2023 on several occasions for claims regarding their social media posts.

Despite these administrative and governmental efforts to control online issues through existing regulatory measures, challenges in cyberspace continue to persist, indicating a significant increase in such incidents. In 2021, the Sri Lanka Computer Emergency Readiness Team (SLCERT) observed the reporting of a number of incidents associated with issues arising out of cyberspace, as indicated in Table 10.1 (Sri Lanka CERT, 2023).

The high incidence of problems related to social media, as compared to other reported issues, underscores the urgent need for regulation. Despite the existence of some regulatory frameworks, these incidents highlight the limitations of current legal measures in effectively overseeing social media platforms (SMPs). This situation calls for enhanced regulatory approaches to address these challenges.

Establishing a clear boundary for moderating social media content and comprehensively regulating such platforms has proven difficult in the absence of a specific regulatory framework. From another perspective, the push toward exerting authoritarian control over the digital space has led to blurred lines, often resulting in violations of fundamental human rights, including the freedom of speech and expression, and the manipulation of information in various contexts. This situation has necessitated a swift move toward more formal regulation, as evidenced by the recent enactment of the Online Safety Act in Sri Lanka.

[32] See https://www.dailymirror.lk/breaking_news/Social-Media-activist-Darshana-Handungoda-arrested-at-BIA/108-253629.

[33] See https://www.adaderana.lk/news/91524/social-activist-piyath-nikeshala-arrested.

10.5 Online Safety Act of Sri Lanka (OSA)

10.5.1 Background of the OSA

The Online Safety Act emerged as a regulatory response to the Sri Lankan government's concerted efforts following the *Easter Sunday attacks*. These efforts included the temporary shutdown of Internet access to curb the dissemination of fake news and hate speech, particularly targeting minority communities in the country. After a prolonged initiative, the proposed bill was gazetted on September 18, 2023, and subsequently tabled in Parliament on October 3, 2023. However, the bill has faced significant criticism, primarily concerning its purported infringement upon online free speech and expression. Within a short span of time, more than 30 petitions were lodged in the Supreme Court (SC) of Sri Lanka, challenging various provisions of the bill. Yet the Act was passed on January 24, 2024, by a margin of *108–62 votes* at the Parliament, and came into effect after the Speaker endorsed it.[34]

10.5.2 Salient Features of the Act

The Online Safety Act of Sri Lanka comprises 57 provisions divided into eight parts. Serving as a model for external regulation of social media governance (Gauja, 2021), it draws from Singapore's Protection from Online Falsehoods and Manipulation Act (POFMA). The Act's objectives include creating the Online Safety Commission, restricting the online dissemination of specific factual statements, curbing the use of online and inauthentic accounts for prohibited activities, establishing mechanisms for identifying and declaring online spaces used for prohibited purposes, and suppressing funding and support for false statements of fact.[35] This objective is commendable as it enables the counteraction of sponsored manipulative content proliferating across Internet platforms, including social media. Through Section 2, the OSA's application extends beyond Sri Lanka's borders, allowing the regulation of content shared across platforms in specific instances.

As a regulatory framework, the Act provides[36] explicit definitions for key terms, including "fact," "false statement," "internet intermediary," and various technical terminologies. Part I outlines the establishment of the Online Safety Commission, with Section 5 specifying the President's authority to appoint up to five members possessing expertise in information technology, law, governance, or related domains. Subsequent provisions detail procedural aspects of the Commission, covering membership, meetings, and the official seal.

[34] See https://www.bbc.com/news/world-asia-68163414.

[35] Online Safety Act 2024, s 3.

[36] Online Safety Act 2024, s 56.

Part II authorizes the powers and functions of the Commission, granting it 17 powers to issue notices and directives to stakeholders; conduct investigations;[37] register Internet platforms, including SMPs;[38] and specify declared online locations, with recommendations to disable access to information disseminated through them.[39]

Part III delineates offenses within the legislation's purview, imposing stringent penalties for various violations, including the communication of false statements, contempt of court,[40] provocations leading to riots,[41] disturbance of religious assemblies,[42] outrage of religious feelings,[43] causing harassment,[44] and imputing offenses against the state.[45]

Further, as an integral facet of online safety, the Act extends its reach to encompass offenses such as cheating,[46] child abuse,[47] and, notably, the utilization of bots to commit offenses,[48] reflecting the implications of artificial intelligence (AI).

By virtue of Part IV, the Act outlines procedural and administrative matters among the Commission, Internet intermediaries, users, and the court of law. Part V of the Act delves into the concept of declared online locations, aiming to permanently disable online platforms that persistently communicate or disseminate prohibited statements within Sri Lanka three or more times within the last 6 months. Typically, this declaration is made by a Magistrate's Court. Part VI of the OSA addresses countering inauthentic online accounts and the coordination of such deceptive behaviors. In Sri Lanka, inauthentic online accounts often involve misleading uses related to the account's identity. Coordinated inauthentic behavior entails two or three online accounts connected together for the same purpose and controlled by a single individual.

Overall, the Online Safety Act of Sri Lanka provides a comprehensive framework for addressing challenges posed by online content and behavior, safeguarding the integrity of online spaces, and protecting users from harmful activities. However, there are several problems within the OSA that could potentially undermine the objectives of the Act and lead to concerns regarding authoritarianism, similar to what Sri Lanka has witnessed in other regulatory frameworks, such as the ICCPR Act and PTA. These issues are discussed below.

---

[37] Online Safety Act 2024, s 11(i).

[38] Online Safety Act 2024, s 11(k).

[39] Online Safety Act 2024, s 11(h).

[40] Online Safety Act 2024, s 13.

[41] Online Safety Act 2024, s 14.

[42] Online Safety Act 2024, s 15.

[43] Online Safety Act 2024, s 16.

[44] Online Safety Act 2024, s 22.

[45] Online Safety Act 2024, s 21.

[46] Online Safety Act 2024, s 18.

[47] Online Safety Act 2024, s 23.

[48] Online Safety Act 2024, s 24.

10.6 Impacts of the OSA Explained

On a positive note, the Act represents one of the most efficient attempts in Sri Lankan legislative history due to its comprehensive nature. It has adeptly identified and addressed various concerns within the Internet space, effectively bridging the gaps left by the previous CCA. Particularly noteworthy are the updates, including provisions related to *bots*, as identified under this Act. These updates align with the contemporary nature of the legislation, showcasing a forward-looking approach that ensures relevance in addressing issues related to online safety and cyber activities (Soorya, 2023).

The OSA draws insights from the POFMA of Singapore—Bill 10 of 2019. POFMA, considered one of Singapore's most *controversial* bills, faced both local and global criticisms for granting extensive powers to the government and imposing what was perceived as arbitrary restrictions on online *free speech.* Despite the contentious nature of POFMA, in hearing the case of *The Online Citizen Pte Ltd v Attorney-General and Another Appeal, and Other Matters*,[49] the Court of Appeal upheld the constitutionality of the POFMA Act, asserting its alignment with Article 14 of the Singaporean Constitution. In summing up, the court identified the following:

a) Subject statements identified by the Minister are constitutionally protected until they are judicially determined to be false.
b) Correction Directions (CDs) do not inherently restrict constitutional free speech, as the statement-maker has the freedom to qualify the subject statements. Any purported restrictions are deemed justifiable under Article 14.
c) POFMA correctly anticipates that false subject statements can lead to actual or potential harms, even when taken out of context.
d) The current proportionality analysis, based on the requirement of "the least restrictive means," is not presently applicable in Singapore (Chan, 2022).

However, criticisms persist that POFMA carries a greater threat to the free speech regime of Singapore, such as extensive and broad provisions, discretionary powers of ministers, and the lack of judicial insights. Against this backdrop, Sri Lanka has modeled its OSA after the POFMA framework.

Though legislators claim that OSA is largely influenced by POFMA, significant differences exist between the frameworks of Singapore and Sri Lanka (Rajapakse, 2023). While both Acts focus on prohibiting the communication of false statements of fact, the Sri Lankan legislation encompasses a broader range of offenses compared to its Singaporean counterpart. The OSA extends the scope of the Act to cover religion, contempt of court, rioting, cheating, intent to provoke a breach of peace, and, importantly, offenses related to military personnel.[50]

[49] *The Online Citizen Pte Ltd v Attorney-General and Another Appeal, and Other Matters* [2021] SGCA 96.

[50] Online Safety Act 2024, s 21.

However, I argue that the extensive coverage of offenses would not undermine free speech—as long as it serves a rational objective, and the application and enforcement mechanisms are in accordance with established standards.

In addition to these divergent features from POFMA, the OSA has many other significant issues with its substantive and procedural features.

10.6.1 Vague and Broad Provisions of the OSA

While POFMA defines a false statement as "false or misleading, wholly or in part, and which a reasonable person would consider to be a representation of fact,"[51] the OSA of Sri Lanka adopts a broader approach and defines a false statement as:

> a statement that is known or believed by its maker to be incorrect or untrue and is made especially with intent to deceive or mislead but does not include a caution, an opinion or imputation made in good faith.

It provides a subjective criterion in the case-by-case analysis and envisions a danger in how the provision can be applied and interpreted—particularly in a majoritarian space like Sri Lanka, where minority voices are often suppressed through labeling with legislative frameworks, as done under the ICCPR Act.

The definitions provided in the Act for certain terminologies are *vague*, posing a risk of subjective interpretation, particularly within the context of stifling online discussions. For instance, the wording surrounding the "communication of false statements" in Section 12 is both *vague* and *overly broad*, potentially allowing for selective application or targeting to silence online media and dissenting voices. This ambiguity may result in consequences akin to those of the Prevention of Terrorism Act in cyberspace. The Office of the United Nations High Commissioner for Human Rights (OHCHR) has expressed concern regarding the ambiguous definitions within the OSA (OHCHR, 2023).

This alarm stems from the potential for subjective interpretations and arbitrary applications, as highlighted by the UN body. A similar situation arose in the United Kingdom (UK), where the ambiguous clause "legal but harmful" was removed from the Online Safety Act of the United Kingdom (MacCarthy, 2022). This removal was deemed necessary due to the perceived threats it posed to free speech and the digital economy. Drawing parallels to this case, it is crucial to reassess and refine the language used in the Act to prevent unintended consequences, particularly the suppression of online discussions. Failure to address these concerns could lead to a scenario reminiscent of the challenges posed by the PTA in the digital realm.

Compared with the UK Online Safety Act, the UK Bill, argues Sajini Wickramasinghe, includes provisions directing the Office of Communications (OFCOM) to protect the freedom of expression and privacy. Section 69 mandates

[51] Protection from Online Falsehoods and Manipulation Act 2019, s 2(2).

OFCOM to consult individuals with expertise in equality issues and human rights when producing transparency report guides for service providers. Section 144 requires OFCOM's annual report to include a statement on the steps taken to ensure that online safety functions are compatible with the freedom of expression and privacy. The absence of similar provisions in the Sri Lankan Act that actively protect democratic rights and freedoms is noted as a concerning disparity (Wickramasinghe, 2023).

This Act also raises fears that the law could be employed to tighten control over civic space, suppress opposition, and crack down on critics. As a country with a history of human rights violations, crackdowns on protests, and heavy-handed regulations, this provision may be weaponized on many occasions, including during elections, in Sri Lanka (Amnesty International, 2024). These provisions have a chilling effect on free speech and expression across social media platforms, potentially leading to a shrinkage of civic space online (Ashwini Natesan, 2023).

In January 2024, before the Act was passed, several local and international organizations joined forces and submitted an open letter to the Government of Sri Lanka, urging the withdrawal of the proposed online safety bill.[52] The letter alleges that the bill has sparked widespread concerns among scholars, experts, and civil society due to its perceived severe implications on human rights and democratic values. Additionally, iProbono points out that the provisions of the bill, while appearing to enhance security, may not effectively regulate the core problems and could potentially be manipulated to silence women's voices (iProbono, 2024). The extensive list of offenses outlined in the bill raises the risk of censorship or punitive actions against advocacy or critical discussions on gender-related issues.

10.6.2 Online Safety Commission

A salient aspect of this Act is the establishment of the Online Safety Commission, which is comprised of five members appointed by the president of the commission. However, this provision has come under scrutiny from numerous human rights defenders and organizations. The concentration of absolute authority in the president's hands regarding appointments and removals has been criticized for its potential risks to accountability and the abuse of power. It is essential to highlight that this commission holds exclusive authority over a wide array of issues related to online safety, including issuing directives, registering social media and users, conducting investigations, and summoning individuals, among other responsibilities. Entrusting such extensive powers to a commission appointed by the head of the executive branch raises concerns of replicating a scenario reminiscent of previous government regimes that, during certain incidents, imposed Internet bans in Sri Lanka—actions

[52] See https://www.accessnow.org/press-release/open-letter-sri-lanka-must-withdraw-online-safety-bill/.

widely condemned as human rights violations. Placing such broad authority in a *nonindependent* commission without adequate *oversight* mechanisms may have detrimental consequences. It could impede the free flow of information, particularly during electoral periods and peaceful assemblies, where the commission's expansive powers may be weaponized. This potential abuse of authority could lead to restrictions on essential democratic processes, raising further concerns about the protection of human rights and freedoms.

10.6.3 Penal Provisions

After the landmark decision of *Sinha Ratnatunga v. The State*,[53] Sri Lanka abolished *criminal defamation* through the Penal Code (Amendment) Act, No. 12 of 2002. In this case, the editor of the "Sunday Times" newspaper was accused under Section 480 of the Penal Code[54] of publishing or causing to be published an excerpt regarding Her Excellency the President. The article appeared in the gossip column of editions, city-wide and provincial-wide. The article was published in *The Sunday Times* on February 19, 1995, under the heading *Anura: Sootin Says Courting Days Are Here.* In the High Court, the defendant was held guilty of the offense of criminal defamation; the appeal also upheld the decision of the High Court. The case influenced the government to form a committee in January 1995 consisting of R.K.W. Goonasekera (chairman), Shirani Bandaranayake, Rohan Edrisinha, Jayampathi Wickremaratne, K. Javid Yusuf, Victor Gunwardena, and Lucien Rajakarunanayake. The committee was appointed to find out what legal reforms were necessary to ensure media freedom and to make necessary recommendations (Victor Ivan, 2000). The report containing the recommendations of that committee was handed over to the media minister on May 27, 1996. The recommendation of the committee was that the law of criminal defamation should be abolished, or the procedures must be brought to the level of those existing in England so that there would not be any room for arbitrary prosecution. This amendment repealed Chapter XIX of the Press Council Law, thereby eliminating penal sanctions for defamation in Sri Lanka. While the removal of criminal defamation from the Penal Code safeguarded media freedom in Sri Lanka, it concurrently had adverse implications on the freedom of the country's citizens in light of the evolving Internet and cyberspace landscape.

However, the newly passed OSA endorses various penal sanctions for the communication of a "prohibited statement of fact," ranging up to 20 years of imprisonment. The penalties in this Act should adhere to the standards of "proportionality," a principle that is lacking in the current legislation as the prescribed

[53] *Sinha Ratnatunga v. The State* [2001] 2 Sri L.R 172.

[54] "Whoever defames another shall be punished with simple imprisonment for a term which may extend to two years or with fine or with both."

penalties are severe. The chilling effect of these provisions may be exacerbated as the penalties are unduly harsh. Moreover, several offenses outlined in the OSA are duplicative, with identical or similarly worded offenses found in other laws, such as the Penal Code of Sri Lanka. The existence of duplicative offenses not only generates uncertainties but also opens the possibility of selectively applying different legal frameworks based on the accused party (Ratnayake & Lafir, 2023). Simultaneously, proposing a vague penal law for online publication may lead to curtailing online speech and media freedom. While the protection of online safety is paramount, the articulation and application of certain provisions in the penal legislation require careful consideration. Broad and vague provisions may result in a failure to strike a balance between competing rights. In particular, these penal provisions may be weaponized to suppress public outcry and protests, as witnessed in previous instances, such as the "GotaGoGama" movement.

10.6.4 Failure in Lawmaking

Beyond the fact that the OSA has substantive and procedural issues integrated with human rights and media freedom, the framework also carries failures accompanied by the process of lawmaking that may lead to the repeal the OSA.

Considering the severe nature of the Act, the bill was challenged in the Supreme Court of Sri Lanka, according to Article 121(1) of the Constitution of Sri Lanka. The Supreme Court has determined that if specific sections of the bill are amended during the committee stage, the bill can be passed with a simple parliamentary majority. However, if these sections remain unchanged, a special majority in the Parliament is required for the bill's passage, as per Section 84(2) of the Constitution.[55]

However, it is claimed that the Parliament of Sri Lanka has failed to incorporate the recommendations of the Supreme court in lawmaking. The Human Rights Commission of Sri Lanka, an independent body overseeing human rights implementation, has raised concerns about the Official Secrets Act (OSA) and the Parliament's failure to amend specific sections that require a special majority for enactment (Human Rights Commission of Sri Lanka, 2024). The Center for Policy Alternatives (CPA) also expressed concerns regarding the OSA, citing the previous examples of the Personal Data Protection Act and the Right to Information Act, and urges the government to reevaluate both the process and content of the legislation (Center for Policy Alternatives, 2024).

In this regard, in the history of Sri Lankan politics, a suit was instituted for the *very first time* against the speaker by a member of the Parliament. Parliamentarian Hon. M.A. Sumanthiran filed a fundamental rights petition in the Supreme Court against Speaker Mahinda Yapa Abeywardana and Attorney General (AG) Sanjay

[55] See https://economynext.com/sri-lankas-online-safety-bill-can-be-passed-with-simple-majority-subject-to-31-amendments-138573/.

Rajaratnam, alleging that the Speaker wrongly certified the Online Safety Bill (OSB) and that the AG provided negligent advice regarding the same. The petitioner highlighted that the Supreme Court had determined certain clauses of the bill to be inconsistent, requiring a two-thirds majority for enactment. The SC also noted that specific amendments, if incorporated, would allow the bill to pass with a simple majority. However, the government's proposed committee-stage amendments did not fully address SC recommendations, leading to concerns about compliance with the Constitution. Despite opposition concerns, the Speaker approved the amendments, citing compliance with the SC's determination.[56] The suit is now pending before the Supreme Court of Sri Lanka for a final determination.

10.6.5 Emerging from the Trauma of Bloodshed

The analysis highlights the current inadequacies in Sri Lanka's legal, policy, and institutional frameworks for regulating social media platforms. These structures have demonstrated inconsistencies, selective enforcement, and potential misuse. The absence of safeguards and regulatory mechanisms to hold *tech companies* accountable for the content on their platforms is a significant drawback that needs to be addressed to advance the regulation of social media platforms in the Global South. While achieving this goal will require considerable effort, time, and attempts, it is essential to ratify the OSA in the future. This would ensure effective regulations with inclusive platform participation and prevent potential government abuse through heavy-handed approaches that stifle human rights, including free speech, across platforms. Also, the blend elements of public and private governance would be practically essential in navigating through the complex social media content governance or moderation. As the Online Safety Act of the UK suggests, the hybrid environment of regulatory measures would assist this goal; meanwhile, that would keep the government controls away from individual content analysis.

The OSA should also be amended to align with the standards recognized in the international and domestic legal framework, including the Constitution of Sri Lanka, especially concerning limitations on free speech and expression online. The *three-part test*—(a) prescribed by law, (b) pursuing a legitimate aim, and (c) being necessary for a democratic society—should be adhered to in establishing clear-cut provisions, particularly those related to penal sanctions.

Although Sri Lanka has also enacted the OSA, which resembles external regulation models similar to those of India and Germany, discussed in previous chapters of this book, it differs significantly in its framework. Despite being categorized under broader regulatory approaches, each of these frameworks is distinct and unique. Sri Lanka shares several similarities with India, yet the IT Rules in India differ notably from the OSA. Both countries, emerging from the Majority World and operating

[56] See https://www.themorning.lk/articles/EBqKwaCKz1lZA95CSHco.

within multicultural South Asian contexts, have implemented regulatory measures that reflect their individual needs and circumstances. India's IT Rules demand specific roles from platforms, a requirement that is not addressed by Sri Lanka's OSA. This difference may be influenced by the different user base sizes in each country.

Moreover, India's IT Rules exhibit flexibility by leaning toward a coregulation model, as evidenced by its publication of a Code of Ethics—a feature that Sri Lanka has not adopted. As discussed in Chap. 6, Sri Lanka's framework aligns more closely with the digital authoritarianism model observed in China, differing markedly from India's approach.

I argue that for a jurisprudence like Sri Lanka's, merely leaving the potential regulatory penumbra without the inclusion of platforms, the judiciary, or any other independent oversight mechanisms could result in the potential abuse of regulatory frameworks aimed at curbing free speech online. Therefore, *a multiplayer role* in the regulatory regime is not only enriching but also essential for Sri Lanka.

Additionally, a *norm-based* framework would be sustainable amid the changing landscape of technology, especially concerning content moderation. By particularly involving platforms and developing a *conditional immunity* model of regulatory approach, which entails invoking the duty of care from private platforms, we can maximize the free speech of users while holding platforms more accountable and keeping extreme censorship at bay.

As a country from the Global South, undergoing regulatory change is deemed necessary, and Sri Lanka should carefully consider competing values. The chapter examines the social media landscape and narratives from a *postwar* context, analyzing how social media platforms amplified voices across virtual platforms. While the OSA exhibits a few progressive features, it raises concerns, particularly regarding the balance of free speech online. However, the study identified potential pitfalls of the Act, such as the vague and broad nature of the provisions, the formation of the online safety commission, penal provisions, and procedural fallacies that can potentially be weaponized against online speech, similar to the previous ICCPR Act and PTA. Consequently, there is a need for amendments that incorporate various suggestions within this spectrum, including proposing a *norm-based* regulatory framework, encouraging inclusive platform participation, invoking oversight mechanisms, and incorporating universally accepted standards, such as the *three-part test* recognized under international law. The model of the OSA should be revisited with major changes, addressing concerns of free speech and expression, as the present Act carries the danger of major blows on them, particularly as a fragile democratic state navigating through the *transitional justice* era. Such revisions would contribute to making the Internet space in Sri Lanka resilient, reliable, and conducive to freedom, ushering in an era of digital democracy.

References

Afef Abrougui & Access Now. (2021). *Internet shutdowns and elections handbook.* Access Now.

Amarasingam, A., & Rizwie, R. (2020). *Turning the tap off: The impacts of social media shutdown after Sri Lanka's Easter Attacks.* International Centre for Counter-Terrorism.

Amnesty International. (2024, January 24). *Sri Lanka: Online Safety Act major blow to freedom of expression.* Retrieved from Amnesty International: https://www.amnesty.org/en/latest/news/2024/01/sri-lanka-online-safety-act-major-blow-to-freedom-of-expression/

Anuradha Rao. (2018). *#RiseUpSL: The role of social media and citizen.* NUS Institute of South Asian Studies (ISAS).

Ashwini Natesan. (2023, September 28). *Online Safety Bill in Sri Lanka- Thoughts and potential concerns.* Retrieved from Sri Lanka Press Institute (SLPI): https://slpi.lk/2023/09/28/online-safety-bill-in-sri-lanka-thoughts-and-potential-concerns/

Bischoff, P. (2023, October 16). *Internet Censorship 2024: A global map of internet restrictions.* Retrieved from CompariTech: https://www.comparitech.com/blog/vpn-privacy/internet-censorship-map/#Will_online_censorship_become_the_norm

Byman, D., & Joshi, A. (2021). Preventing the next social-media genocide. In D. D. Allin (Ed.), *In Survival December 2020–January 2021: A world after Trump* (pp. 125–152). Routledge.

Center for Policy Alternatives. (2023). *A brief analysis of the Aragalaya.* Colombo.

Center for Policy Alternatives. (2024, February 7). Statement on the Online Safety Act No. 09 of 2024. Colombo.

Chan, G. K. (2022). Online falsehoods, constitutional free speech and its limits. *Singapore Journal of Legal Studies*, 166–176.

Commonwealth Observor Group. (2019). *Sri Lanka Presidential Election.* Commonwealth Observer Group.

Dasanayaka, D. (2023). *Abuse of power under the guise of the ICCPR ACT.* Right to Life Human Rights Centre.

Data Reportal. (2024). *Digital 2024: Sri Lanka.*

Democracy Reporting International. (2020). *Social media monitoring analysis of the discourse on Facebook before and after Sri Lanka's 2019 Presidential Election.* Democracy Reporting International.

Democracy Reporting International. (2021). *Facebook and Sri Lanka's Easter Sunday Attacks: Constructing narratives and scapegoats.* Democracy Reporting International.

DeVotta, N., & Ganguly, S. (2019). Sri Lanka's post–civil war problems. *Current History, 118*(807), 137–142.

Freedom House. (2024). *Freedom on the Net 2023 - Sri Lanka.* Freedom House.

Gauja, A. (2021). Digital democracy: Big technology and the regulation of politics. *University of New South Wales Law Journal, 44*(3), 959–982.

Grewal, K. K. (2023). The epistemic violence of transitional justice: A view from Sri Lanka. *International Journal of Transitional Justice, 17*(2), 322–338.

Gunatilleke, G. (2017). Two faces of Sri Lankan media: Censorship and resistance. In S. U. (Eds.), *Media as politics in South Asia* (pp. 143–159). Routledge.

Gunatilleke, G. (2021). Is Section 3 of Sri Lanka's ICCPR Act fit for purpose? *The Bar Association Law Journal*, 156–162.

Gunatilleke, G. (2023). Limitations on fundamental freedoms in Sri Lanka: Majoritarian influence of constitutional practice. *International Journal of Law in Context, 19*(3), 334–351.

Hattotuwa, S., Wijeratne, Y., & Serrato, R. (2018). *Weaponising 280 characters-What 200,000 tweets and 4,000 bots tell us about state of Twitter in.* Center for Policy Alternatives.

Herath, V. (2022). Incidents and trends in media freedom in Sri Lanka. In C. f. (CPA), *Human rights and democracy in Sri Lanka: Threat to journalists, human rights defenders and civil society* (pp. 63–69). Center for Policy Alternatives (CPA).

Hewage, K., & Weerasekera, H. (2021). *Social media for business.* Institute of Policy Studies of Sri Lanka.

Human Rights Commission of Sri Lanka. (2024, February 08). Observations on the Online Safety Act, No. 9 of 2024. Colombo.

Human Rights Watch. (2024). *World Report 2024*. Human Rights Watch.

iprobono. (2024, January). *Decoding the Sri Lankan Online Safety Bill*. Retrieved from iprobono: https://i-probono.com/articles/decoding-the-sri-lankan-online-safety-bill/

Jayasuriya, N. A., Azam, S. F., & Ferdous, M. (2017). The impact of social media marketing on brand equity: A study of fashion-wear retail in Sri Lanka. *International Review of Management and Marketing, 7*(5), 178–183.

Law & Society Trust. (2018). *Fact-finding report on the anti-Muslim violence in the Kandy district March 2018*. Law & Society Trust (LST).

MacCarthy, M. (2022, December 21). *U.K. government purges "legal but harmful" provisions from its revised Online Safety Bill*. Retrieved from Brookings: https://www.brookings.edu/articles/u-k-government-purges-legal-but-harmful-provisions-from-its-revised-online-safety-bill/

Mihlar, F. (2019). Religious change in a minority context: Transforming Islam in Sri Lanka. *Third World Quarterly, 40*(12), 2153–2169.

Nayakarathna, S. (2021, August 1). *Sri Lanka's fight against the 'Infodemic' during the pandemic*. Retrieved from Friedrich Naumann Foundation: https://www.freiheit.org/sri-lanka/sri-lankas-fight-against-infodemic-during-pandemic

Nifra, N. (2022). *The role of social media in the Sri Lanka Protest Movement*. Retrieved from https://vocal.media/: https://vocal.media/pride/the-role-of-social-media-in-the-sri-lanka-protest-movement

OCHCR. (2022). *Human Rights Council Fifty-first session*. Office of the United Nations High Commissioner for Human Rights.

OHCHR. (2023, October 13). *Human rights concerns over two draft laws in Sri Lanka*. Retrieved from OHCHR: https://www.ohchr.org/en/press-briefing-notes/2023/10/human-rights-concerns-over-two-draft-laws-sri-lanka

OOSGA. (2023, October 30). *Social media in Sri Lanka - 2023 Stats & Platform Trends*. Retrieved from OOSGA: https://oosga.com/social-media/lka/.%20%20

Rajapakse, C. (2023, September 22). *Sri Lanka's new Bill on Online Safety: Comparison with Singapore*. Retrieved from Lirne Asia: https://lirneasia.net/2023/09/sri-lanka-online-safety-bill

Ratnayake, N., & Lafir, T. (2023, December 6). *Sri Lanka's Proposed Online Safety Bill: Regulation, but at what cost?* Retrieved from Media Diversity Institute: https://www.media-diversity.org/sri-lankas-proposed-online-safety-bill-regulation-but-at-what-cost/

Satkunanathan, A. (2020). Sri Lanka: Minority rights within shrinking civic space. In T. S. *Collective, South Asia State of Minortities Report* (pp. 196–229). South Asia Collective.

Soorya, B. (2021). Revitalizing 'Digital Democracy': Regulating social media discourses in Sri Lanka. In *Proceedings of SLIIT International Conference on Advancements in Sciences and Humanities* (pp. 423–432). Faculty of Humanities and Sciences, SLIIT.

Soorya, B. (2023, December 07). *Falsehood vs. Free Speech: Competing Narratives of the Online Safety Bill*. Retrieved from Ground Views: https://groundviews.org/2023/12/07/falsehood-vs-free-speech-competing-narratives-of-the-online-safety-bill-in-sri-lanka/

Sri Lanka CERT. (2023). *Annual Report 2021*. Sri Lanka CERT.

Statista. (2023, November). *Social Media Advertising - Sri Lanka*.

Tazamal, M. (2021, February 8). *For Sri Lanka's Muslims, discrimination even in death*. Retrieved from Bridge: https://bridge.georgetown.edu/research/for-sri-lankas-muslims-discrimination-even-in-death/

Victor Ivan. (2000, December 24). *Criminal defamation Vs. Media freedom*. Retrieved from Sunday Times: https://www.sundaytimes.lk/001224/news3.html

Wattegama, C. (2021). *Digital economy of Sri Lanka: National goals and lessons from the South.* In United Nations Conference on Trade and Development. UNCTAD/BRI PROJECT/RP15. UN (United Nations), New York, USA.

Wickramasinghe, S. (2023, October 4). *UK and Sri Lanka: A comparison of two Online Safety Bills.* Retrieved from Ground Views: https://groundviews.org/2023/10/04/uk-and-sri-lanka-a-comparison-of-two-online-safety-bills/

Chapter 11
Conclusion and a Way Forward

This book set out to answer the question: *How do different social media content regulatory models, from Western to Majority world contexts, impact online free speech?*

In addressing the central question, it became evident that a global trend is emerging in the regulation of social media platforms, manifesting through various proposed regulatory models. Internal regulations, typically implemented by the platforms themselves, ostensibly diminish the authoritarian powers of states (governments). However, this approach presents significant challenges, primarily stemming from private *decision-making* processes and algorithmic discrimination. On the other hand, the external regulation model appears to be selectively applied, often serving as a tool to suppress voices and restrict free speech within online spaces, particularly as an extension of authoritarian regimes in fragile democratic states. Therefore, among the three models, *coregulation* emerges as more convincing as it strives to strike a balance between public and private actors—governments and platforms—establishing a regulation based on principled considerations.

I have explored four distinct jurisdictions—the United States, Germany, India, and Sri Lanka—to understand how cultural norms, public power, and the power asymmetry between platforms and governments influence social media regulations. These countries offer perspectives from North American, European, and majoritarian world backgrounds.

Upon analyzing the regulatory frameworks proposed by various jurisdictions, it is evident that Section 230 of the Communications Decency Act in the United States exemplifies the self-regulation model. In contrast, frameworks such as the Network Enforcement Act (NetzDG) in Germany, the Information Technology (Intermediary Guidelines and Digital Media Ethics Code) Rules in India, and the Online Safety Act in Sri Lanka are based on the external regulation model. However, there are notable differences among these frameworks with regard to standards, procedures, and institutional mechanisms, influenced by a myriad of factors discussed throughout the book.

S. Balendra, *Free Speech in the Puzzle of Content Regulation*, Law, Governance and Technology Series 70, https://doi.org/10.1007/978-3-031-75813-3_11

Indeed, the treatment of free speech within these proposed frameworks reflects distinct jurisprudential approaches. The US stance, exemplified by Section 230, strongly emphasizes free speech protection, adopting a rights-based approach that grants significant immunity to platforms and Internet intermediaries. While this amplifies online free speech, as acknowledged under the First Amendment, contemporary studies indicate a noticeable imbalance in accommodating other competing rights and values. The broad immunities granted to platforms often lead to a lack of transparency in decision-making, creating challenges that have been identified in both scholarly and policy discussions. This urges a reevaluation of the immunities given to Internet intermediaries. Although these immunities can amplify online freedom of speech, it is also essential for the Internet to preserve other rights related to regulatory models that may conflict. Making significant changes to Section 230 would create legal repercussions; meanwhile, keeping them broader also would end up with these challenges.

In stark contrast, Germany's Network Enforcement Act (NetzDG) takes a divergent approach to free speech. It shifts certain responsibilities to platforms for determining the admissibility of content but faces criticism for its excessive punishments, transparency requirements, and prolonged decision-making time frames. Scholars and experts argue that this approach results in the "over removal" of content, a severe violation of online free speech. The NetzDG is also criticized for the decision-making power given to private entities and the concerns about free speech and the lack of safeguards in its implementation. As the EU's Digital Service Act is applied to Germany, the provisions of the NetzDG are replaced with full effect from February 2024.

In India, one of the top global markets, social platforms are widely used for various purposes, including as sanctuaries for political discussions and speech, involving figures as prominent as the Prime Minister. In 2021, India introduced a new regulatory framework, the Intermediary Guidelines and Digital Media Ethics Code, which incorporates new *safe harbor* provisions to limit the liability of Internet intermediaries. While the additional monitoring mechanisms for intermediaries are commendable, the short deadlines and institutional arrangements, especially the vesting of authority in government organs, raise concerns about the potential threat to online free speech and media rights. Although India's approach, as a representative of the Global South in regulating and moderating online content, has been seen as a role model, its shortcomings should be addressed without undue delay to fully utilize the proposed framework. Also, as we have identified, along with the form of external regulations, the publication of the ethics code based on the model seems to show that India is marching toward some aspect of coregulation—which is a good indication.

Sri Lanka's regulatory model, the Online Safety Act (OSA), while progressive in some respects, raises concerns about the balance of free speech online. The study highlights issues such as vague and broad provisions, the formation of the Online Safety Commission, penal provisions, and procedural errors, which could be used against online speech, similar to past legislation. Sri Lanka, being a jurisdiction with a fragile democracy that approaches human rights with heavy-handed legislation, the

Online Safety Act is also considered "old wine in a new bottle." The study suggests the need for amendments, including a norm-based regulatory framework, inclusive platform participation, oversight mechanisms, and alignment with internationally recognized standards like the *three-part test*.

In addressing the question, the study suggests that achieving the global regulation of social media content appears to be impractical due to significant differences in jurisdictions, which range from majoritarian countries to Western nations. While many regulatory models fall under the external regulation category, there are stark variations in standards and approaches. For instance, although both EU and Chinese models represent external regulation, the study highlights significant contrasts in their application, particularly concerning free speech.

Further, the study highlights that while the Western jurisprudence approach to social media regulation significantly differs from that of the Majority World and although the three broader regulatory models vary in their treatment of content and their interplay with free speech, the approach to regulation is not solely determined by these model variations and geographical distinctions. For instance, despite the similarities between India and Sri Lanka as emerging countries from the Majority World, their regulatory frameworks—India's IT Rules and Sri Lanka's OSA—are shaped by internal factors, such as authoritative approaches, political dynamics, and market size. These factors play a crucial role in influencing their respective regulatory approaches.

This analysis establishes that the coregulation model offers a radical approach to addressing these challenges. However, it must be developed further to overcome the pitfalls identified in this study, such as the model's nonbinding nature, the lack of accountability, and inconsistent enforcement measures.

Finally, I emphasize three concluding statements on the social media regulations within the context of safeguarding free speech online.

11.1 The Nature of Technology and Law

Social media, a product of technological evolution, provides an expansive digital arena for interpersonal interaction. However, the ever-evolving nature of technology presents a formidable challenge for regulation through a purely legislative lens. A prime example of this complexity lies in the rapid emergence of artificial intelligence (AI) on a global scale, where striking a regulatory balance becomes an intricate task. The notion of a *legal lag* encapsulates the struggle to keep pace with technological advancements through legislative means. While technology evolves swiftly, altering regulatory regimes involves procedural complexities that impede a nimble response. The dynamic landscape of AI underscores the inherent difficulty in formulating and adapting regulations to keep pace with its rapid development. In light of these challenges, it becomes evident that relying solely on legislative measures may prove insufficient. Herein lies the importance of incorporating ethical guidelines alongside legal frameworks. By complementing legal arrangements with ethical considerations, there is an opportunity to bridge the gap left by the legal lag, albeit to a certain extent. Ethical guidelines serve as a flexible and adaptive tool, allowing for a more immediate response to emerging technological trends without the procedural hurdles associated with legislative changes. Rather than exclusively pursuing tightly fitted regulations, which may be challenging to implement universally within the realm of common jurisprudence, a more pragmatic approach involves a dual focus on legal and ethical considerations. This combined strategy acknowledges the inherent challenges posed by the rapid evolution of technology, emphasizing the importance of a dynamic and multifaceted approach to navigating the intricate landscape of social media regulation in an era dominated by technological innovation.

Given the complexities in the regulation of governments in regulating SMPs, the traditional regulatory methods are futile in countering the content moderation challenges in the era of AI. Therefore, in order to overcome a broader range of ethical, human rights, and societal values, I suggest the adoption of *soft law* measures, together with a fundamental framework, that would assist the platforms and enforcement authorities in overcoming this challenge. Despite their imperfections and lack of direct enforceability, these soft law measures are seen as necessary to fill the regulatory gap in the short term and manage the challenges posed by technology. While many aspects of soft law are already present in platforms, extending these toward a legislative effort that requires a minimal level of compliance could be a viable alternative to the heavy-handed legislative frameworks that often stifle free speech and hinder online innovations. For example, jurisdictions, instead of passing regulatory frameworks to take down or remove content online, may issue some kind of guidelines or code of ethics or any similar instruments to platforms that operate in their jurisdictions to establish standards and guidelines on the content shared across the SMPs. I trust, it would help to mitigate the potential risks on the nature of the content in the social media platforms, while facilitating the amplification of free speech, by establishing common standards.

For example, rather than passing regulatory frameworks that mandate the take-down or removal of online content, jurisdictions could issue guidelines, codes of ethics, or similar instruments to platforms operating within their territories. These would establish standards for content on social media platforms. I believe this approach would help mitigate potential risks associated with the nature of the content on SMPs while facilitating the amplification of free speech by establishing common standards.

11.2 Principle-Based Regulations and Process

Establishing a principle-based regulatory regime is fundamentally imperative for formalizing the foundational values inherent in its application, particularly within the inherently dynamic nature of the Internet. The study elucidates a critical observation, emphasizing that while the coregulation model is often referred to as a principle-based approach, its application and procedural implementation frequently fall short within this context. This discrepancy has notably hindered the effectiveness of the model, preventing it from achieving its intended objectives within the jurisprudence of both Germany and India. In light of these challenges, there is a compelling argument for the incorporation of principles not only into the regulatory framework but also into the application processes. This proposition contends that the adoption of principles throughout the regulatory process is essential despite potential resistance from institutional arrangements. By embedding principles into the entire regulatory life cycle, it becomes possible to overcome the shortcomings observed in the application of models. This shift toward a principled approach is particularly crucial for the preservation and fortification of free speech in online environments. While facing resistance, integrating principles into the regulatory process serves as a means to align proposed guidelines and regulations with their intended objectives. This holistic adoption of principles facilitates a more effective and consistent application of regulations, thereby enhancing the likelihood of achieving the overarching goal of maintaining and strengthening free speech in the digital realm.

11.3 Promotion of Inter-/Multidisciplinary Research

Regulating social media necessitates a holistic approach that extends beyond the confines of legal frameworks. Given the dynamic nature of social media and the Internet, it is imperative to consider both internal and external dimensions in formulating a comprehensive regulatory sphere. Understanding the intricacies of social media requires a multidimensional perspective that encompasses communication, computer science, data science, humanities, social sciences, and legal and policy studies. Consequently, interdisciplinary or multidisciplinary studies should be actively promoted to develop nuanced and effective regulatory strategies.

A convincing regulatory approach must account for the diverse cultural, technological, and human values inherent in the social media landscape. To achieve this, it is essential to foster research collaborations across these disciplines. By incorporating insights from communication, computer science, data science, humanities, social sciences, and legal and policy studies, a well-fitted regulatory framework can be crafted. This approach ensures that regulations around the social media apparatus align with the complexity of the digital sphere, encompassing cultural diversity, technological advancements, and fundamental human values.

Recognizing the significance of protecting competing values in the digital realm, various organizations and institutions have initiated research collaborations across disciplines. Notable examples include the Oxford Internet Institute, the Berkman Klein Center for Internet & Society at Harvard University, and the Information Society Project at Yale Law School. These initiatives underscore a collective commitment to understanding and addressing the multifaceted challenges posed by social media, with the ultimate goal of striking a balance that preserves essential values, including the paramount principle of free speech. Currently, most research initiatives are concentrated in Western jurisdictions, with a few exceptions, such as the National University of Singapore. This trend may be attributed to factors such as limited resources and a shortage of experts in other regions. However, it is crucial for countries in the majority world to step forward and take a leading role in research initiatives within their own jurisdictions.

In conclusion, addressing the challenges and limitations inherent in social media regulations necessitates a shift toward a principle-based approach, informed by ethical considerations and supported by the promotion of interdisciplinary research studies. This comprehensive strategy opens new avenues for mitigating drawbacks, allowing for a more nuanced and adaptable regulatory framework. This multifaceted approach not only rectifies shortcomings but also enables the establishment of a balanced framework that harmonizes competing values. It emphasizes the preservation of free speech as a central tenet, serving as the backbone for a socially responsible media environment. Such an approach contributes to the cultivation of social media platforms characterized by integrity, trust, and resilience, reinforcing their role as vital components of contemporary communication. Moreover, this framework will uphold the freedom of speech beyond geographical distinctions, extending from the West to the South and across territorial borders from Sri Lanka to the United States.

Correction to: Free Speech in the Puzzle of Content Regulation: Insights from the West and the Global South

Correction to:
S. Balendra, *Free Speech in the Puzzle of Content Regulation*, Law, Governance and Technology Series, https://doi.org/10.1007/978-3-031-75813-3

The book was inadvertently published with an incorrect volume number of "20", whereas it should be "70". The volume number has been updated in the book.

The updated version of this book can be found at
https://doi.org/10.1007/978-3-031-75813-3

S. Balendra, *Free Speech in the Puzzle of Content Regulation*, Law, Governance and Technology Series 70, https://doi.org/10.1007/978-3-031-75813-3_12

List of Cases

- Animal Defenders International v. United Kingdom [2013] ECHR 362, (2013) 57 EHRR 21
- Anuradha Bhasin v. Union of India AIR 2020 SC 1308
- Ashlesh Biradar v. State of West Bengal PA (RB) WPA (P) 104/2022
- Bantam Books, Inc. v. Sullivan, 372 U.S. 58 (1963)
- Blumenthal v. Drudge, 992 F.Supp. 44 (D.C.D.C., 1998)
- Brentwood Academy v. Tennessee Secondary School Athletic Association, 531 U.S. 288 (2001)
- Cengiz and Others v. Turkey (2015) 48226/10 and 14027/11
- Cubby, Inc. v. CompuServe Inc., 776 F.Supp. 135 (S.D.N.Y. 1991)
- David L. Hudson Jr., Zeran v. America Online, Inc. (4th Cir.) (1997)
- Doe v. MySpace, Inc., 528 F.3d 413 (5th Cir. 2008)
- Facebook LLC v. Union of India, W.P.(C) No. 7281/2021
- Fair Housing Council of San Fernando Valley v. Roommates.com, LLC, 521 F.3d 1157 (9th Cir. 2008)
- Fields v. Twitter., 16-cv-00213-WHO
- Force v. Facebook, Inc., 934 F.3d 53 (2nd Cir. 2019)
- Gentry v. eBay, Inc., 121 Cal. Rptr. 2d 703 (Cal. Ct. App. 2002)
- Glawischnig-Piesczek v. Facebook Ireland, Limited Case C-18/18 (2019)
- Gonzalez v. Google LLC, 598 U.S. 617
- Google France, Google Inc. v. Louis Vuitton Malletier, C-236/08
- Google Inc., v. Equustek Solutions Inc. [2017] 1 S.C.R. 34 (Can.)
- Google LLC v. Equustek Solutions Inc., 2017 WL 5000834 (N.D. Cal. Nov. 2, 2017)
- Google Spain SL and Google Inc. v. Agencia Española de Protección de Datos (AEPD) and Mario Costeja González (2014) C-131/12
- Handyside v. United Kingdom (5493/72)
- Jones v. Dirty World Entertainment Recordings LLC, 755 F.3d 398 (6th Cir. 2014)

S. Balendra, *Free Speech in the Puzzle of Content Regulation*, Law, Governance and Technology Series 70, https://doi.org/10.1007/978-3-031-75813-3

- KS Puttaswamy v. Union of India, AIR 2017 SC 4161
- L'Oréal SA v. eBay International AG, C-324/09
- Maneka Gandhi v. Union of India (1978) 1 SCC 248
- Marsh v. Alabama, 326 U.S. 501 (1946)
- Maughan v. Google Tech., Inc., 49 Cal. Rptr. 3d 861 (Cal. Ct. App. 2006)
- New York Times Co. v. Sullivan, 376 U.S. 254
- Oakmont, Inc. v. Prodigy Services Co., 1995 WL 323710
- Packingham v. North Carolina, 582 U.S. 98 (2017)
- Prager University v. Google LLC, 951 F.3d 991, 997 (9th Cir. 2020)
- Raju Prosad Sarma v. The State of Assam WP (C)/5527/2022
- Reno v. American Civil Liberties Union, 521 US 844 (1997)
- Savva Terentyev v. Russia, 10692/09 ECHR (2018)
- Shreya Singhal v. Union of India, AIR 2015 SC 1523; Writ Petition (Criminal) No. 167 OF 2012
- Sinha Ratnatunga v. The State [2001] 2 Sri L.R 172
- Smith v. California, 361 U.S. 147 (1959)
- The Online Citizen Pte Ltd v. Attorney-General and Another Appeal, and Other Matters [2021] SGCA 96
- Twitter, Inc. v. Taamneh, 598 U.S. 471 (2023)
- Whatsapp v. Union of India, W.P.(C) No. 7284/2021
- X Corp. v. Union of India (W.P. No. 13710 of 2022)
- Yahoo!, Inc. v. La Ligue Contre le Racisme et L'Antisemitisme, 169 F.Supp.2d.
- Zeran v. America Online, Inc., 129 F.3d 327 (4th Cir. 1997)

The manufacturer's authorised representative in the EU is Springer
Nature Customer Service Centre GmbH, Europaplatz 3, 69115 Heidelberg,
Germany. If you have any concerns regarding our products, please
contact ProductSafety@springernature.com

Printed and bound by CPI Group (UK) Ltd, Croydon, CR0 4YY
30/09/2026
02225589-0005